WEAPONS, DRUGS & MONEY

Crime, Corruption, and Community Based Liberation in the U.S./Mexico Neoliberal Military Political Economy

WEAPONS, DRUGS & MONEY

Crime, Corruption, and Community Based Liberation in the U.S./Mexico Neoliberal Military Political Economy

by **Simón Sedillo**

edited by
**Carolina Saldaña &
Samara Almonte**

COMUNICACIÓN COMBATIVA

Weapons, Drugs, and Money

This edition © 2022 Comunicación Combativa (Austin, Texas)
(Paperback) ISBN: 979-8-9853776-0-6 (Ebook) ISBN: 979-8-9853776-1-3
(PDF) ISBN 979-8-9853776-2-0
Library of Congress Control Number: 2022904508

Comunicación Combativa
306 Provines Drive
Austin, TX 78753
USA
combativa.org

The completion of this book was made possible by the
2021 Radical Imagination Grant offered by the NDN Collective.

Edited by Carolina Saldaña and Samara Almonte
Cover design by Seth Goodman
Book design by Sari Dennise

Table of Contents

Foreword

By Samara Almonte

When talking to Simón about how neoliberalism has directly impacted his life and the factors that drove him to become a community rights defense organizer, filmmaker, and now author, there was a particular factor that struck me the most. He accredits his lifelong work of dismantling neoliberalism to walking this Earth with the rage of his ancestral trauma and lived trauma. How many of us are feeling rage at this moment that is so powerful it almost seems to transcend time? And how many of us have been criminalized by political, carceral and even educational institutions for expressing this rage? For Black and Indigenous people across the world this criminalization happens since the day we are born on this Earth. Knowing Simón for quite some time now and having the privilege to witness his transition into fatherhood, I have seen how someone can transform anger into action, but more importantly, combat anger with actions driven by radical love, community-based liberation and radical imagination.

In this book, I believe Simón not only prepares us with the tools necessary to understand our anger towards the injustices we witness every day in our lives and society at large, but also provides a sense of hope and the opportunity to imagine a different world. I believe he speaks from a place of radical love because he loves with a critical heart that shows us compassion throughout our radicalization journey. And this book in particular speaks from a place of community-based liberation because Simón's work is based on Indigenous principles that can be seen across so called "Mesoamerica." Simon "walks by asking," meaning that his work is informed and led by the people he is in community with. The knowledge and tools shared in this book are rooted in community-based liberation, because Simón "teaches by learning." As much as Simón has been a mentor and teacher for me, we both can agree that I have taught him a thing or two, and his daughters also have so much to teach us. And lastly, Simón writes this book from the Indigenous principle of "propose not impose." The purpose of this book isn't to propose that all racialized people, and especially not white people coming across this book, try to impose these community-based strategies directly into their own context. But rather that these examples from Indigenous and non-indigenous communities in so-called Mexico, serve to educate and perhaps even inspire similar movements among Black, Indigenous and other racialized communities in "North America" and across the world. This is not to say that communities outside of the "Americas" have not historically and currently practiced forms of self-determination and community-based liberation; in fact, Simon hopes that this book will bring readers, scholars and community organizers across the world together as we build upon the ideas presented in these chapters, and even develop new analyses and solutions from this text.

Simón's main goal for writing this book from an educational perspective is to demystify our understanding of neoliberalism, clarify how the spectrum of institutional U.S. and Mexican politics from left to right participates in neoliberalism, and demonstrate the devastating effect that neoliberalism has on communities in general. What sets this book apart, or more importantly what sets Simón apart as an author on the topic of neoliberalism, is that this book is written from theory based on lived experiences and that Simón's identity as a reconnecting Indigenous person and self-identified Chicano provides him with the frameworks to understand and document the violence perpetuated by neoliberalism on Indigenous communities both across Mexico and the United States. Simón made it clear to me from the first day I met him that he does not see his work as work meant to "give voice to the voiceless," but rather to "pass the mic" and uplift others' stories and work when they have different lived experiences from his own. For example, in this book we see a mention of the Prison Industrial Complex (PIC) as a main characteristic of neoliberalism, yet he doesn't dive deep into this topic because he would rather point people to Michelle Alexander's book, *The New Jim Crow*, which he believes does a phenomenal job of documenting this history. Also when diving deeper into the history of US colonialism against the Native peoples of the so called USA, he defers to Jimmy Lee Beason the II, a Native Pahuska from the Eagle Clan of the Osage Nation, and a professor in the Indigenous / American Indian Studies Department at Haskell Indian Nations University in Lawrence Kansas.

I feel honored to be part of Simón's journey as an author and more importantly to call him a friend and mentor in my life. Thinking about my own anger as a young racialized woman and looking back at my own reconnecting and healing journey, I realize how much of the fire within me was ignited from the time I met Simon when I was barely 19 years old. So many of the lessons and stories that Simón has shared with me since then have been compiled into this book, so that other young people may know how to nurture their own fire in a way that doesn't leave them burned out. I know that Simón, alongside his amazing partner and beautiful daughters, will continue fighting for liberation until the day he becomes an ancestor of this world. However, I also hope that he knows how much of a foundation he has created for the generations to come so that we can dream even further for the liberation of our people. In the words of Simón himself, "It's not ambitious to believe we can engage in our own liberation, that we can carry out our own liberation, and [implement] models of self-governance that bring liberation from this construct we are living in." Thank you for your work Simón, may the generations continue feeding the spirit of our liberation and transcend our own notions of what it means to be loved and cared for in this world.

Preface

The purposes of this book are firstly to demystify our understanding of neoliberalism, clarify how the entire spectrum of
institutional U.S. and Mexican politics from left to right participates in neoliberalism, and demonstrate the devastating effect
that neoliberalism has on communities in general. Certainly
this book will help us understand the effects of neoliberalism
on the rest of the world as well; however, the glaring examples
of ongoing state sponsored violence condoned and encouraged
directly by U.S. foreign policy, transnational activity, economic
interests, the consumption of narcotics in the USA, and subsequent militarism in Mexico are profound enough to merit a
book dedicated to just the military political economy between
the USA and Mexico itself.

Secondly the purpose of the book is to share several specific
struggles in Mexico for grassroots community-based liberation
through self- determination, self-defense, and autonomy. These
are specific examples from both Native and non-Native communities in Mexico, but it is truly my belief that these examples can
serve to educate, inspire, and perhaps even spark similar movements among Black, Native, and other racialized communities
in both countries, if not the world.

By no means, however, do we assume that these specific
communities and geographies are the only ones doing so, or
that these are the only viable strategies for liberation. In fact
I think in order for us to have a much broader perspective to
adequately draw from, we must also take a look at similar communities and strategies from around the world.

Unfortunately the vast majority of literature on the subject of neoliberalism is hyper intellectualized and overly complicated. It is inaccessible to readers just trying to figure out what neoliberalism is, how it works, how it affects them both directly and indirectly, and most importantly, how to resist and ultimately dismantle it.

The book has been broken up into 20 short chapters. Quite a lot of the information, though not everything in the book, is either common knowledge or could perhaps even be considered a simplification to academics specializing in geopolitics and political economy. However, it's not at all common knowledge for average everyday folks trying to understand these complicated and intertwined aspects of the neoliberal military-political economy as a common enemy of Black, Indigenous and other racialized communities everywhere. This should allow diverse readers to pick and choose what they feel they already know and go to sections they want to read about specifically. It should also facilitate anyone wishing to reference specific sections of the book for teaching or research purposes.

The book will most certainly be incomplete and will require further critical analysis, research, and the filling in of gaps, which I hope readers will undertake and share. There also may very well be errors, misconceptions, or changes that occur, which readers can clarify with further research, analysis, and updating. I do not believe the information is infallible, and hopefully we can work together as a community to strengthen or even challenge arguments given, so that the end result can be as useful as possible to readers and their communities.

Finally as an educator and mentor I must recognize that the next generations are smarter and better equipped to undertake political economic and geopolitical analysis of this nature. I hope this book can serve young people to push these arguments to new and unforeseen areas of investigation, research, and, more importantly, towards community-based direct action for self-defense, self-determination, and autonomy.

PART ONE: NEOLIBERALISM

PART ONE
NEOLIBERAL LIE

Chapter 1
What is Neoliberalism?

In the United States in particular there is a terminological dilemma that complicates and confuses the true meaning of neoliberalism. To begin with, at its core, the meaning of the word liberal has almost totally been transformed. Liberal in the United States today nearly always refers to center-left leaning political beliefs, while liberal in the rest of the world refers to the economic system of free market (or laissez-faire) capitalism.

More specifically, liberal in the United States is associated with everything to the left of the Republican political party, including the Democrats, civil rights, human rights, social programs, multiculturalism, identity politics, environmentalism, equality, and honestly, a very watered down version of socialism.

Liberal in the United States however, apparently does not include basic internationally recognized leftist concepts such as communism and anarchism, much less any traditional Indigenous strategies for grassroots community-based liberation through self-determination, self-defense, and autonomy. In essence what the United States defines as liberal is actually quite far from what the rest of the world defines as leftist. The meaning of the word liberal has become a very limited replacement of much broader, reality encompassing leftist politics throughout the world. Liberal is defined primarily in diametrical opposition to right-wing politics, or what in the United States is referred to as conservative politics.

So again, the word liberal in neoliberalism refers to economic liberalism, or what is known as free market liberalism. This is an economic term, which is not directly related to what is referred to as liberal politics in the United States although there is a correlation between political liberalism as defined in the United States and economic liberalism. This does not surprise most people.

However, what does surprise most U.S. Americans who identify as politically liberal is how much of their politics is actually rooted in a neoliberal framework. The only apparent contribution to social change by liberal or institutional left politics in the United States is an ongoing validation of electoral politics, the non-profit industrial complex, and the global NGO (Non-Governmental Organization) phenomenon. Yet the primary function of most non-profits and NGOs is to provide a false sense of peace, tranquility, and comfort, while never actually offering dignity, justice, and liberty.

Colonialism has always justified itself through ingenuous attempts at "saving savages" from themselves. The primary method of "saving" communities has come about through different types of acculturation and assimilation. The non-profit industrial complex locally and non-governmental organizations globally have been telling us that they are saving us (mainly from our savage selves) without ever actually giving us the means for self-liberation, much less for self-determination and autonomy.

Arundhati Roy said it best in her essay "Public Power in the Age of Empire."

> It's important to turn our attention away from the positive work being done by some individual NGOs, and consider the NGO phenomenon in a broader political context...
>
> ...Their real contribution is that they defuse political anger and dole out as aid or benevolence what people ought to have by right. They alter the public psyche. They turn people into dependent victims and blunt the edges of political resistance...
>
> ...in the long run, NGOs are accountable to their funders, not to the people they work among. They're what botanists would call an indicator species. It's almost as though the greater the devastation caused by neoliberalism, the greater the outbreak of NGOs. Nothing illustrates this more poignantly than the phenomenon of the United States

preparing to invade a country and simultaneously readying NGOs to go in and clean up the devastation....

...Eventually – on a smaller scale, but more insidiously – the capital available to NGOs plays the same role in alternative politics as the speculative capital that flows in and out of the economies of poor countries. It begins to dictate the agenda.

It turns confrontation into negotiation. It depoliticizes resistance. It interferes with local people's movements that have traditionally been self-reliant. NGOs have funds that can employ local people who might otherwise be activists in resistance movements, but now can feel they are doing some immediate, creative good (and earning a living while they're at it).

Charity offers instant gratification to the giver, as well as the receiver, but its side effects can be dangerous. Real political resistance offers no such short cuts.

The NGO-isation of politics threatens to turn resistance into a well-mannered, reasonable, salaried, 9-to-5 job. With a few perks thrown in.

Real resistance has real consequences. And no salary." (1)

This is one of the most glaring flaws of liberal politics in the United States. In terms of right-wing politics, there is a misconception that conservative politicians are so very different from liberal politicians, and nothing could be further from the truth. Many believed that the arrival of the Trump presidential administration in the United States was a swift move away from neoliberalism towards fascism. However it is clear that neoliberalism has always been, and continues to be fascist at its core, regardless of whether liberals, conservatives, or outright fascists are in U.S. political office. (2)

To be clear, Reagan, Bush Sr., Clinton, Bush Jr., Obama, Trump, and Biden all serve neoliberal interests in the end, regardless of whether they call themselves liberals or conservatives, or act like fascists.

The same can be said for the Mexican presidents De la Madrid, Salinas de Gortari, Zedillo, Fox, Calderon, Peña Nieto, and Lopez Obrador.

In short, both so called liberals and conservatives in the U.S. political spectrum participate in, propagate, and perpetuate neoliberalism. And furthermore, though neoliberalism is an economic term or in its purest form an economic theory, it is in fact today a fully functioning system of political economy: the neoliberal political economy.

Neoliberalism is a system of political economy. A system of political economy is a system of government and a system of economics working together. Simply put, political economies are systems of power and money. Neoliberalism is a system of power and money.

Neoliberalism is a system of power and money that prioritizes the political and economic interests of wealthy and powerful nations, their transnational corporations, their financial institutions, and some very wealthy and influential individuals. And it does not simply prioritize these political and economic interests; it enforces them with a variety of very specific, political, economic, and military strategies.

Therefore, a more complete definition would clarify that neoliberalism is a system of military-political economy that prioritizes and enforces the interests of wealthy and powerful nations, their transnational corporations, financial institutions, and some very wealthy and influential individuals. In fact, it has become the most aggressive and prevalent system of social, political, and economic organization in the world today.

It is also important to de-intellectualize the term and clarify that neoliberalism is just a pretty way of saying and practicing capitalist imperialism. In fact, neoliberalism is nothing more than the most recent incarnation of capitalist imperialism.

Capitalism is an economic (financial) system for making money. Imperialism is a political system or strategy for gaining power. While capitalism is a system for making money by any means necessary, imperialism literally means the taking of land, labor and resources by force for power. When we say capitalist imperialism, what we are actually saying is: the taking of land, labor, and resources by force for money and power.

As the most recent incarnation of capitalist imperialism, neoliberalism does have several specific characteristics that differentiate it from previous forms of capitalist imperialism, which we will identify throughout the book. For now, one of the factors that truly differentiates neoliberalism from other forms of capitalist imperialism is the series of specific strategies it uses to create the illusion of democracy, freedom, liberty, justice, and social responsibility.

Mexico and the United States serve as excellent examples for analyzing some of these specific neoliberal characteristics and how they are interconnected. A more in-depth analysis and critique of neoliberalism and capitalist imperialism in general, but in Mexico and the United States in particular, has to include a discussion around patriarchy, white supremacy, and Christianity as well.

Patriarchy, white supremacy, and Christianity have been the forerunners and continue to be the underpinnings of the economic, military, and political system of U.S. capitalist imperialism around the world, which again, is devoted to making money and gaining power by any means necessary, including the self-legitimized use of violence and brute force.

The United States is a white, male, Christian, military-political economy that has consistently overvalued the lives of white Christian men above all other lives. As a matter of fact, the natural resources that are extracted from this earth to maintain white, Christian, and male dominance over the planet, are considered more valuable than all lives. Most human life has simply become just another disposable variable in the equation of the neoliberal military-political economy for white, male, Christian wealth and power.

If you are not contributing to white, male, Christian wealth and power, then you are considered disposable. If you are creating real alternatives, or worse yet, challenging and confronting the wealth and power of white, male Christian supremacy, then you are considered a threat. Indeed, successful alternatives and confrontations are treated as military targets.

For example, when it comes to Israel and Judaism, the Zionist nation-state of Israel absolutely maintains U.S. based white, male, Christian power in Palestine. To this end, Israel is protected by the U.S. military-political economy of neoliberalism.

The military-political economy under which we exist is classist, racist, patriarchal, fascist, supremacist, and genocidal at its core. Black and Indigenous communities, in particular women from these communities, have been living under a continuous colonialism built upon humiliation, torture, slavery, and genocide.

What the neoliberals, in particular left-leaning neoliberals, would have us believe is that they have finally figured out a democratic and socially responsible way of engaging in capitalist imperialism. This is the ultimate lie of neoliberalism, and one of the primary characteristics that differentiates neoliberalism from other forms of capitalist imperialism. Neoliberals love to present themselves as persons involved in democratizing society.

It is impossible to forcibly take people's land, labor, and resources for power and money in order to maintain white male, Christian, supremacy around the world in a "democratic" and socially responsible way. It simply cannot be done.

The propaganda and mass-media manipulation that champion this military-political economy as a democracy or democratizing endeavor, are fundamental elements of neoliberalism just as paramilitary death squads are; both exhibit yet other specific characteristics of neoliberalism as they perpetuate its "deniable atrocities." (3)

The United States in particular has been living on a manufactured political pendulum, which supposedly swings left and right. That pendulum, however, has only swung far enough to the left to force it to swing to the extreme right over and over again. That left swing is and always has been a lie because it has continued to maintain a military-political economy through white, male, Christian, supremacy. Yes, even with a Black president, who dropped nearly three bombs an hour on racialized communities around the world for eight years, and deported more undocumented people than any other president in U.S. history.

All presidents and their political parties are nothing more than managers of a store owned by very powerful corporate and banking mafias, who again, maintain power and wealth through white, male, Christian supremacy and a military-political economy.

Absolutely no type of political or legislative reform or political party or platform is ever going to end this.

Neoliberalism does a wonderful job of propagating the illusion of democracy, inclusion, diversity, liberty, and freedom while in fact maintaining quite the opposite by systemically opposing grassroots community-based liberation through self-determination, self-defense, and autonomy.

Community-Based

Community can be defined in a variety of ways. For the purposes of this book in particular, when I say community-based, I am referring specifically to a group of individuals sharing a geographic space or territory with some sort of identity or connection to that territory. In this book, the specific examples presented are of students, residents of a city or town, and Indigenous Peoples each with a shared territory. The ability to engage in community-based self-determination, self-defense, and autonomy, however, is not limited to these sub-groups, but rather includes any group of people sharing a territory.

Community-based self-determination exists when a community has the collective power to decide what is in its own best interest. Community-based self-defense exists when a community has the means, strategies, and tactics necessary to collectively defend its right to self-determination.

Community-based autonomy exists when a community achieves its ability to collectively carry out and build upon the decisions it has made in its own collective self-interest. Though community-based autonomy is the goal, even among the examples presented in the book, none of the communities is completely autonomous, but rather all either walked or are currently walking towards autonomy.

Chapter 2
How Did it Come to Be?

In order to talk about the roots of neoliberalism today we have to take a serious historical look at the roots of U.S. American capitalist imperialism. These roots are colonialism, genocide, human trafficking, and slavery. These are the true forefathers of the United States.

The other so-called forefathers of the United States who signed the Declaration of Independence, were of course, overwhelmingly slave owners. Yes, including George Washington, Thomas Jefferson and Ben Franklin. (1)

The elementary school fable about George Washington's "wooden dentures" is a lie as they were not wooden at all, but rather were actual teeth extracted and sold at a low cost from Black human beings owned as slaves. (2)

Thomas Jefferson spent years raping and fathering children with Sally Hemmings, a Black woman he owned as a slave. (3)

Andrew Jackson, the seventh president of the United States was a slaver who justified the genocide of Indigenous tribes across the territory through legislation and specific acts of military brutality to enforce the laws that he promoted. (4)

Abraham Lincoln is recognized as having signed the Emancipation Proclamation, which on paper ended slavery in the United States, yet he ordered the hanging of 38 Sioux warriors on December 26, 1862, right in the middle of the U.S. Civil War, but never ordered the execution of any of the Confederate officials or generals. (5)

These are only a few of so many other historical white male Christian supremacist roots of the birth of the so-called USA. What is clear, however, is that in order for the United States to have become the modern day "superpower" that it is today, all of this must be factored in. What has in fact "made America great" above all else is greed, and the unbridled violence necessary to feed that greed. It is this same greed and unbridled violence that is at the core of neoliberalism today.

Selling neoliberalism to U.S. Americans

From 1970 to 1996 a television talk show by the name of "Donahue" hosted by its protagonist Phil Donahue ran over 7000 episodes of daytime TV covering a range of topics of interest to American families across the board. The Donahue show preceded the ever famous Oprah Winfrey show by 16 years. At the time, the show had the tremendous power of changing public opinion around a variety of issues.

On two different occasions, once in 1979 and once in 1980, Donahue hosted a special guest by the name of Milton Friedman, an economist and statistician. This was the first time that this goofy yet very charismatic economist had the opportunity to be heard by average everyday Americans on a syndicated national television platform, as opposed to being heard only in academic or political circles.

Though there are many other fathers of neoliberal economic theory and neoliberal political economic praxis, Friedman is the only one who was featured on daytime TV before a nationwide audience in the United States.

Donahue, standing in awe of Friedman's way of thinking, introduces him and paraphrases his book *Free to Choose* (6):

> We have too much government. We are not allowing the free enterprise system to work as your favorite historical figure Adam Smith had suggested it would work, if we just left things alone. We have too much government intervention. It is interrupting the wonderful work that the invisible hand does if we leave it alone, but it is also depriving people of personal liberties.

Friedman followed this introduction up with:

> There is a very important role for the government to play, but there is such a thing as too much of a good thing, and the government has been growing beyond bounds... The government is too big. It is too intrusive. It restricts what we can do. It is becoming our master instead of our servant. We've got to act against it and cut it down to size.

As their conversation progresses with camera shots cutting to the faces of predominantly white middle-class American moms in the studio audience, Donahue plays the role of the concerned citizen and asks Friedman how, with zero government intervention, are we supposed to prevent monopolies from happening? To which Friedman responds:

> If you want to catch a thief you send a thief. If you want to catch a businessman monopoly you send another businessman to break it down. You don't send a government civil servant after them. The most effective anti-monopoly legislation you could possibly have would be free trade.

Towards the end of the show after Friedman explicitly argues against any government intervention with regards to illegal drug use, Donahue cites the fact that if Ronald Reagan, who was set to be the next U.S. President, were to take on Friedman's absolute laissez-faire approach to government he would undoubtedly lose the presidency, to which Friedman's response was:

> Fortunately, one of the great virtues of being a college professor is that you can say exactly what you believe and what you mean. I am not running for office, I've never run for office, I have no desire to run for office, and so I regard it as a great luxury that I can be irresponsible.

To the sound of a great applause, which was most probably prompted by the show's producers, the show cuts to a commercial. (7)
What is clear is that through his visits on the Donahue show,

Friedman was able to make some very unpopular ideas about politics and economics significantly more popular than ever before. Though his laissez-faire approach to government (for example the legalization of all drugs and narcotics) as a whole would be too radical for the staunchly Christian and conservative Ronald Reagan presidency from 1981 to 1989, what would be adopted and implemented with all the power of the law and military might, would be free market capitalism or specifically free trade, privatization, austerity measures, and a foreign policy based upon the imposition of a neoliberal military-political economy around the world.

What exactly is free market capitalism and free trade?

Free market capitalism, also known as laissez-faire capitalism, basically means unregulated capitalism (making profits by any means necessary, without restriction). Laissez-faire is French for "let it be." The basic idea is that governments should not intervene in business and thus, the markets will regulate themselves through the power of the consumer's right to choose. The reality is that proponents and benefactors of laissez-faire capitalism, or free market capitalism are almost always big business, i.e. transnational corporations and international financial institutions or banks, and the very few billionaires who rake in the profits.

Free trade, simply put, is laissez-faire capitalism applied to international trade. So this would specifically entail the deregulation of the manufacture, importation and exportation of goods, services, and raw materials. We will look at the effects of free trade in particular in the chapter on the effects of neoliberalism.

The word "free" in free market capitalism and in free trade is in direct relation to the freedom of transnational corporations and financial institutions to conduct business for profit with the least amount of regulation or intervention into their activities. This refers specifically to taxes, tariffs, and regulations such as environmental, and labor regulations that are intended to protect the natural environment from pollution, contamination, or devastation, and protections for workers in terms of wages, labor rights, and working conditions. Though it is never explicitly mentioned, this would also include freedom from the intervention of individuals or communities directly or indirectly affected by the for-profit activities of transnational corporations and financial institutions.

Privatization

One of the most fundamental functions of capitalist imperialism, and neoliberalism is the maintenance of private property and the privatization of resources and services available to citizens of a nation-state. In the United States, private property and privatization are at the core of the nation-state's foundation, beginning with the colonization of the territory and the legal use of slave labor. Private property and privatization are so ingrained in U.S. history that today, with the exception of some Indigenous reservations, and very few community gardens, the fact that public spaces have been reduced to nothing more than public parks, and libraries is a normal aspect of daily life in the United States. Even so, public green spaces are subjected to heavy surveillance by a police state that may enact violence on homeless people and other marginalized communities. The concept of communally or collectively owned land or organizing spaces is so foreign at this point, that it is associated with un-Americanism.

For the benefactors of neoliberalism, the privatization of higher education, health care, and public services such as electricity, water, and transportation has become synonymous with freedom, liberty, and independence; any alternative is now synonymous with "socialism" or "outright communism."

What is particularly contradictory here is that it takes a tremendous amount of government, effort, legislation and tax money to employ all of these austerity measures that generate poverty and trauma among the general population, leading to further spending on policing and militarizing communities in response to this poverty and trauma. **(8)** This is not a broken system. It is a system that is working perfectly well to keep poor people poor, and make rich people richer with violence and brute force.

The U.S. government in particular is spending more and more

on policing, while simultaneously cutting the mental health and social services that would be necessary to effectively and efficiently address the effects of extreme poverty: low wages, high rents, alcohol and drug addiction, domestic violence, and mental health crises, just to mention a few clear examples.

In terms of foreign policy, the imposition of the austerity measures brought forth by the neoliberal political economy is enforced by militarism. While U.S. military spending far exceeds that of any other nation-state, it is simultaneously exporting a culture of militarism to nation-states such as Mexico through direct weapons sales, financing, training, and equipment. What in turn is taking place in Mexico is a strategy of internal defense wherein the military itself is being used as the primary public security force with a particular offensive against Indigenous communities engaging in grassroots liberation through community-based self-determination, self-defense, and autonomy.

Based on the way in which the debate for or against neoliberalism is set up, however, one would either have to be for government intervention in business and public life, which is also known as Keynesian economics or protectionism, or one would have to be against government intervention, a hands-off approach to business in particular. Third, fourth, or fifth options do not even enter the debate. The fundamental problem with the framework of this debate is that it assumes the legitimacy, legality, and honesty of governments and businesses to begin with, while in reality governments and businesses are at the very least corruptible if not absolutely inherently corrupt.

As far as this book is concerned, supporting either argument would require succumbing to the corrupt nature of governments and businesses. We are clearly in a global political and economic situation in which transnational corporations, banking institutions, and governments have been allowed to pretend to take care of us and Mother Earth; this has been devastating and must be critically re-evaluated immediately.

The Birth of Neoliberalism

The current incarnation of neoliberalism began as a fascist military-political economy under the dictatorship of Augusto Pinochet in the South American nation of Chile from September 11, 1973 to 1990. The democratically elected socialist government of Salvador Allende was overturned by a military coup that was supported by the U.S. government with direct involvement by the Central Intelligence Agency at the command of at least two major U.S. based transnational corporations: International Telephone & Telegraph (ITT) and the Anaconda Mining Corporation. **(9)**

Immediately after Salvador Allende was assassinated, his administration was replaced by a military dictatorship led by General Augusto Pinochet. Pinochet would go down in history as an absolute tyrant who, among his many atrocities, had dissidents thrown alive from helicopters. His opponents were detained in concentration camps, murdered, and tortured relentlessly by military forces with commanding officers who had received training at the U.S. Army School of the Americas or S.O.A. **(10)** I have dedicated an entire chapter to the S.O.A. later in the book.

In 1973, as Pinochet took power by force with the use of S.O.A. trained military officials, a group of Chilean economists who were educated at the University of Chicago's School of Economics (under the auspices of economic theorists such as Milton Friedman) simultaneously returned to Chile with an economic and political model for the military government of Chile. They came back home with a book titled *The Brick: Foundations of the Political Economy of the Chilean Military Government.* **(11)** The book is a compilation of research and discussions on political economy among these Chilean economists and academics from the Chicago School of Economics. This book in essence imposed a military, political, and economic model based upon the interests of transnational corporations and financial institutions over the basic human and civil rights of the Chilean people in the middle of a fascist military dictatorship. The neoliberal military-political economy was literally born. In Chile, and later throughout the Americas, the military-political economy of neoliberalism would become known as "the model." It is imperative to note that U.S. President Richard Nixon and U.S. Secretary of State Henry Kissinger absolutely supported and aided the military dictatorship in Chile. U.S. support of repressive governments that imposed the U.S. military-political economy was and continues to be constant and unwavering. Today, after some decades of flirting with a facade of democracy in the post Dirty War era, neoliberalism is returning to its military and fascist roots. It would make even more sense to argue that neoliberalism has been military and fascist all along.

Since this era of "anti-communist" military dictatorships established throughout South and Central America, Mexico, and the Caribbean, known as the "Dirty War Era," neoliberalism has consistently attempted to give the illusion of progress towards social responsibility and "democracy" while in fact, intentionally engaging in quite the opposite. I put the words anti-communist in quotations because much more than anti-communist, the dictatorships were pro-neoliberalism in general and pro U.S. foreign policy in particular. Chile has since been touted as a stellar example of how neoliberalism can be a great success for democracy, and Friedman himself even referred to it as "Chile's Miracle." **(12)** This, however, has never been true for average everyday Chilean people or for the entirety of the working poor throughout the Americas either.

The popular uprising that we saw in Chile in 2019 happened because neoliberalism has continued to benefit the top 1% of the population, the Chilean elite, and is devastating the nation's poor and working class. Neoliberalism in Chile still consists of a fascist dictatorship, except that now it is international, financial, transnational, and corporate, pretending to be democratic while generating a tremendous wealth gap. In Chile, this is what democracy looks like. And it is not only true for Chile and all of Latin America, but for the whole world. The roots of neoliberalism are fascist military dictatorships, and though neoliberalism has tried to give the illusion of democracy, it has continued to be economic, political, and military fascism. Today we are undoubtedly seeing a worldwide shift towards unabated, full-blown right-wing fascism wherein authoritarian governments wish to impose a military-political economy by using even more brute force with less theatrics.

Chapter 3
Who is Responsible?

The most profitable industries in the world are those backed by the institutions, and governments that benefit the most from the neoliberal military-political economy. These include, but are not limited to mining, pharmaceuticals, weapons, real estate, prison, manufacturing, food and agriculture, mainstream media industries and, of course, international financial and banking institutions. I would also venture to say that the individuals who benefit most from the neoliberal military-political economy are the 2755 billionaires around the world. Together these industries, institutions, governments, and individuals make up the global oligarchy responsible for the neoliberal military-political economy. (1)

In addition to this vast oligarchy that benefits the most from neoliberalism, the average everyday citizens from the privileged political class of the wealthiest countries in the world also benefit greatly. Though they do not rake in the profits, they do enjoy a certain peace, tranquility, and comfort that the rest of the world certainly does not. They don't experience the constant brute force that militarized communities live through day in and day out. They have "basic" things like drinking water, running water, hot water, air conditioning and heat, electricity, food, medicine, education, and shelter. They have a semblance of democracy in which they seem to believe. This is not to say for example, that all U.S. citizens or residents have the same privileges, and comforts, but rather that enough of the citizens with political agency in these countries enjoy the benefits of neoliberalism enough to have kept it alive and well all this time.

In the most powerful countries in the world, neoliberalism provides products and merchandise to its citizens who have little or no consciousness of their origin: watches, phones, computers, tablets, video games, automobiles, airplanes, gasoline, shoes, clothes, jewelry, chocolate, coffee etc.

There is a long list of minerals that must be mined in order to produce and maintain cutting-edge communications technology. Where are these mines? Whose communities are affected by them? Are there environmental consequences to mining? Who is doing the actual mining? Are workers paid a fair wage? Are neighboring communities affected? Does mining have health consequences?

In terms of fashion, it is no secret that the cotton industry exploits land and labor around the world. What about the laborers working to make your new blue jeans? Are they paid a fair wage, or are they exploited to provide you with a cheaper pair? You might say, "But wait, my jeans aren't cheap and I work hard to buy them." What if I told you that most laborers in denim factories around the world would have to work two whole months in order to afford one pair of your jeans? How expensive do they feel now?

How about all that bling? Where do gold, silver, diamonds and platinum come from? Are there children mining it? What effect does its extraction have on the natural environment? Whose blood, sweat, and tears went into making that tennis bracelet, or those diamond studs that you got on sale at the mall?

And yet, with all of these products and merchandise, most citizens of wealthy countries are not reaping the billions in profits from these sales. (2) In fact it would seem that most citizens are simply living blindly in prisons of their own comfort. Surrounded by the illusion of endless choices, like "which hair gel works best for me," these privileged citizens are kept complacent. And this happens while transnational corporations, financial institutions, billionaires, and politicians make tremendous profits off of the destructive natural resource extraction and exploited labor practices that go into manufacturing all of these products.

All of these things are taken for granted although they have always come on the backs, sweat, and blood of others. Neoliberalism has been able to persist primarily by providing relative peace, tranquility, and comfort to a select group of privileged citizens in the most powerful nations in the world.

The rest of the population, in particular poor people in these powerful countries and average, everyday citizens around the world, are either blinded by their own prisons of consumerist comfort or they no longer believe the lie that the current political economic system is about peace, prosperity, and democracy. Most can clearly and irrefutably see that neoliberalism is a violent and corrupt system of government, business, and finance that truly benefits a highly select few while systemically subjugating and oppressing the rest of the world. Though the evidence is clear, not many people have the political agency and ability to do anything about it.

There are several questions you must answer for yourself about neoliberalism: Where on this spectrum do I stand? Am I one of the select few who truly benefit from neoliberalism? Am I one of the citizens of a country that is kept complacent by the comforts provided to me by neoliberalism? Am I one of the disposable variables in the economic equation of neoliberalism? Am I or is my community targeted by neoliberalism? Am I a threat to neoliberalism? Do I care that I may benefit, although just a little bit, from neoliberalism while others suffer its atrocities? Is my peace, tranquility, and comfort built on the backs, sweat, and blood of others through neoliberalism? Do I want to change this? What am I willing to do to change this?

One of the major difficulties that communities have in confronting neoliberalism is in identifying exactly who or what they are confronting. In a lot of ways neoliberalism is like a headless octopus with many more than eight tentacles. I say headless because there really is no one leader but rather a collective system of powerful countries, government institutions, financial institutions, transnational corporations, industries, billionaires, and I would also add, criminal organizations. **(3)**

The relationship between organized crime and the military-political economy of neoliberalism is more irrefutable now than ever. One could reasonably argue that organized crime is an integral component of neoliberalism. **(4)**

It is important to make a list of specific agents of neoliberalism, discussing briefly how and why each is included in this list. The list will be incomplete, however my hope is that it will help readers to think critically of who and what should be included and why, and therefore more easily identify agents as they may arise or be noticed. Some of the more glaring examples have entire chapters dedicated to them in this book.

The different agents of neoliberalism I would like to discuss can mostly be broken down into what are known as "industrial complexes." According to Wikipedia, an industrial complex

> is a socioeconomic concept whereby businesses become entwined in social or political systems or institutions, creating or bolstering a profit economy from these systems. Such a complex is said to pursue its own financial interests regardless of, and often at the expense of, the best interests of society and individuals. Businesses within an industrial complex may have been created to advance a social or political goal, but mostly profit when the goal is not reached. The industrial complex may profit financially from maintaining socially detrimental or inefficient systems.

The Political Industrial Complex would include the complex systems of local, state, and federal institutional governments of nation-states, and their political parties around the world. A critical analysis of the Political Industrial Complex has to include a critique of electoral politics in and of itself, political parties and their candidates as a whole, and institutional forms of governance as a whole as well, but in particular, centralized forms of institutional governance. This industrial complex is in essence omnipresent and would include virtually all the other industrial complexes within it; however, it contains within itself factors such as campaign financing, gerrymandering, voter suppression, lobbying, and a legal and legislative framework, which together are the bases for the legitimized institutional political corruption of all the other industrial complexes.

The Business Industrial Complex would include transnational corporations and the business industries in which they engage. This is the most diverse of the industrial complexes in that it includes all of the manufacturing industries, such as weapons, transportation, consumer goods, electronics, chemicals, pharmaceuticals, paper, printing and publishing, plastics, industrial equipment, furniture and fixtures, building materials, fashion, sporting goods, toys, household goods, etc. It would also include the entire food and animal feed industry, such as agriculture, food processing, food packaging, food storage and transportation, etc. There is also the entire media communications industry, including telecommunications, TV, film and video, photo, radio, newspapers magazines and books etc. The Business Industrial Complex is such a giant that it has to be broken down into several smaller parts in order to be digested, however when treated as its own entire independent industrial complex, we can fathom the vastness of its political and economic power, scope, and influence.

The Banking Industrial Complex would include all banks and international financial institutions, as well as financial regulatory agencies and institutions, chambers of commerce, international trade and investment, the stock market, and monetary regulating institutions. It is important to note that banks usually hold controlling interest in most transnational corporations as well, and are the largest holders and purveyors of private property in the world. One way or another, banks and financial institutions also hold and benefit from all business activity, be it public or private, legitimate or criminal.

The Military Industrial Complex would include all weapons and weapons technology manufacturers, all armed forces and police, all private military police and security contractors, and the local, state, and federal governments that employ them. (The Military Industrial Complex in particular is simultaneously part of the Business Industrial Complex and the Political Industrial Complex.)

The Prison Industrial Complex would include the entire prison industry, both private and public, as well as the entire justice system including the courts, the police, bail bonds, and probation and parole industries. An excellent book on the Prison Industrial Complex is Michelle Alexander's *The New Jim Crow*. (5)

The Media Industrial Complex which would include telecommunications (cell phone and internet), TV, film and videos, photos, radios, newspapers, magazines, and books, etc.

The Legal Industrial Complex overlaps with the prison industrial complex but also includes the wide variety of lawyers outside of the criminal justice system. It also overlaps with the Political Industrial Complex in terms of legislation and public policy and regulations.

The Agricultural Industrial Complex is included in the Business Industrial Complex but is vast enough in its political and economic power, scope, and influence that it must be designated as its very own industrial complex.

The Food Manufacture Industrial Complex is also included in the Business Industrial Complex but is vast enough in its political and economic power, scope, and influence that it must be designated as its very own Industrial Complex.

The Natural Resource Extraction Industrial Complex (mining, biodiversity, lumber and water, gas, oil) is also included in the Business Industrial Complex but is vast enough in its political and economic power, scope, and influence that it must be designated as its very own industrial complex.

The Academic Industrial Complex includes all educational institutions, but particularly higher learning institutions such as colleges and universities, their administrators and professors, and the industries they work with or feed into directly and indirectly. In countries like the United States and Chile, for example, the private higher education industry also includes its own student debt industry which stands aside from the Banking Industrial Complex because of its relationship to higher education.

As a critical thinker, one turns to academia to attempt to decipher and make a little bit of sense out of the complex reality of the world around us, and again, academia predominantly falls short of feeding knowledge back into communities outside of academic circles so that they may self-evaluate and flourish. Knowledge has become the specialty of a privileged few, who instead of spreading, sharing, and building more knowledge through community work, have concentrated knowledge into a competitive, for-profit industry, a knowledge industry if you will.

At the end of the day, when it comes to grassroots community liberation through self-determination, self-defense, and autonomy in particular, most academics have spent a lot more time intellectualizing than actually liberating, pontificating instead of contributing, and publishing instead of acting. In the realm of academia, with very few exceptions, traditional Indigenous forms of grassroots community liberation are treated as obsolete and extinct; therefore, any historical reference to this type of liberation is almost always reduced to a footnote, spectacle, or is rendered completely inadmissible to the discussion.

The Healthcare and Pharmaceuticals Industrial Complex would include the entire healthcare industry, including hospitals, clinics, private practices, doctors, nurses, and administrators as well as the entire pharmaceutical industry, biomedical engineering, and research and development industries. It should be noted that the pharmaceutical industry also merits its own chapter in this book as a primary culprit of narcotics addiction in the USA.

The non-profit Non-Governmental Organization (NGO) Industrial Complex includes all nonprofits and NGOs, their executive officers, their staff, their funders, the government agencies and philanthropic organizations that they are associated with, and all of their activities. Though there is a lot of very good work being done by many nonprofits and NGOs, the nonprofit and NGO phenomenon is an integral component of the neoliberal military-political economy.

The Organized Crime Industrial Complex would include all organized criminal enterprises; the criminal activities in which they engage, including the manufacture, marketing, and sale of narcotics, weapons, security, protection, human trafficking, human organ trafficking, the transportation and storage of all illegal substances; and the legitimizing businesses, industries, and even banking institutions that "launder" criminal profits for them.

The Billionaire Industrial Complex may not be considered an industrial complex in itself by other analysts; however, in addition to benefiting from one or another of the other industrial complexes, these 2755 billionaires merit their own personal mention because of the amount of wealth and power concentrated among such a small number of individuals in the world.

The U.S. American, Canadian, and European people in particular are not an industrial complex unto themselves either, but in general they benefit from one or many of the industrial complexes in terms of privilege, wealth, political access, peace, tranquility, and power. Though one could argue that ignorance is the primary driving force behind their participation in the global military-political economy, I would argue that apathy, comfort, individualism and complacency play a much larger role in their continuous consent and participation in the neoliberal military-political economy in particular, and in capitalist imperialism in general.

These are very few and very brief examples, but they can help us begin to understand the complexity and headless multi-tentacled nature of the global military-political economy. I am certain that each reader will be able to think of other examples, and may wish to join in a teaching and learning exercise of sharing and expanding upon this list and deepening our basic understanding of the different agents of neoliberalism today.

Chapter 4
How Does Neoliberalism Affect Communities?

What neoliberalism does in fact do, is commodify life itself. The worth of human lives and of all living things on this earth is quantified. What is put on the neoliberal scale is the worth of natural resources over the worth of life. On one end of the scale we have all living things on this earth, including human beings and Mother Earth herself. On the other end of the scale we have the economic value of natural resources and the desire to extract them for the wealth and power of white male Christian supremacists. Our current climate crisis rests primarily on the shoulders of neoliberal extractive and manufacturing policies with no regard for the environment whatsoever.

Neoliberalism, like capitalist imperialism, has always reduced life as we know it into disposable variables in an economic, political, and military equation. All forms of life on earth are considered disposable in this equation whose sole purpose is to gain wealth and power through the control of territory, extraction of natural resources, and exploitation of labor. Neoliberalism is, in essence, a global system of oligarchy: a small group of people who have taken absolute control over the earth, its people, and its natural resources.

Entire ecosystems and sectors of society are considered disposable in this military-political economy. Workers, students, teachers, farmers, peasants, Black people, Indigenous people, other People(s) of Color, Muslims, women, young people, poor people, and in particular Black and Indigenous women are considered disposable and displaceable in this political economic equation. If one or several of these sectors of society begin to organize successfully for grassroots liberation through community-based self-determination, self-defense, and autonomy, they cease to be considered mere disposable variables, and are transformed into threats and, therefore, specific military targets.

What we have collectively learned through decades of surviving neoliberalism is that contrary to the dominant media narrative, the greatest threat to this military-political economy has never been communism, terrorism, the narcotics trade, or so called "organized crime," but rather grassroots liberation through community-based organizing for self-determination, self-defense, and autonomy. This is particularly true when it comes to a community defending a specific territory that holds an economic interest for governments, financial institutions, transnational corporations, and capitalists in general.

Another irrefutable fact is that the vast majority of these territories are being defended by Indigenous people across the globe. And to be absolutely clear, the vast majority are being defended by Indigenous communities that have traditional cultural practices, strategies, and self-governing models for grassroots liberation through community-based self-determination, self-defense, and autonomy.

The North American Free Trade Agreement (NAFTA)

The North American Free Trade Agreement was first signed and sent for ratification in 1992 by Canada, the USA, and Mexico, and was officially ratified in 1993. (1) It is important to note that the idea of NAFTA in the USA was originally initiated by the presidency of Ronald Reagan, a Republican, was signed by George Bush Sr., a Republican, and was brought into fruition under the presidency of Bill Clinton, a Democrat. (2) Their participation in making NAFTA a reality demonstrates that all three presidents were proponents of the neoliberal military-political economy.

Therefore again, the word "Free" in the North American Free Trade Agreement refers specifically to freedom from taxes, tariffs, and regulations protecting the environment or laborers; measures intended to protect the natural environment from pollution, contamination, or devastation; and initiatives for the protection of workers in terms of wages, labor rights, and working conditions. Though it is never explicitly mentioned, this would also include freedom from the intervention of individuals or communities directly or indirectly affected by the for-profit activities of transnational corporations, financial institutions, and the local business political elite. In Mexico, this really is where the horror story begins.

After the initial signing of NAFTA in 1992, then Mexican President Carlos Salinas de Gortari reformed Article 27 of the Mexican Constitution. This constitutional article had granted very specific protections for ownership of communal land by Indigenous Peoples in Mexico. In essence the Article made it law that the lands held by Indigenous Peoples would be held communally and would never be exposed to privatization and/or the sale of individual lots to anyone, particularly not to foreign investors. **(3)**

The Mexican Constitution of 1917 was ratified by the government that came about as a result of the Mexican Revolution, and Article 27 was one of the most important aspects of the Constitution for Indigenous communities. Unlike the reservation system in the United States, Indigenous Peoples in Mexico were granted communal or collective ownership of the territory upon which they had resided up to that historical moment. **(4)**

What the constitutional reform to Article 27 did was reverse these protections and make it legal for the communally held lands (or *ejidos*) to be parceled into individual lots and titled as private property by individual "heads of households" who could, in turn, do whatever they wanted with their parcels. This specifically made it legally possible to sell the parcels to individuals, businesses, transnational corporations, and/or national and international investors from outside the local Indigenous communities. **(5)**

The constitutional reform of Article 27 was followed up immediately by a government program known as PROCEDE: Program for Certification of Rights to Ejido Lands, which was put into place to certify and convert the formerly communal owned land into individual lots and parcels of private property. **(6)**

It is important to note that primarily due to Indigenous cultural roots, values, world-views, and communal self-governing structures, as well as militancy in the Indigenous communities that understand the significance and importance of communal land ownership for their very survival, the constitutional reform and

PROCEDE program have been largely unsuccessful to date in privatizing Indigenous land in Mexico. This is so true that what the Mexican government, transnational corporations, local land barons, and criminal organizations began to enact and are enacting as I write this book are violent strategies of displacement and land expropriations, which we will discuss further in the chapter about militarism. Nonetheless, the reform of Article 27 and the PROCEDE program were regarded as major threats to Indigenous self-determination, self-defense, and autonomy in all of Mexico. (7)

An equally alarming threat to the Indigenous farm-working population throughout Mexico had to do specifically with the Free Trade importation of U.S. corn to Mexico. Here it is important to understand the historical roots, importance, and significance of corn to Mexican Indigenous populations. Corn was first domesticated by and became the primary staple crop of Indigenous Mesoamerican populations. In simpler terms, one could say that Indigenous communities in Mesoamerica, which includes Mexico, basically invented corn. There has been absolutely no need for corn from the United States, in particular genetically modified yellow or white corn, to be imported to Mexico at all.

The following question is, if Mexico's Indigenous population invented corn, has produced corn for thousands of years, and has made it the staple crop for the survival of its communities to this very day, how did the United States manage to import corn to Mexico and make it available at a cheaper price than Mexico's own Indigenous people could? The answer is that the U.S. corn agribusiness received a ridiculous number of government tax write-offs and direct subsidies to produce corn that was cheaper. The government paid U.S. agribusiness corn producers to produce corn cheaper than they could without that government support.

Why? By undercutting the price of corn produced by Indigenous farmers in Mexico, corn production for them is rendered an unviable means of survival, which in essence makes communal ownership of Indigenous land economically unsustainable in an imposed free market economy. This, coming on the heels of the reform of Article 27 of the Mexican Constitution, was a not so subtle act of genocide. Today, similar political economic strategies have been applied to coffee, beans, and other staple crops of Indigenous communities throughout Mexico.

There are many other examples of how NAFTA was a direct threat to Mexico's Indigenous communities, but with these two, we have more than enough to understand how this trade agreement embodies some of the worst aspects of neoliberalism.

A final detail about NAFTA that I find absolutely devastating to average everyday folks, but in particular to Indigenous communities that wish to defend and protect their territories not just in Mexico, but in Canada and the United States, as well, has to do with a specific stipulation in the NAFTA document called Chapter 11. Most U.S. Americans think of a bankruptcy law when they hear Chapter 11, but this is something completely different.

The entire NAFTA document is 1700 pages long. Of these, 741 pages are the treaty document itself, 348 pages are dedicated to annexes, and 619 are dedicated to footnotes and explanations. Needless to say it is a tedious and boring document. The section of the document dedicated to Chapter 11 under NAFTA is 27 pages long. It in and of itself is a tough legalese read, but is critical for understanding the political and economic imposition it explicitly entails. **(8)**

Chapter 11 stipulates that the free trade agreement is intended to allow for 1. the unrestricted and unregulated flow of capital investment, and 2. the unrestricted and unregulated undertaking of the business activity for which the investment was made. Therefore, no entity, industry, institution, agency, individual, community or local, state or federal government itself has any legal recourse to hinder, halt, or prevent said investment activity from taking place regardless of environmental, labor, or even human rights measures that are afflicted by the activity. **(9)**

If any entity, industry, institution, agency, individual, community or local, state and federal government does anything to hinder, halt, or prevent said investment activity from taking place, the investor, in most cases a transnational corporation, has the right to sue the entity, industry, institution, agency, individual, community or local, state and federal government hindering said investment activity.

So if a transnational corporation that has invested in a territory to engage in agricultural practices, mining activity, or anything that can have adverse effects on the natural environment or on the health of workers, or a community and its members in proximity to the investment territory, is in anyway hindered or halted from continuing said activity, Chapter 11 of NAFTA grants the investor the right to legally sue whomever is doing the hindering or halting, again, even if it is the federal government of the nation itself.

In essence Chapter 11 is an absolutely legally binding subversion of national sovereignty in favor of the investor regardless of the threat posed to the natural environment, the well-being of workers, or the well-being of individuals and communities in proximity to the investment activity. As a subversion of national sovereignty it is an absolute annihilation of an individual's or a community's right to halt threats to their well-being, for example, by a mining operation that is polluting or devastating primary sources of drinking water.

However, there is a method through Chapter 11 that allows entities, industries, institutions, agencies, individuals, communities or local, state and federal governments to be heard when a concern arises. They can each appeal to a NAFTA Chapter 11 tribunal, which in practice has honestly been consistently partial to the investors to date.

Under the Trump administration NAFTA was rewritten, changed, and ratified as the USMCA: the U.S., Mexico, Canada Agreement. One fundamental change in the USMCA is that Canada has opted out completely, and the United States has also further protected itself from the Chapter 11 stipulations, but Mexico, as the primary purveyor of raw materials, natural resources and cheap labor of the agreement, must continue to adhere to most of the rules of Chapter 11 when trading with the U.S.A. **(10)**

So the rich countries were tired of having their national sovereignty subverted by transnational corporations, but Mexico was literally bullied with the threat of a trade blockade if it did not agree to the USMCA and continued adherence to Chapter 11 stipulations. **(11)**

In response to the privatization and austerity measures within

NAFTA, the revocation of Article 27 of the Mexican Constitution, the introduction of foreign crops through transnational agro-industries, the natural resource extractivism, the labor exploitation, and the Chapter 11 stipulations of NAFTA that threaten national sovereignty and Indigenous autonomy, there has been a tremendous amount of community-based organizing and resistance in communities throughout Mexico and in particular Indigenous communities. This resistance has been met with a variety of state-sponsored strategies, including low intensity warfare to carry out deniable atrocities through the use of paramilitary forces. **(12)**

Paramilitaries are armed civilians who receive training, support, and financing, or simply receive impunity from official entities such as a political party, a government administration, the police, or the military. A paramilitary organization may also be generated and supported by non-governmental institutions including corporations, banks, or individuals such as wealthy local land owners or the political elite as well.

Paramilitary forces use violence to carry out social, political or economic objectives against a target civilian population that is either considered a disposable variable, a barrier, or a direct threat to a given political, economic, or military interest.

The primary purpose and function of paramilitarism is to generate and exploit what are known as "deniable atrocities". That is to say, its forces carry out atrocities such as extrajudicial executions, kidnappings, beatings, rape, and torture against a civilian population in such a way that governments, police, or the military can deny involvement in and/or responsibility for those atrocities once committed. These atrocities are used to dissuade social, political, or economic opposition.

A key calling card of paramilitarism is the implementation of its atrocities with total impunity. It is impunity of this nature that further delegitimizes governments and their justice systems all together.

When a paramilitary group is generated from a local population to cause internal conflict in a target region, oftentimes ideological, political, religious, cultural, geographic, or social differences between opposing groups are exploited to generate violent confrontations.

A common end result of the deniable atrocities carried out by heavily armed paramilitaries around the world is the formalized militarization, policing, and criminalization of a community, organization, group, or individual being targeted.

Chapter 5
The Zapatista National Liberation Army - EZLN

In Mexico, the North American Free Trade Agreement (NAFTA), was a direct hit to Indigenous autonomy. The day that NAFTA went into effect, January 1, 1994, was the same day that multiple Indigenous nations including individuals from the Tzeltal, Tzotzil, Chol, Tojolabal, Mam, and Zoque nations in the southeastern Mexican state of Chiapas organized an armed uprising as the Zapatista National Liberation Army or EZLN. This was not at all a mere coincidence, but rather was directly related to NAFTA. The Zapatistas declared NAFTA a death sentence for Indigenous farmworker communities throughout Mexico. **(1)**

The Zapatistas had begun organizing in 1982. This was a twelve year process of, first and foremost, speaking, listening, and organizing, then of training and arming themselves. The Zapatistas are predominantly Catholic, and early on they also had the counsel and the ear of the local Catholic Archbishop Samuel Ruiz. The Zapatistas called him "Grandfather." Samuel Ruiz was a liberation theologian who participated in the 1968 Medellin Conference on liberation theology. Liberation theologians have historically been allies of leftist indigenous movements throughout Mexico, Central, and South America. Samuel Ruiz was no exception.

At some point after the Zapatista uprising, then Mexican General in command of the area General Jose Ruben Rivas Peña, wrote an analysis of the conflict in Chiapas in which he stated: "The Vatican is the indirect cause of the conflict in Chiapas with its contaminated thread of liberation theology." **(2)**

The real causes for the Zapatista uprising, in addition to systemic marginalization, were the attempted privatization of communally owned Indigenous lands, the influx of subsidized U.S. corn into the Mexican market, and Chapter 11 stipulations of NAFTA that gave Indigenous communities little to no recourse to defend their territories and their people from the threat of transnational contamination and natural resource extraction.

The Zapatistas had an incredible advantage that protected them and made them significantly more effective. This advantage was the internet. The *New York Times* called them "The First Post Modern Revolution." **(3)** Their uprising was accompanied with simultaneous and continuous online declarations, communiques, statements, rebuttals, interviews, stories, poetry, artwork, children's stories, imagery, etc. The words from the Clandestine Indigenous Revolutionary Committee–General Command of the Zapatista National Liberation Army EZLN, were heard around the world immediately. **(4)**

> You threaten us with prison, but we are already in prison.
> You threaten us with death, but we are already dead.

The Zapatistas took 12 years to organize their uprising, 12 years to speak and listen, 12 years to come to a consensus about how, when, where, why, and who. By January 1, 1994, the Zapatistas had prepared themselves militarily, prepared a media strategy, made a formal declaration of war, and followed the Geneva Convention Rules of War to the letter of the law. They developed an identifiable uniform, declared a territory and a variety of ethnic identities, treated captives with respect and dignity, and turned over the injured to the Red Cross. **(5)**

The Mexican federal government was absolutely blindsided by the level of discipline, clarity, professionalism, and strategy employed by the EZLN. At first the government claimed there were no more than 200 insurgents, when in fact the 3000 + Zapatista insurgents were so well trained that though only about half of them had real firearms, the other half went to battle with wooden rifles painted black to give the appearance of force while awaiting the opportunity to recover weapons from the enemy army in combat. **(6)**

The Zapatistas released their first communique online titled:

The First Declaration from the Lacandon Jungle

TODAY WE SAY: ENOUGH IS ENOUGH!
TO THE PEOPLE OF MEXICO
MEXICAN BROTHERS AND SISTERS:

We are a product of 500 years of struggle: first against slavery, then during the War of Independence against Spain led by insurgents, then to avoid being absorbed by North American imperialism, then to promulgate our constitution and expel the French empire from our soil, and later the dictatorship of Porfirio Diaz denied us the just application of the Reform laws and the people rebelled and leaders like Villa and Zapata emerged, poor men just like us. We have been denied the most elemental preparation so they can use us as cannon fodder and pillage the wealth of our country. They don't care that we have nothing, absolutely nothing, not even a roof over our heads, no land, no work, no health care, no food nor education. Nor are we able to freely and democratically elect our political representatives, nor is there independence from foreigners, nor is there peace nor justice for ourselves and our children.

But today, we say ENOUGH IS ENOUGH. We are the inheritors of the true builders of our nation, the dispossessed. We are millions and we thereby call upon our brothers and sisters to join this struggle as the only path, so that we will not die of hunger due to the insatiable ambition of a 70 year dictatorship led by a clique of traitors that represent the most conservative and sell-out groups. They are the same ones that opposed Hidalgo and Morelos, the same ones that betrayed Vicente Guerrero, the same ones that sold half our country to the foreign invader, the same ones that imported a European prince to rule our country, the same ones that formed the "scientific" Porfirista dictatorship, the same ones that opposed the Petroleum Expropriation, the same ones that massacred the railroad workers in 1958 and the students in 1968, the same ones that today take everything from us, absolutely everything.

To prevent the continuation of the above and as our last hope, after having tried to utilize all legal means based on our Constitution, we go to our Constitution to apply Article 39 which says:

"National Sovereignty essentially and originally resides in the people. All political power emanates from the people and its purpose is to help the people. The people have, at all times, the inalienable right to alter or modify their form of government."

Therefore, according to our constitution, we declare the following to the Mexican federal army, the pillar of the Mexican dictatorship that we suffer from, monopolized by a one-party system and led by Carlos Salinas de Gortari, the maximum and illegitimate federal executive that today holds power.

According to this Declaration of War, we ask that other powers of the nation advocate to restore the legitimacy and the stability of the nation by overthrowing the dictator.

We also ask that international organizations and the International Red Cross watch over and regulate our battles, so that our efforts are carried out while still protecting our civilian population. We declare now and always that we are subject to the Geneva Accords, forming the EZLN as our fighting arm of our liberation struggle. We have the Mexican people on our side, we have the beloved tri-colored flag highly respected by our insurgent fighters. We use black and red in our uniform as our symbol of our working people on strike. Our flag carries the following letters, "EZLN," Zapatista Army of National Liberation, and we always carry our flag into combat.

Beforehand, we refuse any effort to disgrace our just cause by accusing us of being drug traffickers, drug guerrillas, thieves, or other names that might be used by our enemies. Our struggle follows the Constitution which is held high by its call for justice and equality.

Therefore, according to this declaration of war, we give our military forces, the EZLN, the following orders:

• First: Advance to the capital of the country, overcoming the Mexican federal army, protecting within our advance, the civilian population and permitting the people in the liberated area the right to freely and democratically elect their own administrative authorities.

• Second: Respect the lives of our prisoners and turn over all wounded to the International Red Cross.

• Third: Initiate summary judgments against all soldiers of the Mexican federal army and the political police that have received training or have been paid by foreigners, accused of being traitors to our country, and against all those that have repressed and treated badly the civil population and robbed or stolen from or attempted crimes against the good of the people.

• Fourth: Form new troops with all those Mexicans that show their interest in joining our struggle, including those that, being enemy soldiers, turn themselves in without having fought against us, and promise to take orders from the General Command of the Zapatista Army of National Liberation.

• Fifth: We ask for the unconditional surrender of the enemy's headquarters before we begin any combat to avoid any loss of lives.

• Sixth: Suspend the robbery of our natural resources in the areas controlled by the EZLN.

To the People of Mexico: We, the men and women, full and free, are conscious that the war that we have declared is our last resort, but also a just one. The dictators have been applying an undeclared genocidal war against our people for many years. Therefore we ask for your participation, your decision to support this plan that struggles for work, land, housing, food, health care, education, independence, freedom, democracy, justice and peace. We declare that we will not stop fighting until the basic demands of our people have been met by forming a government of our country that is free and democratic.

JOIN THE INSURGENT FORCES OF THE ZAPATISTA ARMY OF NATIONAL LIBERATION

—General Command of the EZLN, 31 December 1993 (7)

The Zapatistas proceeded to take control of seven municipalities throughout the state of Chiapas. The success of the uprising was quickly met by a major military offensive by the Mexican Army leaving several Zapatistas dead and wounded. Several of these deaths would soon be unveiled as criminal extrajudicial executions of prisoners of war at the hands of the Mexican Military, particularly the well documented Massacre at the Ocosingo Market, in which eight Zapatistas were murdered with shots fired at close range to the head. The Mexican General in charge of the first military response to the Zapatista uprising, Juan López Ortiz had received two infantry courses at the U.S. Army School of the Americas from the 12th of October to the 9th of December, 1959. (8)

The extrajudicial executions were in fact investigated by the Mexican Army. According to a June 1995 Human Rights Watch report on the Military investigation of the Ocosingo Massacre, the military investigation identified Second Lt. Arturo Jiménez Morales as the sole culprit of the murders. Jiménez Morales is said to have taken his own life hours after his confession. The military closed the case on the murders. No one has ever been prosecuted for the Ocosingo Massacre. **(9)**

After 12 days of fire fights and major national and international protests in favor of the Zapatistas, but against a civil war, a cease-fire was negotiated and peace talks were initiated between the Mexican Federal government and the Zapatistas.

The peace talks would quickly prove to be as much of an illusion as 64 years of democracy under one party rule (The Institutional Revolutionary Party - PRI would go on to rule as a single party for a total of 71 years). At the time of the uprising the Mexican president was Carlos Salinas de Gortari of the PRI. Salinas de Gortari was absolutely instrumental to signing and approving the North American Free Trade Agreement (NAFTA).

Three months after the uprising began, on March 23, 1994, the PRI candidate slated to become the next Mexican President, Luis Donaldo Colosio was assassinated at a rally in Tijuana, Baja California. **(10)** With only four months left until the presidential elections, the PRI chose Ernesto Zedillo to become the next Mexican president. **(11)** Though Colosio's assassination is shrouded in a variety of possible conspiracies, including versions that involve the PRI and Salinas de Gortari, for me what is much more important to notice, is how from Gortari to Colosio, to Zedillo, the U.S. federal government was consistently unwavering in its support for the PRI's one party rule. **(12)**

It is at this point where we can begin to see clearly the way in which the neoliberal military-political economy that began under a fascist military dictatorship in 1973 in Chile, continued to function under a political party dictatorship in Mexico in 1994. However, instead of the Chilean graduates of the Chicago School of economics known as the "Chicago Boys," we have Ivy League graduates. Gortari himself is a Harvard graduate with a Masters in Public Administration, a Masters in Political Economy, and a Doctorate in Political Economy and Government. Zedillo is a Yale graduate with a Doctorate in Economic Sciences. He is currently (2022) the Director of the Yale Center for the Study of Globalization; Professor in the Field of International Economics and Politics; Professor of International and Area Studies; and Professor Adjunct of Forestry and Environmental Studies at Yale University. So with Salinas de Gortari and Zedillo in office in Mexico from 1988 - 2000 instead of "Chicago Boys", Mexico got its very own Harvard Boy and its very own Yale boy, both from the Institutional Revolutionary Party (PRI).

Chase Manhattan Bank

On January 13, 1995, a consultant for Chase Manhattan Bank by the name of Riordan Roett published a memo titled "Mexico-Political Update, Chase Manhattan's Emerging Markets Group Memo." At the time Roett was the head of the Latin American Studies Department in the Paul H. Nitze School of Advanced Studies at Johns Hopkins University. Also at the time, the Dean of the School of Advanced Studies was Paul Wolfowitz (from 1994 to 2001). From 2001 to 2005 Wolfowitz would be George W. Bush's Deputy Secretary of Defense and he would be considered a primary orchestrator of the Iraq invasion. From 2005 through 2007 Wolfowitz would serve as the 10th President of the World Bank Group. Therefore, under the tutelage of this historically shady personality, Riordan Roett consulted the Emerging Markets Group of Chase Manhattan Bank, and within his memo, the subject of Chiapas, and the Zapatistas was directly addressed:

Chiapas:

The uprising in the southern state of Chiapas is now one-year old and, apparently, no nearer to resolution. The leader, or spokesman, of the movement, sub-commandante (sic) Marcos, remains adamant in his demand that the incumbent PRI governor resign and be replaced by the PRD candidate who, Marcos argues, was deprived of victory by government fraud in the recent election. Marcos continues to lobby for widespread social and economic reform in the state. Incidents continue between the local police and military authorities and those sympathetic to the Zapatista movement, as the insurgency is called, and local peasant groups who are sympathetic to Marcos and his cronies.

While Zedillo is committed to a diplomatic and political solution to the stand-off in Chiapas, it is difficult to imagine that the current environment will yield a peaceful solution. Moreover, to the degree that the monetary crisis limits the resources available to the government for social and economic reforms, it may prove difficult to win popular support for the Zedillo administration's plans for Chiapas. More relevant, Marcos and his supporters may decide to embarrass the government with an increase in local violence and force the administration to cede to Zapatista demands and accept an embarrassing political defeat. The alternative is a military offensive to defeat the insurgency which would create an international outcry over the use of violence and the suppression of indigenous rights.

While Chiapas, in our opinion, does not pose a fundamental threat to Mexican political stability, it is perceived to be so by many in the investment community. The government will need to eliminate the Zapatistas to demonstrate their effective control of the national territory and of security policy. (13)

Less than 4 weeks after the publication of the Riordan Roett Memo, on February 9, 1995, Ernesto Zedillo, the Yale Doctorate, and President of Mexico under the PRI, ordered a military offensive against the Zapatistas. **(14)**

Sixteen years after the fact, the undeniable truth about the military offensive was revealed in a February 4, 2011 article by Gilberto López y Rivas in the Mexican newspaper *La Jornada*. However the truth had always been there, and continues to be there, in plain sight for anyone to see. Not only the Zapatistas, but also a number of human rights and community rights organizations, activists, and students documented and made public every single atrocious strategy employed in the "Campaign Plan of the General Command of the 7th Military Region of the Mexican Secretary of National Defense." In 2011, Gilberto López y Rivas shared some details from a leaked manuscript of the Campaign Plan. **(15)** The Zapatistas themselves had since its inception, already dubbed the military campaign plan, "Plan Chiapas 94."

Low Intensity Warfare

Plan Chiapas 94 was headed by the Mexican general José Rubén Rivas Peña. From the 25th of February to December 12, 1980, Rivas Peña took a Command and Staff course at the U.S. Army School of the Americas. **(16)** What Gilberto López y Rivas' 2011 article in *La Jornada* exposes, is an official strategy of what is known as "Low Intensity Warfare." Again, the Zapatistas and their supporters consistently made the world aware of the ongoing strategy of Low Intensity Warfare, which they have continued to endure for nearly three decades. **(17)**

In López y Rivas' article what is most importantly exposed about Plan Chiapas 94 is the creation, training, and support for paramilitary organizations:

> Secretly organize certain sectors of the civilian population, among others, cattle ranchers, private property owners, and individuals characterized by their sense of patriotism (sic), who will be employed by orders in support of our operations. **(18)**

Further along in the document several annexes are mentioned but not included with the actual document. However one of the descriptions of one of the annexes is included, and it states as follows:

> Describes the army's activities as training and support for the self-defense forces or other paramilitary organizations, which could be the primary fundamental mobilization for military operations and development. It also includes assistance and aid which is given to other government

> entities and officials on a local, municipal, state and federal
> level. In the case of non-existent self-defense forces it will
> be necessary to create them. (19)

Paramilitary forces are armed civilians who receive training, support, and financing, or simply receive impunity from official entities such as a political party, a government administration, the police or the military. A paramilitary organization may also be generated and supported by non-governmental institutions such as corporations, banks, or individuals such as local land barons, or the political elite as well. In this case the paramilitary organizations are being trained, equipped, and financed by the Mexican Army.

Paramilitaries use violence to carry out social, political or economic objectives against a target civilian population that is either considered a disposable variable, a barrier, or a direct threat to a given political, economic, or military interest. In this case the paramilitaries have been consistently used against unarmed Zapatista support base communities.

The primary purpose and function of paramilitarism is to generate and exploit what are known as "deniable atrocities." That is to say, the purpose of paramilitarism is to carry out atrocities such as extrajudicial executions, kidnappings, beatings, rape, and torture against a civilian population in such a way that governments, police, or the military can deny involvement in and/or responsibility for those atrocities once committed. These atrocities are used to dissuade social, political, or economic opposition. In the end these deniable atrocities are used to justify the further militarism of a target region.

So while Riordan Roett's Chase Manhattan memo recognized the political danger of an all-out military offensive against the Zapatistas, it did call for their elimination. **(20)** The use of paramilitaries and other strategies to erode the Zapatista support base fits in perfectly with Roett's recommendations.

According to a January 20, 2004 National Security Archive Electronic Briefing by Kate Doyle, titled: "Rebellion in Chiapas and the Mexican Military," despite both the U.S. and Mexican federal governments' denial of knowledge of the Zapatistas, between April 28, 1992 and May 30, 1995 there are at least 41 declassified documents from the Defense Intelligence Agency, the State Department, the Army Intelligence and Security Command, and the CIA Directorate of Intelligence that expose constant knowledge, awareness, and analysis on the Zapatista uprising and the Mexican military response.

According to Doyle, and I absolutely have to agree:

> When the U.S. government considered the rebellion in Chiapas, it did so through the twin lenses of its primary national interests: money and power. (21)

In a document dated circa January 1, 1994, titled "Guerillas Capture Key Towns in Chiapas, Mexico," the Defense Intelligence Agency, admits that the uprising was:

> ...coordinated, well-planned and executed. (22)

In another document dated January 5, 1994, titled "DIA Weekly Intelligence Forecast," the Defense Intelligence Agency states:

> The January 1st incident demonstrated highly professional planning, leadership, and operational competence of the Rebel Zapata Army of National Liberation (EZLN) that took control of four towns in Chiapas.
>
> While the insurgents are not strong enough to face the Army, neither is the Army capable of eradicating the rebels in hiding. The government will seek to restrain the army to avoid local complaints of Army human rights abuse. A standoff with recurring violence could frighten foreign investors and embarrass the government, affecting the presidential elections in August. The government will beef up security in the region, and could be tempted into repressive tactics. (23)

Immediately after the Zapatista uprising began, the U.S. military intelligence community was aware of and concerned about the fear it might spark in foreign investors, as well as the embarrassment it might cause the Mexican government.

Over the coming years, the Zapatistas would respect the peace accords and ceasefire with the Mexican federal government although they, in turn, have been consistently policed and harassed by military troops and, over time, attacked by paramilitary organizations created by the Mexican armed forces. The paramilitary violence against the Zapatistas would peak on December 22, 1997, with a massacre of 45 unarmed Tzotzil Natives from Zapatista support base communities. The Tzotziles were in a church in the community of Acteal in the municipality of Chenalho. Of the 45, only 11 were men, and the rest were women and children. They were gunned down and hacked to pieces with machetes. The paramilitary organization that carried out the murders was named *Mascara Roja,* or "Red Mask." By the time of the Acteal Massacre the U.S. Army School of the Americas graduate Jose Ruben Rivas Peña, also the Mexican general in charge of Plan Chipas 94, and responsible for the creation of paramilitary organizations such as *Mascara Roja,* would already be working in the states of Oaxaca and Guerrero. These two states would see an increase in paramilitary activity as of the date of his arrival. **(24)**

For me, the Massacre of Acteal marks a transition in Mexican neoliberalism from a military-political economy into a paramilitary-political economy. That is a system of money and power which uses armed thugs to carry out its dirty work. Among many lessons the Zapatistas would share over the years, however, is their confirmation that strategies such as paramilitarism are acts of desperation when the state is placed in a social, political or military checkmate.

The Zapatistas stand very much apart from the traditional "Latin American" guerrilla movements. The primary characteristic that sets the Zapatistas apart is, first and foremost, their diverse Indigenous ethnic identity. The Zapatistas have consistently contested the pigeon-holing of their political ideology into classical

Eurocentric categories. Though they sympathize with Marxism and anarchism, they root themselves in grassroots horizontal community-based organizing for self-defense, self-determination and autonomy. From the onset, the Zapatistas made clear their intention to support Indigenous autonomy without seeking power or a separate sovereign state. Rather the Zapatistas have sought to build Indigenous autonomy within the framework of the Mexican nation-state. Originally the Zapatistas were most concerned with ending the political party dictatorship of the Institutional Revolutionary Party (PRI), which they refer to as the Party-State. They called upon Mexicans and Mexican institutions to uphold the Mexican Constitution, and demand an untainted democratic electoral process to save the nation from the tyranny of the PRI.

In the year 2000 for the first time in 71 years, Mexico elected a presidential candidate from a party other than the PRI. Vicente Fox of the National Action Party (PAN) was elected president, and though he was not a PRI party member, his resume did not set him far apart from the neoliberal Mexican elite political class. As a former executive for Coca Cola and a Harvard educated businessman, Fox, it turns out, would continue to propagate the neoliberal military-political economy as yet another Harvard Boy. However there is no doubt that the Zapatista uprising was instrumental in pushing the entire nation towards this profound initial political transition away from the political party dictatorship of the PRI.

Though in the First Declaration of the Lacandon Jungle, the Zapatistas stated their intention to advance towards Mexico City, this never occurred as part of the EZLN's military operations. As the movement transitioned into a peaceful movement of hearts and minds and public opinion, however, on March 10, 2001, the Zapatistas did organize an unarmed march of several Zapatista delegates including commanders from the EZLN, and a massive national mobilization to Mexico City. The mobilization had as its primary purpose a demand for the recognition of the original peace accords signed with the Mexican government, the removal of military bases in proximity to Zapatista territory, and the unification of their struggle with the struggle of Indigenous nations across Mexico. En route to Mexico City, the Zapatistas stopped at the first National Indigenous Congress in the P'urhépecha community of Nurio, Michoacán. It was at this meeting that Indigenous nations from throughout Mexico agreed to join the Zapatistas in their struggle for Indigenous autonomy with peace, justice, and dignity.

President Fox said upon his election that he would resolve the conflict in Chiapas in 15 minutes, and though he claimed to understand and respect the plight of the Indigenous rebels, when the Zapatistas came to Mexico City, and presented themselves before the nation's Congress, all three of the political parties –the Institutional Revolutionary Party (PRI), National Action Party (PAN), and even the Democratic Revolution Party (PRD)– decided not to agree to any of the Zapatista demands. **(25)** Together they passed a very watered down version of the original peace accords. Fox said he would remove military bases from Zapatista territory, and many were moved, but merely kilometers away. In May of 2000 it became clear that Fox would continue to uphold the counterinsurgency strategy of low intensity warfare. After a paramilitary attack against the Zapatistas support base, Fox sent the new militarized police, the Federal Preventive Police (PFP), created by the PRI's Ernesto Zedillo in the previous administration, into the region. The Zapatistas and several independent organizations viewed the PFP's presence as harassment and a clear provocation. **(26)**

This series of circumstances and the lack of results in working with the institutional forms of government certainly pushed the Zapatistas into focusing on their ongoing building of the Indigenous autonomy for which they rose up in the first place. In August of 2003, the Zapatistas announced major changes in their organizational framework and strategy. This would be a truly historic moment for armed insurgencies around the world. What the Zapatistas showed was that despite maintaining a military strategy of armed self-defense and a political strategy of negotiation and dialogue with institutional forms of government, they never lost touch with the most important strategy of all, grassroots community-based liberation through the actual construction of autonomy. To this end, the EZLN made it very clear that they understood that in order to build autonomy, they would need a democratic form of government. They also made public that up to this point it had been the EZLN, the military branch of the organization, that had been making all of the decisions, and that this could not be democratic because as a matter of strategy and tactics, armies cannot be democratic. Therefore the EZLN literally stepped down from power in order to give birth to what became known as the *Caracoles,* distributed geographically in Zapatista controlled territory, and the *Juntas de Buen Gobierno* or Good Governance Councils, that would be traditional Mesoamerican Indigenous rotating structures for self-governance. In effect, since the institutional government made no advances in providing the conditions for Indigenous autonomy, the Zapatistas decided to build that autonomy themselves from the bottom up. In 2003 the Zapatistas created five Caracoles, encompassing 27 Autonomous Zapatista Municipalities. In 2019 the Zapatistas announced the addition of seven more Caracoles totaling twelve.

The Zapatistas have slowly but surely transitioned from a purely military organization into a grassroots community-based organization for demanding self-determination, practicing self-defense, and engaging in the construction of autonomous communities without the help or permission of the institutional government. Today in 2022 there are a total of 47 Zapatista centers or municipalities within the 12 Caracoles, with approximately over 300,000 Zapatistas holding almost half of the state of Chiapas. To this day, the Zapatistas have not given up any of their weapons, and in the face of the neoliberal military and paramilitary political economy, it is all too clear that the Zapatistas are not just surviving; they are thriving in terms of Indigenous autonomy and actual land returned to the hands of Indigenous people without any form of institutional government control. These numbers are absolutely unprecedented across the so-called Americas. As a result of their tremendous success, unarmed Zapatista support base communities continue to suffer an increase in state-sponsored displacement through ongoing paramilitary attacks even today in 2021 under the supposed "leftist" government of President Andres Manuel Lopez Obrador. **(27)** The Zapatistas continue to be a reference point for Indigenous autonomy, grassroots liberation, and a community-based analysis of the neoliberal military-political economy everywhere.

I recommend reading all six of the of the Zapatista Declarations from the Lacandon Jungle, and staying attuned to ongoing Zapatista communications and events on the website ***https:// enlacezapatista.ezln.org.mx/*** There you can scroll down to find translations in multiple languages of all the different Zapatista communications, which have been and continue to be launched through the internet. I included the entire 1994 First Declaration from the Lacandon Jungle towards the beginning of this chapter, and I want to close the chapter with an excerpt from the 2005 Sixth Declaration from the Lacandon Jungle. The Zapatistas were my first teachers on the subject of neoliberalism, and I think this excerpt is a perfect small example of those teachings:

Excerpt from the Sixth Declaration
from the Lacandon Jungle

How We See the World

Now we are going to explain to you how we, the zapatistas, see what is going on in the world. We see that capitalism is the strongest right now. Capitalism is a social system, a way in which a society goes about organizing things and people, and who has and who has not, and who gives orders and who obeys. In capitalism, there are some people who have money, or capital, and factories and stores and fields and many things, and there are others who have nothing but their strength and knowledge in order to work. In capitalism, those who have money and things give the orders, and those who only have their ability to work obey.

Then capitalism means that there are a few who have great wealth, but they did not win a prize, or find a treasure, or inherit it from a parent. They obtained that wealth, rather, by exploiting the work of the many. So capitalism is based on the exploitation of the workers, which means they exploit the workers and take out all the profits they can. This is done unjustly, because they do not pay the worker what his work is worth. Instead they give him a salary that barely allows him to eat a little and to rest for a bit, and the next day he goes back to work in exploitation, whether in the countryside or in the city.

And capitalism also makes its wealth from plunder, or theft, because they take what they want from others, land, for example, and natural resources. So capitalism is a system where the robbers are free and they are admired and used as examples.

And, in addition to exploiting and plundering, capitalism represses because it imprisons and kills those who rebel against injustice.

Capitalism is most interested in merchandise, because when this is bought or sold, profits are made. And then capitalism turns everything into merchandise, it makes merchandise of people, of nature, of culture, of history, of conscience. According to capitalism, everything must be able to be bought and sold. And it hides everything behind the merchandise, so we don't see the exploitation that exists. And then the merchandise is bought and sold in a market. And the market, in addition to being used for buying and selling, is also used to hide the exploitation of the workers. In the market, for example, we see coffee in its little package or its pretty little jar, but we do not see the campesino who suffered in order to harvest the coffee, and we do not see the coyote who paid him so cheaply for his work, and we do not see the workers in the large company working their hearts out to package the coffee. Or we see an appliance for listening to music like cumbias, rancheras or corridos, or whatever, and we see that it is very good because it has a good sound, but we do not see the worker in the maquiladora who struggled for many hours, putting the cables and the parts of the appliance together, and they barely paid her a pittance of money, and she lives far away from work and spends a lot on the trip, and, in addition, she runs the risk of being kidnapped, raped and killed as happens in Ciudad Juárez in Mexico.

So we see merchandise in the market, but we do not see the exploitation with which it was made. And then capitalism needs many markets...or a very large market, a world market.

And so the capitalism of today is not the same as before, when the rich were content with exploiting the workers in their own countries, but now they are on a path which is called Neoliberal Globalization. This globalization means that they no longer control the workers in one or several countries, but the capitalists are trying to dominate everything all over the world. And the world, or Planet Earth, is also called the "globe," and that is why they say "globalization," or the entire world.

And neoliberalism is the idea that capitalism is free to dominate the entire world, and so you have to resign yourself and conform and not make a fuss, in other words, not rebel. So neoliberalism is like the theory, the plan, of capitalist globalization. And neoliberalism has its economic, political, military and cultural plans. All of those plans have to do with dominating everyone, and they repress or separate anyone who doesn't obey so that his rebellious ideas aren't passed on to others.

Then, in neoliberal globalization, the great capitalists who live in countries that are powerful, like the United States, want the entire world to be made into a big business where merchandise is produced like a great market. A world market for buying and selling the entire world and for hiding all the exploitation from the world. Then the global capitalists insert themselves everywhere, in all the countries, in order to do their big business, their great exploitation. Then they respect nothing, and they meddle wherever they wish, as if they were conquering other countries. That is why we Zapatistas say that neoliberal globalization is a war of conquest of the entire world, a world war, a war being waged by capitalism for global domination. Sometimes that conquest is by armies who invade a country and conquer it by force. But sometimes it is with the economy, in other words, the big capitalists put their money into another country or they lend it money, but on the condition that they obey what they tell them to do. And they also insert their ideas, with the capitalist culture which is the culture of merchandise, of profits, of the market.

Then the one that wages the conquest, capitalism, does as it wants; it destroys and changes what it does not like and eliminates what gets in its way. For example, those who do not produce, nor buy nor sell modern merchandise, get in their way, or those who rebel against that order. And they despise those who are of no use to them. That is why the Indigenous get in the way of neoliberal capitalism, and that is why they despise them and want to eliminate them. And neoliberal capitalism also gets rid of the laws that do not allow them to exploit and to have a lot of profit. They demand that everything be bought and sold, and, since capitalism has all the money, it buys everything. Capitalism destroys the countries it conquers with neoliberal globalization, but it also wants to adapt everything, to make it over again, but in its own way, a way that benefits capitalism and doesn't allow anything to get in its way. Then neoliberal globalization, capitalism, destroys what exists in these countries. It destroys their culture, their language, their economic system, their political system, and it also destroys the ways in which those who live in that country relate to each other. So everything that makes a country a country is left destroyed.

Then neoliberal globalization wants to destroy the nations of the world so that only one nation or country remains, the country of money, of capital. And capitalism wants everything to be as it wants, in its own way, and it doesn't like what is different, and it persecutes it and attacks it, or puts it off in a corner and acts as if it doesn't exist.

Then, in short, the capitalism of global neoliberalism is based on exploitation, plunder, contempt and repression of those who refuse. The same as before, but now globalized, worldwide.

But it is not so easy for neoliberal globalization, because the exploited of each country become discontented, and they will not say "Well, too bad." Instead, they rebel. And those who remain and who are in the way resist, and they don't allow themselves to be eliminated. And that is why we see, all over the world, those who are being screwed over, engaged in resistance, not putting up with it. In other words, they rebel, and not just in one country but wherever they abound. And so, as there is a neoliberal globalization, there is a globalization of rebellion.

And it is not just the workers of the countryside and of the city who appear in this globalization of rebellion. Others also appear who are much persecuted and despised for the same reason, for not letting themselves be dominated, like women, young people, the indigenous, homosexuals, lesbians, transsexual persons, migrants and many other groups who exist all over the world but who we do not see until they shout Ya basta! Enough of being despised! And they rise up, and then we see them, we hear them, and we learn from them.

And then we see that all those groups of people are fighting against neoliberalism, against the capitalist globalization plan, and they are struggling for humanity.

And we are astonished when we see the stupidity of the neoliberals who want to destroy all humanity with their wars and exploitations, but it also makes us quite happy to see resistances and rebellions appearing everywhere, such as ours, which is a bit small, but here we are. And we see this all over the world, and now our heart learns that we are not alone. (29)

PART TWO: WEAPONS

Chapter 6
The Military Industrial Complex

Before talking about the military industrial complex, we have to talk about militarism in and of itself and more specifically U.S. militarism. Over the last 15 years I have consistently asked my students the same question: Who was the first official enemy of the U.S. government and therefore the first official military target of the U.S. armed forces? The answer has varied quite a lot over the last 15 years and I am glad to say that today my students are answering both correctly and faster than ever before.

The first official enemy of the U.S. government and first military target of the U.S. armed forces were the original Indigenous inhabitants of the territory so-called the United States. **(1)** Indigenous People(s). That's who. Not the British Red Coats, not the Spanish, not the French, not Mexico, but Indigenous People(s), were the first military target. The U.S. armed forces not only aided westward expansion into Indigenous territory, but also participated in removal strategies that ranged from intentionally spreading disease, to massacres, to forced relocation. The geographical girth of the United States, spanning an area that includes two major oceans on its coastlines; its diverse topography; and its natural resources, have been and continue to be primary factors in its global political and economic power. **(2)** The territory was stolen from Indigenous nations over the course of a century through the moral and legally binding justification of white, male, Christian supremacy, otherwise known as the Doctrine of Discovery. **(3)**

On August 3, 1492, an Italian man by the name of Cristoforo Colombo set sail from Palos, Spain on ships funded by the Spanish Monarchy. On October 12, 1492 Cristopher Columbus's expedition reached land, probably in the Bahamas. Seven months later, on May 4, 1493, the Catholic Pope Alexander VI issued a Papal Bull known as the "Inter Caetera." **(4)** A Papal Bull is an official type of public decree made by a Pope. In the Inter Caetera the Pope declares that Christians had the divine right to "discover," claim, and exploit any lands inhabited by non-Christians. The Papal Bull was clearly made with tremendous expediency in order to validate, under God, the Spanish conquest of the Americas. Over time the same Papal Bull would be recognized and applied by other European nations claiming territories throughout the Americas, then eventually by the U.S. government under what is known as Manifest Destiny. **(5)**

I only know this because of an amazing Indigenous educator and friend. It has been a true honor for me to know and have the opportunity to speak with Jimmy Lee Beason the II, a Native Pahuska from the Eagle Clan of the Osage Nation, and a professor in the Indigenous / American Indian Studies Department at Haskell Indian Nations University in Lawrence, Kansas. Jimmy's statements do not reflect the opinion of Haskell Indian Nations University. When it comes to U.S. militarism and military strategies against the Indigenous nations across the so called USA, Jimmy teaches and writes about it all:

> All federal Indian law reinforces the Doctrine of Discovery. In 1823, in the case of Johnston v. M'Intosh, John Marshall, the Chief Justice of the U.S. Supreme Court ruled against Native claims to their land and specifically referred to the Doctrine of Discovery as justification for the taking of indigenous land. One of the most recent times the Doctrine of Discovery was cited in a U.S. court case was in 2004 with the City of Sherrill v. Oneida Indian Nation of New York.

The bedrock precedent cited in the opinion of the court, which was delivered by Justice Ruth Bader Ginsburg, was in fact the Doctrine of Discovery. **(6)**

> Every act of state violence to continually control and counteract any native resistance, is all steeped in that Euro-American Christian religious ideology. That concept

of supremacy. We've seen it today when you had Trump in there and these groups like the Proud Boys. Well, that comes from a very long time ago.

In terms of U.S. military intervention against Indigenous nations, a lot of those first initial fights, battles, and conflicts started under (George) Washington. Washington had a whole policy about fighting native people. And the policy basically was to keep pushing further West, and when native people started defending themselves and attacking white settlers, it would be the excuse to bring in the military. That was how they operated. During the Northwest Indian War, which refers to the old Northwest that consisted of Indiana and the Ohio valley, a lot of the top military people were also land speculators. They had made promises to their soldiers in the revolutionary war that they would be given land. That provided their justification for just taking land, acre by acre, step by step. That was pretty much how the USA rolled from that point on; sending in colonial settlers. When a conflict with Natives would occur, that would be the justification to send in the army.

Native people were dealt with under the War Department. Anything having to do with Natives was dealt with by the War Department. So you had generals negotiating treaties and terms etc. Most reservations originally started off as Prisoner of War (POW) camps. When you think about Geronimo and different resistance leaders or resistance groups, that was where they were sent, because they were considered Prisoners of War. Geronimo was a POW up until the day he died. So the military was the enforcer of those policies when it came to the land, which speaks to the conquest and colonization of our territories. That was the beginning, when the Northwest Indian wars were the first huge Native resistance to U.S. expansion.

The particular history of the colonization of the Osage

nation itself was that Natives did not deal with the U.S. Army head on. What happened was part of the strategy of the United States through Thomas Jefferson to move native people in the East, across the Mississippi River. The Jefferson administration, Meriwether Lewis, and William Clarke of "Lewis and Clarke," were involved in supplying, encouraging, and providing provisions to these eastern tribes that were being forced West and given the resources and ammunition to fight Osages so that they could begin moving into that area. This is the very beginning of paramilitaries in America. It was basically almost like a proxy war in which they were like military auxiliaries. They just used them like that.

There is another component to this as well. Thomas Jefferson had blatantly talked about pacification through commerce. He thought the best way to control tribes in these areas was not necessarily through military force, but by forcing them to become reliant on trade. So he talked about the factory systems where Osages would start to get their goods, European tools, guns, and all that stuff, and over the course of 100+ years a lot of Osage people had become reliant on all that. So they used that factory style trade mechanism to make them more pliable to their demands: "If you don't do what we say, we are not going to give you this anymore." (7)

So-called "Indian Boarding Schools"

Another key element of the war against Indigenous people that the U.S. Army coordinated along with the church as of 1879, was the forced assimilation of Indigenous children in a military strategy infamously known as "Kill the Indian, Save the Man." This entailed the kidnapping of Indigenous children from their homes, the forced relocation of these children to concentration camps that were inappropriately named "boarding schools," and the systemic acculturation and assimilation of these children into the norms of white Christian U.S. American society. For a nation championed as a civilization by its historians, there is nothing civilized about a society that would allow and endorse this particular military strategy.

Through diligent militance in uncovering the true history of what went on at these so called Indigenous boarding schools, it has now become inarguably clear that rampant abuse including sexual violence, beatings, and murder were commonplace at these U.S. (and Canadian) concentration camps.

While white residents in proximity to U.S. Army Indigenous boarding schools would return runaway Indigenous children who had escaped their official captors, the U.S. Armed Forces before the Civil War simultaneously upheld slavery, quelling rebellions by enslaved people with a military presence, and returning runaway enslaved Black people to their so-called "proper owners."

So to be clear, at its roots, the U.S. Army is a white male Christian supremacist institution that upheld the continued subjugation of Indigenous Peoples and enslaved Black people across the land. We cannot have a critical dialogue about U.S. militarism or the U.S. military-political economy, without first acknowledging these two very basic historical facts.

Expansion, Wars, and the Military Industrial Complex

The following significant factor which undoubtedly launched the United States into becoming a global military superpower, was the victory against Mexico in the Mexican-American War. The territorial gains from Mexico would grant the United States a vast global geopolitical advantage, but yet again, these lands were stolen Indigenous lands to begin with. What are now known as the states of Arizona, California, New Mexico, Texas, Colorado, Nevada, and Utah were once Apache, Yaqui, Tongva, Coahuiltecan, Shoshone, Goshute, Pueblo, Diné, Caddo, Hopi, Karankawa, Tonkowa and many other Indigenous people's land.

In 1898 the United States broke from its isolationist non-interventionist approach to the former European colonies, and intervened militarily in the Cuban revolution against the Spanish

Crown. In three months, three weeks, and two days on August 13, 1898, the United States won the war.

According to the U.S. State Department's Office of the Historian this is the moment when the United States began to become a global superpower:

> The global equilibrium, which had allowed the United States to grow and prosper in virtual isolation since 1815 was gone forever as the result of a short but shattering war. In 1898, U.S. domestic support for the independence of Cuba enmeshed the United States in a struggle with Spain over the fate of the island nation. The decision to aid the Cuban resistance was a major departure from the traditional American practice of liberal nationalism, and the results of that decision had far-reaching consequences. The 1898 Treaty of Paris ending the war gave Cuba its independence and also ceded important Spanish possessions to the United States —notably Puerto Rico, the Philippines, and the small island of Guam. The United States was suddenly a colonial power with overseas dependencies.

> This assumption of colonial responsibilities reflected not only the temporary enthusiasms of 1898, but also marked a profound change in the diplomatic posture of the United States. The foreign policies of the early 19th century had less relevance at the dawn of the 20th century because the nation had changed. The United States had almost all the attributes of a great power —it stood ahead or nearly ahead of almost all other countries in terms of population, geographic size, its location on two oceans, economic resources, and military potential. (8)

Immediately after the U.S. victory against Spain in the Spanish-American war, the U.S. capitalist and imperialist military-political economy would be imposed through direct military interventions from 1898 to 1934 in Panama, Honduras, Nicaragua, Mexico,

Haiti, and the Dominican Republic in what would later become known as the Banana Wars. (9) Here, the use of military force for the purpose of securing political and economic interests in the region could not be more explicit and overt.

Between 1934 and 1938, under the auspices of Franklin D. Roosevelt the U.S. government attempted to redefine its image throughout Latin America and the Caribbean and to challenge stereotypes about Latin Americans in the United States through what would be called the "Good Neighbor Policy." The policy began with the withdrawal of U.S. Marines stationed in Haiti and basically ended with the nationalization of foreign-owned oil assets in Mexico.

Internally the Good Neighbor Policy was more about branding Latin America as an opportunity for trade and investment for Americans, and in order to carry this out, Roosevelt created the Office of the Coordinator of Inter-American Affairs (OCIAA). In August of 1940, Nelson Rockefeller, the businessman and politician was appointed to head the Office. The (OCIAA) was basically a propaganda tool for reframing the image of Latin American countries and their people to a U.S. audience. The real purpose was to foment trade and U.S. investment in Latin America. It is here that we begin to see a strategic shift from direct U.S. military intervention in Latin America to one of both covert intervention and the propagation of national military security forces used for "Internal Defense" throughout Latin America. This strategy would intensify significantly after the Second World War, entering the Cold War era.

Though U.S. history classes and documentaries paint the U.S. military as the primary victor in the Second World War, this could not be further from the truth. The United States only became involved in the war well after the fighting was all but done. The former Soviet Union was clearly responsible for crippling and decimating the Nazi's military forces to the point that when the United States finally was fully engaged in the war, there was little left to accomplish. The historical record is only skewed in U.S. history, while the rest of the world is clear about the facts. The reduced U.S. involvement in the world war is also evident by the lack of serious material losses inside the territorial United States, which further projected the United States into superpower status as Europe was left in absolute ruins.

The actual role of the USA leading up to its eventual involvement in WWII was that of U.S. corporations manufacturing and selling weapons, fuel, and industrial supplies to both sides for profit, even well after the United States became engaged in the war. As a matter of fact, several U.S. corporations such as ITT received compensation for the Allied bombings of their manufacturing plants in Nazi Germany. **(10)**

This fact, along with other for-profit weapons ventures by U.S. corporations in conflicts around the world, led Dwight D. Eisenhower, the WWII Supreme Allied Commander in Europe and the 34th President of the USA to address the issue with grave public concern in his presidential farewell speech on January 17, 1961:

> Until the latest of our world conflicts, the United States had no armaments industry. American makers of plowshares could, with time and as required, make swords as well. But we can no longer risk emergency improvisation of national defense. We have been compelled to create a permanent armaments industry of vast proportions. Added to this, three and a half million men and women are directly engaged in the defense establishment. We annually spend on military security alone more than the net income of all U.S. corporations.
>
> Now this conjunction of an immense military establishment and a large arms industry is new in the American experience. The total influence—economic, political, even spiritual—is felt in every city, every Statehouse, every office of the Federal government. We recognize the imperative need for this development. Yet, we must not fail to comprehend its grave implications. Our toil, resources, and livelihood are all involved. So is the very structure of our society.

In the councils of government, we must guard against the acquisition of unwarranted influence, whether sought or unsought, by the military-industrial complex. The potential for the disastrous rise of misplaced power exists and will persist. We must never let the weight of this combination endanger our liberties or democratic processes. We should take nothing for granted. Only an alert and knowledgeable citizenry can compel the proper meshing of the huge industrial and military machinery of defense with our peaceful methods and goals, so that security and liberty may prosper together. (11)

What in fact did happen and is continuing to happen is that the so-called Military Industrial Complex has absolutely begun to dictate the weaponized global reality in which we exist today. The United States has approximately 800 military bases in countries around the world. It has the world's largest military spending budget in the world as well, outspending the combined military budgets of the next 15 countries. Between the war in Vietnam and most recently the war in Afghanistan, the United States has proven that the profitability of war to the Military Industrial Complex, does not require a victory, nor the restoration of any sort of democracy. War is profitable regardless of the victors, and regardless of the social, political, and economic outcome of the war.

Though there is a tremendous amount of rhetoric and historical posturing about the spreading of democracy and freedom around the globe, it is clear that what is actually being spread is a for-profit military-political economy rooted in transnational imperialism. Mexico is no exception to those affected and may well be one of the clearest examples of how the United States is able to intervene politically, economically, and militarily in a country while appearing not to do so.

Chapter 7
The U.S. Army School of the Americas - SOA

The U.S. Army School of the Americas (SOA) is a training school that was originally located in the Central American nation of Panama, and later moved to Columbus, Georgia, U.S.A. at Fort Benning. Today the school has changed its name to the Western Hemisphere Institute for Security Cooperation (WHINSEC), but throughout Mexico, Central America, and South America, it is still known as the School of the Assassins.

The SOA is known for training military officials throughout Mexico, Central America, and South America in military counter-insurgency strategies that include the use of violence, torture, coercion, political and mass media manipulation, and the imposition of several military dictators. If you want to learn more about the SOA check out the SOA Watch at SOAW.ORG, which is a watchdog organization that has exposed many of the SOA's deepest secrets.

Among the many opponents of the SOA there have been several different religious communities, in particular radical leftist Catholic Jesuits. The primary reason for this is the fact that in several countries throughout Central and South America, SOA graduates specifically targeted religious leaders and organizers who garnered support for leftist community leaders, organizations, and rebels.

Among these, perhaps the most famous cases come from El Salvador, according to the SOA Watch:

> In 1993, the United Nations Truth Commission Report on El Salvador cited the officers responsible for the worst atrocities committed during that country's brutal civil war. Over two-thirds of those named were trained at the School of the Americas.

Their crimes include the assassination of Archbishop
Oscar Romero (1980), the murder of four U.S. church wom-
en (1980), the El Mozote Massacre (1980) with more than
900 killed, the Sheraton Hotel murders of labor leaders
(1981), the Lake Suchitlan Massacre (1983) with 117 killed,
the Las Hojas Massacre (1983) with 16 killed, the Los
Llanitos Massacre (1984) with 68 killed, the San Sebastian
Massacre (1988) with 10 killed, and the University of Central
America Massacre (1989) with 8 killed. Six of the eight persons murdered at the University of Central America in 1989
were Jesuit priests. (1)

According to the SOAW in Chile:

Augusto Pinochet is not a graduate of the School of the
Americas, yet his influence is held in high esteem there. In
1991, visitors (to the SOA) could view a note from Pinochet,
and a ceremonial sword donated by him, on display in the
office of the Commander.

Graduates of the School of the Americas have comprised
one out of every seven members of the command staff of
DINA, the notorious Chilean intelligence agency responsible for many of the worst human rights atrocities during
the Pinochet years. (2)

Neoliberalism began as a fascist military-political economy under the dictatorship of Augusto Pinochet in Chile from September
11, 1973 to 1990. The military coup was supported by the U.S.
government with direct involvement by the Central Intelligence
Agency and U.S. based transnational corporations.

DINA is the National Intelligence Directorate, which in effect
was Pinochet's secret police between 1973 and 1977. It was
responsible for assassinations, kidnappings, disappearances,
rape, and torture. It was known as Pinochet's Gestapo. (3)
I have had the tremendous fortune of meeting amazing warriors from Chile who have shared their experiences from inside

of Pinochet's concentration camps. I will spare the details; however, I will say this: the level of torture, in particular the sexual torture of both men and women in the camps was absolutely horrific.

This is precisely where we can begin to understand the true functionality of a military-political economy, in this case directly under a fascist military dictatorship.

The SOA in Mexico

Unfortunately SOA graduates are not old news. We continue to unmask their presence to this day, and Mexico is absolutely no exception.

According to the SOA Watch:

> Consistently the countries with the worst human rights records have sent the most students to the SOA during the peaks of repression. Given that history, it is no coincidence that Mexico is now among the top clients of the SOA. In the first 49 years of the School, Mexico sent very few students—766 total—to be trained at the SOA. That number escalated sharply in 1996 and rose to 333 students in 1997, 1,177 in 1998 and close to 700 in 1999. Proponents of the SOA claim that this training is necessary because of Mexico's increased involvement in the "war on drugs"; however, that is just a smokescreen. The truth is that in 1997, only 10% of Mexican students took counter-narcotics courses. No Mexican soldiers were slated for the counter-drug operations course in 1999. However, 40 were projected to take military intelligence training.
>
> The Mexican general in charge of the first military response to the Zapatista uprising, Juan López Ortiz received two infantry courses at the U.S. Army School of the Americas from the 12th of October to the 9th of December, 1959. He was the commanding officer of soldiers responsible for the

Massacre at the Ocosingo Market, where eight Zapatistas were murdered with shots fired at close range to the head.

The sudden rise in Mexican graduates corresponds to the growing movement for economic justice in Mexico. The voices of and for the poor —represented by leaders like Bishop Samuel Ruiz from Chiapas— threaten the powerful and wealthy. Thus, it is not surprising that SOA graduates have come out against the Church. One SOA graduate, General Jose Ruben Rivas Peña, wrote an analysis of the conflict in Chiapas in which he stated: "The Vatican is the indirect cause of the conflict in Chiapas with its contaminated thread of liberation theology." This rhetoric is frighteningly similar to that used in El Salvador prior to the assassination of Archbishop Romero by SOA graduates in 1980. (4)

Rivas Peña was also responsible for the creation of paramilitary death squads that carried out the December 22, 1997 assassination of 45 civilians from the Zapatista support base communities in Acteal, Chiapas, who were attending a Catholic mass. Eleven of those murdered were men, the rest were women and children. They were all unarmed. Several SOA graduates sent to Mexico post- 1994, when the Zapatista uprising began, were specifically being trained in Psychological Operations. (5)

Though the exact number of Mexican SOA graduates is unknown, we have a list of Mexican military personnel trained at the school between 1955 and 2003. Due to the diligent work of SOA Watch, the names and courses taken by these Mexican military personnel have all been made public; however, names of trainees after 2003 continue to be withheld from the public. It is also clear that the list of graduates previous to 2003 is incomplete. The last attempt to release names between 2003 and the present was directly shut down by former U.S. president Barrack Obama's administration.

The 43 Students Who Do Not Want to Disappear

Among the many state-sponsored atrocities that continue to occur in Mexico to this day is one that took place in September of 2014, when 43 male rural Indigenous teacher trainee students from a school in Ayotzinapa, Guerrero, commandeered buses, as they have done every year, to travel to the protests commemorating the October 2, 1968 Tlatelolco Massacre (more on this massacre in the chapter on Militarism in Mexico.) The 43 students were apprehended by local police in cahoots with a local criminal organization. One of the students was murdered on site and had his face literally removed, while the other 42 vanished into thin air. They disappeared, and have yet to reappear.

In early 2015, the Mexican federal government pronounced the missing Ayotzinapa students officially dead. Parents and supporters continue to ignore any official declarations in the matter because the government only had DNA evidence proving the death of one student. Austrian experts at the time of the official declaration cited that the supposed evidence used to declare the deaths of the remaining 42 students was both inconclusive and impossible to work with.

The disappearance of the rural education students in Mexico has garnered major international attention. "Disappearances" have become known as a calling card of the Dirty War era throughout Mexico, Central America, South America and the Caribbean. Disappearances, however, are not just a thing of a painful past; they mark an ever painful present, and an extremely terrorizing future.

And though one of the disappeared student's cell phone tracking device led to a final destination in a military base in the state of Guerrero, and subsequent searches throughout the region uncovered dozens of mass graves that did not belong to any of the students, Alejandro Saavedra Hernández, the military official in charge of the 35th military region in Mexico based in Chilpancingo, Guerrero, which includes the Iguala region (where the disappearances occurred), was given a promotion from Brigadier General to Division General.

His replacement by Brigadier General Raúl Gámez Segovia in the military zone where the students disappeared occurred in December of 2014, when a federal rearrangement of the command of several military zones throughout Mexico was also in motion. Raúl Gámez Segovia is a specialist in military intelligence and a former military professor who teaches subjects such as Irregular Warfare and Civil Unrest.

I checked the list of Mexican SOA graduates myself at the time, and from the 6th of February to the 17th of April in 1995, then Major Raúl Gámez Segovia took a course at the U.S. Army School of the Americas at Fort Benning, in Columbus, Georgia, and was recognized as a distinguished graduate in Military Intelligence for Officers. (6)

The Comunitario Movement in Michoacán

A massive armed rebellion took place across the state of Michoacán against what can only be described as "narco-governance": the relationship of power, money, and control that, exists between narcotics cartels and several institutional structures of local, state, and federal government. We will discuss this historical event and the roots behind it in other chapters throughout the book. For now, in 2009 an Indigenous Nahua community attempted to rise up against narco-governance and was violently repressed into exile. Then in 2011, an Indigenous P'urhépecha community successfully rose up, expelling all institutional forms of government, political parties, and police from their community. They commandeered the municipal police's weapons, surrounded the community with armed checkpoints, and internally erected over 300 campfire barricades throughout the town of 25,000 inhabitants. Within months the community returned to a traditional form of self-governance, which they continue to practice today in 2022. This community is Cherán, Michoacán which we will talk about in more detail in chapter 19.

In 2013-2014 several Indigenous and mestizo communities throughout the state of Michoacán were motivated to rise up as well, in what briefly became known locally as the "Comunitario Movement". In official government declarations and in the mainstream media it was known as the "Autodefensa" movement. Ostula, the Indigenous Nahua community that had unsuccessfully risen up in 2009, was able to successfully rise up in 2014 and has also maintained a structure of traditional self-governance since then.

In January of 2015, one year after the statewide armed uprising which had spread like wildfire throughout the state of Michoacán, Alfredo Castillo the federal envoy in charge of security for the State of Michoacán stepped down and was replaced by General Pedro Felipe Gurrola Ramírez.

Though we were never able to find Gurrola Ramirez on the lists of SOA graduates, he boasted in his public resume about participating in an Army Ranger course at the SOA. This is tremendously significant because it proves that there are other graduates on active duty throughout the Mexican military who are not on the lists that we do have. Therefore we really have no exact idea of in how many graduates there are, and in which atrocities they may have participated or will participate.

Other famous Mexican SOA graduates are today, in fact, members of the very narcotics cartels that are bringing Mexico to its knees. As many as 31 ex-soldiers who were once part of an elite division of the Mexican army –the Special Air Mobile Force Group– deserted their official positions and became the security arm of a major drug cartel, only to later break off and independently create one of the most violent cartels in Mexican history. Mexican military deserters turned cartel hit men are not limited to this one cartel but also include one of Michoacán's own cartels. In a twisted sequence of events, somehow the head of Internal Security in Michoacán, Gurrola Ramirez, was at one point a military general trained at the same U.S. Army institution as some of the most dangerous hit men for one of the most dangerous cartels in the state of Michoacán's history.

Most recently General Luis Rodríguez Bucio has been named the military official commanding the National Guard, a federal military/police national internal security force created on March

26, 2019. Rodríguez Bucio, the commander of this historical military police force created by Mexico's very first supposedly "leftist" president Andres Manuel Lopez Obrador, is also a graduate of the U.S. Army School of the Americas. (7)

Debate with Lee Rials, the Public Affairs officer for WHINSEC, the U.S. Army Western Hemisphere Institute for Security Cooperation

On January 23rd, 2015 I published a short article titled "SOA Graduate Takes Control of Security in Michoacán, Mexico" on the independent news sites elenemigocomun.net and indybay. org. And as a result of the article I received a series of comments from Lee Rials, the Public Affairs officer for WHINSEC, the U.S. Army Western Hemisphere Institute for Security Cooperation, AKA the SOA. The following is our debate on the comment thread of the article on indybay.org. It has been edited for context and to avoid redundancy in content that is included in other chapters.

Missing some facts

by Lee Rials

(lee.a.rials.civ [at] mail.mil) Thursday Jan 29th, 2015 12:57 PM

Mr. Sedillo missed some facts in his discussion, the first being that General Gurrola's name does not appear in the SOAW database of 'graduates.' For another, there is no evidence whatsoever that this series of schools ever taught anything illegal, unethical or immoral, and more importantly, no evidence that anyone used anything learned there for bad purposes. Yes, General Rivas attended the Command and General Staff Course, but that is the same course every Army has for its mid-level officers, preparing them for leading larger units or serving on their staffs. Some of those soldiers who went to work for the cartels did get some training from the United States, but not from the SOA--it never had courses for units, just individuals. The Western Hemisphere Institute for Security Cooperation, which has been in operation for more than 14 years, is open for anyone to see. Visitors may sit in classes, talk with students and faculty, review instructional materials. Anyone can make his/her own evaluation of who we are and what we do. February begins a period of intense activity, with six or seven different courses in session most of the time until October, when the load begins to lessen.

Reply to Mr. Rials regarding WHINSEC
by Simón Sedillo - El Enemigo Común
Thursday Jan 29th, 2015 9:39 PM

Thank you Mr. Rials. There was one mistake and we are working on correcting it asap. It is true that General Gurrola is not on the list of SOA graduates from 1953-1996. As you well know, this list is, however, very incomplete. It does not include names from 1997 to the current date. General Gurrola is cited in the Mexican newspaper article *http://www.quadratin.com. mx/principal/%C2%BFQuien-es-Felipe-Gurrola-Ramirez/* as listing on his resume having received an Army Ranger course at Fort Benning, which is another way of saying "I am an SOA graduate." Mexico has its own list of SOA graduates and that list is slowly beginning to come to light. While WHINSEC may carry out its current activities with a supposed transparency, the SOA Watch *http://soaw.org/* has been instrumental in gathering testimonies of atrocities committed by SOA graduates and has even uncovered training manuals from the SOA that expose the true nature of this military institution. My question to you Mr. Rials is: If WHINSEC is so transparent, why won't you release the names of trainees from 2003 until the current date? Do you have something to hide?

Clarification

by Lee Rials

(lee.a.rials.civ [at] mail.mil) Friday Feb 6th, 2015 8:59 AM

Mr. Sedillo, WHINSEC is a small tenant organization on the huge installation that is Fort Benning. The Ranger School is a component of the Maneuver Center of Excellence, which is the major command of Fort Benning and has not only the Ranger School, but also the Airborne School, the Infantry School, the Armor School, Army Basic Training and Army One-Station Unit Training. The Ranger School is completely unrelated to WHINSEC, although the School of the Americas did offer a 'Commando Course' for a time, based on the Army's Ranger Course. The use of the term 'graduate' is disingenuous, attempting to give a significance to attendance at the SOA that is unwarranted. People took adult, professional courses, then returned to their jobs better prepared to do those jobs. As for transparency, WHINSEC is likely the most transparent of all organizations in the Department of Defense. Anyone can come any workday, sit in classes, talk with students and faculty, review instructional materials. What does knowing by name who has been here tell you about what we teach? Absolutely nothing. You can know everything else about attendees of courses, especially what countries and services they are from. So, I'll offer again, come see who we are and what we do. You are welcome any time.

Final Response to Mr. Rials
by Simón Sedillo - El Enemigo Común

Tuesday Feb 10th, 2015 5:46 PM

The arguments about the violent history of U.S. militarism, in particular covert operations in Latin America, do not reside in the SOA or WHINSEC alone. Nobody is arguing that either institution has that level of importance. However when piecing together a broader history of U.S. militarism, The SOA, WHINSEC, Fort Benning, and many other places such as Ft. Bragg, NC; Ft. Huachuca, AZ; and Ft. Leavenworth, KS., have somehow managed to graduate a disproportionate number of heinous Latin American criminals who used military strategies to impose political and economic foreign policy in Latin America. This line of thinking about Latin America has been going on as formal U.S. foreign policy since the Monroe Doctrine in 1823, way before the SOA and WHINSEC.

SOA graduates however as a whole are an embarrassing bunch of soldiers based upon their military records in their home countries. Graduating from the SOA might not have made these men criminals, but academic, military, and economic support for criminal military operations including military dictatorships in Latin America does make the United States a criminal for supporting these corrupt political regimes.

You might want to fact check yourself or at least have a talk with the institution you are doing PR for. SOA attendees were called graduates by the SOA itself, and apparently each received a diploma for their attendance; the diploma lists them all as graduates as seen here: ***http://imagehost.epier.com/31592/AMERICAS. jpg*** (This Image has since been removed) It is interesting however that today you are trying to shy away from this embarrassing fact.

The SOA is only one small piece of evidence in a much larger puzzle of international human rights abuses. These are war crimes that continue to take place in Mexico today. Mexico is getting ever closer to (Now in 2022 it has surpassed.) Argentina's 30,000 disappeared during the U.S. backed military dictatorship there. Despite ample warning from the UN, the European Union, and countless other international human rights organizations and agencies the U.S. government continues to train individuals and send financial aid and military equipment to nations such as Mexico, where the military is known to be working with organized crime and enforcing repressive internal defense strategies.

The fact that General Gurrola was trained "next door" and "not" at the SOA demonstrates the failure of the U.S. government to deal seriously with the record of the SOA/ WHINSEC, the most intensely scrutinized aspect of U.S. military training in Latin America.

I hope you are bracing yourself for the hail storm of criticisms against the SOA and WHINSEC in the coming months as Archbishop Oscar Romero is officially made a saint by the Catholic church. Oscar Romero's assassins were members of Salvadoran death squads, including two graduates of the School of the Americas. The 1993 United Nations Truth Commission report on El Salvador identified SOA graduate Major Roberto D'Aubuisson as the man who ordered the assassination. SOA graduates murdered this archbishop, four American nuns, six Jesuit priests, their cook and her child all in El Salvador.

The SOA graduates who massacred 16-year old Celina Ramos, her mother Elba Ramos and six Jesuit priests in 1989 at the University of Central America (UCA) in El Salvador, took courses like Urban Counterinsurgency Ops, Commando Operations, Small Unit Training and Management.

We are not just matching up names to lists of graduates. We are consistently matching up names of graduates of this and many other military institutions to real life atrocities and ongoing horror stories.

Another SOA graduate, Jose Ruben Rivas Peña of Mexico, was responsible for the creation of paramilitary death squads responsible for the December 22, 1997 assassination of 45 civilians attending a Catholic mass. Boy do those SOA graduates have a thing against Catholics. You will note that SOA graduates sent to Mexico after 1994 were specifically being trained in Psy-Ops. These facts are problematic and worrisome.

Sources at the [SOA] say that when...soldiers go through the urban combat exercise with blanks in their weapons, half the time the village priest (played by a U.S. Army chaplain) is killed or roughed up.

–Newsweek Magazine, August 9, 1993

Many of the critics [of the SOA] supported Marxism — Liberation Theology — which was defeated with the assistance of the U.S. Army."

–Army School of the Americas web page, June, 1999

In 2005 an SOA graduate by the name of Lt. Col. Geoffrey Demarest engaged in an illegal military mapping scandal in Mexico violating national sovereignty. Demarest entered several Native communities who practice communal land ownership in the states of San Luis Potosi and Oaxaca with a military mapping project obfuscated as academic research by Kansas University. (More on this in the chapter titled "The Demarest Factor)

Demarest believes that traditional forms of land tenure in places like Colombia and Mexico are both criminal and a direct military threat. This is at the core of so many of the major, internationally recognized human rights abuses taking place against Native communities in Mexico right now. The SOA is just one small part of this much larger and very serious issue.

(Here I explained to Mr. Rials the reassignment of SOA graduate Brigadier General Raúl Gámez Segovia to the Iguala region in Guerrero where the Ayotzinapa students disappeared. It has been edited to avoid redundancy)

I don't know about you, but I for one will be paying attention to Brigadier General Raúl Gámez Segovia's movements in the face of mass civil unrest in the aftermath of this horrible human rights atrocity in Guerrero, Mexico.

Other infamous Mexican SOA graduates are now cartel members. That is right Mr. Rials, cartel members once part of an elite division of the Mexican army who deserted their official positions and have since joined cartels, and in one case graduates created one of the most brutal cartels of their own.

How can you claim that "Some of those soldiers who went to work for the cartels did get some training from the United States, but not from the SOA," if you also still want to claim that the U.S. Army is not actually tracking their graduates and that you have no idea what the grads are doing after they leave the institute?

The information about these SOA graduates inside of Mexican cartels is coming from mainstream Mexican media and in-depth independent investigative journalism taking place in Mexico.

The effects of the strategies employed by a disproportionate amount of Latin American soldiers and U.S. advisors graduating from places like the SOA have been and continue to be absolutely devastating to the people of Latin America. These effects are coming to a critical boiling point in Mexico, and the whole world is watching.

Are you really willing to lay your name and your career on the line for an institution that is under serious political fire for these and many many more atrocities by the Pope, religious groups and organizations, world leaders, students, university groups, professors, professionals, collectives, cooperatives, workers, musicians, and average everyday people?

I really wish I had time to get away from my extremely busy and underpaid work schedule to continue this conversation with you, but I simply do not. You see, I don't get paid to troll websites in order to defend a military institution's reputation, and I certainly don't get paid to defend my work against a well-paid troll.

At a time when there are scandals such as Abu Ghraib, Guantanamo Bay, and the evidence of systematic rape and torture at military detention facilities, including cases of soldiers raping young boys in front of their mothers (!!!!????), my guess is that your job must be very well paid.

I know you must provide for your family and I am not one to judge, but I assure you that commenting on blog posts on the weekdays and barbecuing on the weekends is not going to cut it. It is going to take a lot more to clean up the image of the SOA, WHINSEC, Fort Benning, the U.S. Army, and the political and economic interests behind these military strategies.

Thank you for your observations. They have been duly noted.

P.S.
I do want to make sure I read you correctly however. So you're telling me that if we send someone over, you will make public the names of all of the SOA/WHINSEC attendees and the courses they took, including names from 2003 - 2015? If so someone from the SOA Watch SOAW.ORG will be in touch with you so that we can start matching up those names to atrocities since 2003. Thank you.

Mr. Rials never responded and he retired from his position at WHINSEC in August of 2019. **(8)**

Chapter 8
A Brief History of U.S. Backed Militarism in Mexico

In order to begin a discussion around U.S. backed militarism in Mexico we have to start with the Monroe Doctrine. On December 2, 1823, the fifth president of the United States James Monroe gave his annual address to Congress in which he presented, what would by 1850, become known as the "Monroe Doctrine."

In essence Monroe made a declaration to allied European nations stating that the USA would not intervene in any existing European colonies in the Americas; it would, however, consider any extension of those colonies or attempts to colonize already independent nations as acts of aggression against the peace of the United States. Several modern historians have provided clear evidence that the Monroe Doctrine was also very much about the United States protecting its slavery interests throughout the Americas from slave rebellions such as the one in Haiti, and from British abolitionism.

What is specifically significant here in terms of US / Mexico relations is that Mexico had achieved its very own independence from Spain after an 11 year war, on August 24, 1821. Canada would not gain independence from Britain until July 1, 1867. Therefore Mexico was the United States' first neighboring and independent nation-state. As soon as Mexico achieved its independence from Spain, the United States almost immediately recognized the geopolitical significance of the independent nation-state of Mexico.

When the Monroe Doctrine was declared, the United States had little military power to back it up, or pose any real threat to European nations, so in a certain sense the recognition and subsequent protection of Mexican independence was a strategy of strength in numbers. However by 1850 when the doctrine began to be coined as such, it became clear that the United States had its own imperial and neocolonialist intentions as exposed by its military intervention in Mexico.

U.S. Military Intervention in Mexico, 1845

The Mexican-American war was originally instigated by the U.S. annexation of Texas on December 29, 1845. It is important to recall that though the Republic of Texas had declared its independence from the Republic of Mexico on March 2, 1836, Mexico never recognized this declaration and considered Texas part of the Mexican Republic. Therefore the eventual "annexation" of Texas by the United States was certainly perceived as an act of aggression against Mexican sovereignty.

Though eventually the Mexican Republic was reluctantly willing to cede Texas to the United States without further conflict, the boundary between Texas and Mexico would be disputed. Mexico was literally provoked into initiating the war by U.S. troops sent to the disputed territory. On April 25, 1846, what in the United States was called the Mexican War and today is known as the Mexican-American war, began.

In September of 1847 the Mexican capital fell to U.S. forces, and Mexico, and the United States began to negotiate a peace treaty originally named the "Treaty of Peace, Friendship, Limits and Settlement between the United States of America and the Mexican Republic." The treaty was signed on February 2, 1848 and today is known as the Treaty of Guadalupe Hidalgo.

In the treaty, the United States agreed to pay the meager amount of 15 million dollars and gained territorial control over Texas, including the originally disputed boundary with Mexico, as well as the majority of New Mexico and Arizona, and the entirety of Alta California, Nevada, Utah and Colorado. To this day in Mexico, the war is still known as the U.S. intervention in Mexico. Also to this day, the U.S. victory against Mexico is literally celebrated within the very first line of the official hymn of the U.S. Marines:

From the Halls of Montezuma

To the shores of Tripoli

We fight our country's battles

In the air, on land, and sea.

First to fight for right and freedom

And to keep our honor clean;

We are proud to claim the title

Of United States Marines.

The territory acquired by the United States in the U.S. intervention of Mexico would contribute greatly to propelling the country into the Civil War as the legality and future of slavery itself was put into question on the new land as well as on the land simultaneously occupied by U.S. westward expansion. To be clear and leave absolutely no doubt about it, again, all of these lands belonged and continue to belong to the Indigenous Peoples of the region long before the European invasion, long before the birth of the independent nation-states of the Republic of Mexico and the United States of America.

Throughout this entire time period the ongoing genocide, and forced assimilation of Indigenous nations across the lands of so-called Mexico and the so-called United States was continuing to take place at an alarming rate. These key historical territorial occupations contributed greatly to making the United States the political, economic, and military superpower that it is today, all with a clear foundation in the ideology of white, male, Christian, supremacy. The fruits of these territorial occupations would not be reaped until much later, as the American Civil War between 1861 and 1865 clearly devastated the nation-state with a loss of 750,000 citizens, 2.5% of the population.

The Spanish-American War, 1898

On April 21, 1898, the United States in alliance with Cuban independence forces, engaged Spain in what would become known as the Spanish-American War. The United States won the war in three months, three weeks, and two days. The geopolitical significance of the U.S. victory in this war to countries throughout the Americas, but Mexico in particular, would be one of uncovering a northern neighbor that suddenly became a global imperial power and a threat to the sovereignty of nations across the board.

According to the U.S. State Department's Office of the Historian:

> The 1898 Treaty of Paris ending the war gave Cuba its independence and also ceded important Spanish possessions to the United States —notably Puerto Rico, the Philippines, and the small island of Guam. (1)

The geopolitical effect on Indigenous people throughout the Americas, the Caribbean, and the Pacific Islands would be even more devastating. The United States would begin to act militarily against them as other disposable variables in the equation of capitalist imperialism.

The Dictator Porfirio Diaz

At the time of the Spanish-American War, Mexico was in the middle of a military dictatorship under Porfirio Diaz. During this time period, Porfirio Diaz opened the floodgates to foreign investment in Mexico, which was dominated by U.S. businesses and investors but included investors from throughout Europe as well.

Porfirio Diaz used a heavy hand to specifically expropriate communally held land originally collectively owned by the Indigenous nations throughout the territory, and made it available for private purchase to local land barons, but more importantly to foreign investors. Diaz simultaneously granted tax abatements to investors and the security that their newly acquired lands and business ventures would be protected from upheaval and the social political unrest for which Mexico had become known. The foreigners ransacked natural resources such as minerals, rubber, and lumber, while displacing 9.5 million Indigenous farmworkers.

Under a military dictatorship, laissez-faire capitalism, and international investment in free trade, Mexico flourished economically to the extent that at one point the dollar to peso exchange rate was 3.2 dollars to the peso. Mexico's economic strength was comparable to that of France, Great Britain, and Germany. Of course the riches were concentrated among the nation's elite. The majority of the Mexican population and in particular Indigenous farm-working communities that had been dispossessed of their formerly communally held subsistence lands, were forced to become peons of wealthy hacienda owners and the Mexican elite. Those who most benefitted, of course, were close political and business allies of Porfirio Diaz himself, the creme de la creme of the Mexican elite.

In 1910 Porfirio Diaz once again decided not to step down as dictator, but this time he did allow Francisco I. Madero to run against him for the presidency. As Madero, who was himself part of the elite, garnered popular support as a presidential candidate, Diaz had him jailed. The election went forward and though Madero had a tremendous amount of support at this time, Diaz once again declared a near unanimous victory. This was one of the factors leading to the Mexican Revolution, which began on November 20, 1910. Díaz was forced to resign from office on May 25, 1911, and he left the country six days later. He died in Paris, France on July 2, 1915, amidst the ongoing Mexican Revolution.

The Mexican Revolution had a variety of personalities with radically different political perspectives. Among these personalities it is indispensable to mention the Oaxacan anarchist Ricardo Flores Magón, who wrote critically throughout the Mexican Revolution in his own newspaper *Regeneración.* At one point Magón leaves Mexico in political exile for the United States and continues to write and print copies of his newspaper, which are then shipped to Mexico. During his time there he is persecuted by both Mexican and U.S. authorities working in collaboration, and is arrested several times until his final conviction on August 15, 1918. He is sentenced to 20 years for sedition. In November of 1919 Magón was transferred to Leavenworth Prison in Kansas and on November 21, 1922 he was assassinated by a prison guard. **(2)** An absolutely excellent book in English about Ricardo Flores Magón's life and influence on revolutionary Mexican politics to this very day, is *Dreams of Freedom: A Ricardo Flores Magón Reader* edited by Chaz Bufe and Mitchell Cowen Verter. In Spanish the entire Ricardo Flores Magón archive is available at *http://archivomagon.net/*.

One Party Rule (The Political Dictatorship)

The United States, having several economic and political interests in Mexico, intervened politically, financially, and militarily throughout the Mexican Revolution, and in essence assured that whoever ended up in power continued to protect, defend, and secure U.S. political and economic interests, investments, and businesses in Mexico. When the dust settled from the Revolutionary War between 1920 and 1929, what Mexico was left with was over 2 million dead and a single political party that would rule Mexico for 71 years until 2000. After several changes, in 1946 this party was finally named what we know today as the Institutional Revolutionary Party (PRI). To be clear here, the phrase "one party rule" is just a fancy way of saying a political dictatorship. The PRI was a political dictatorship in Mexico for 71 years, and received consistent support and assistance from the U.S. government through covert and overt military and intelligence assistance programs.

According to Mexican author and political analyst Fernando Lobo:

> The PRI political party had an enormous amount of power over the government. We could easily say that the business

classes, major industries, and the bourgeoisie all had to constantly negotiate and make pacts with that PRI government. This was the exact same process through which the neoliberal system was first imposed in Mexico in the 80s, under PRI president Miguel de la Madrid. (3)

U.S. diplomatic relations and foreign policy with Mexico from 1929 to this very day would be marked primarily by an official policy of non-interventionism while simultaneously, U.S. political, economic, and military influence over Mexico would increase significantly in the following decades and would become glaringly evident to Mexico and the world during the Cold War.

Mexico's Federal Security Directorate (DFS)

In 1947, the U.S. Central Intelligence Agency (CIA) assisted Mexico in the creation of the Federal Security Directorate (DFS) as part of the U.S. policy of Soviet containment initiated by the Truman Doctrine. One could reasonably argue that the creation of the DFS in Mexico with help from the CIA marks the true beginning of the Cold War. The DFS was extremely effective in quelling insurgencies and social movements during what is now known as the Dirty War era dated officially from 1964-1987. The DFS did so by committing state-sponsored crimes against humanity and atrocities such as torture, kidnappings, and murder. (4) As these atrocities were uncovered, the Mexican federal government was forced to officially shut down the DFS, while clearly merging its agents and assets with the National Intelligence Center (CISEN), which today continues to function as the Mexican version of the CIA.

Psychological Operations

In 1968, in the middle of the Mexican Dirty War in which the DFS and the Mexican Army were key players, the U.S. Army released a film with the reference number TF33 3972 titled *Psychological Operations in Support of Internal Defense and Development Assistance Programs*. The film is a dramatization of U.S. military assistance programs in a fictional country named "Host-land." The make-up and uniforms of the military officials from Host-land represented in the film are stereo-typically "Latin American." The initial scene is set inside a private meeting between U.S. and Host-land government officials and military personnel, presumably at a U.S. Embassy. The scene concludes with the Host-land officials requesting military assistance with an emphasis on specialists with a particular focus on Psychological Operations.

The film goes on to specify the political and social instability generated by subversive communist insurgencies, and the necessary psychological strategies for counterinsurgency. In a subsequent scene the film describes the use of cultural entertainment teams "to generate controlled interactions, which create a sense of group belonging and assist in the development of national unity."

Finally the film demonstrates how a society under a military psychological operation must be broken down into three groups: the government supporters, the subversives, and "the big group in the middle, the uncommitted civilians." In the film a large target is drawn over this large group in the middle while images of armed individuals stand on either side of it. (5)

The Tlatelolco Massacre

On October 2, 1968, the same year in which the U.S. Army film on psychological operations was released, Mexico suffered one of the most horrifying military atrocities in the nation's history: the Tlatelolco Massacre. Every October 2nd since the massacre there are still major mobilizations, protests, and direct actions commemorating the victims. In Mexico City the protests have often turned into riots.

On October 2, 1968, ongoing tensions erupted between the Mexican government and leftist student organizations engaged in a general strike in Mexico City, at the Plaza de Las Tres Culturas in the district of Tlatelolco in Mexico City. The protest ended in a bloodbath at the hands of infiltrated army provocateurs and the Mexican Army itself under direct orders by the Diaz

Ordaz presidential administration, through the Secretary of the Interior, Luis Echeverría Álvarez.

Infiltrated provocateurs, some of whom were later identified as soldiers of the Army, opened fire at the scene and the military responded by firing as well. Both groups fired into the crowd. The official death toll is 300, but witnesses and participants both claim hundreds more were murdered and disappeared. The military cordoned off the area, illegally entering homes surrounding the plaza to search for students fleeing the massacre.

The massacre occurred just ten days before the 1968 Olympics were to be hosted in Mexico City, and international attention at the time of the Olympics undoubtedly contributed to the government crackdown on the student protest. After the massacre, there was a media blackout that resulted in scarcely any investigative reporting on the matter until years later. The Tlatelolco Massacre is still an ongoing chilling reminder of what the Mexican government is capable of, in the name of internal security.

This would not be the last of these types of coordinated military actions against civilians under the guise of internal security. The Dirty War is officially said to have lasted from 1964 to 1987. Independent researchers have declared that it lasted from 1954 to 2000. I would argue that it began with the formation of the DFS in 1947, and has never ended. What has changed over time is who exactly is presented as the official enemy, and who is used to confront said enemy.

The Tlatelolco Massacre marked a permanent painful reminder in the collective consciousness of Mexico: If your movement gets too big or attracts too much negative attention for the government, there are very serious consequences at stake including, but not limited to, a massacre. The Dirty War would continue in full force in communities throughout Mexico. None of those responsible for the Tlatelolco massacre have ever been charged with anything.

Less than two years later on May 4, 1970, the U.S. Army National Guard would open fire on peaceful protestors at Kent State University, in Kent, Ohio, killing four, injuring nine, and paralyzing one. Though the soldiers responsible for the Kent State massacre were tried, not one was ever charged.

The Mexican Political Elite and the CIA

In 1998, declassified Central Intelligence Agency (CIA) documents exposed a direct relationship between the CIA and key figures involved in the Tlatelolco Massacre and other Mexican Dirty War atrocities. **(6)** Additional declassified documents also demonstrate constant U.S. support for the Diaz Ordaz Government and the subsequent Echeverria presidential administration, both of which were clearly involved in the decision to use military force against the students at Tlatelolco and carry out other acts of state-sponsored violence throughout their presidential administrations. **(7)** This support was garnered along with constant monitoring by the United States of communist threats in Mexico, including those against the student movement. **(8)**

The 1998 declassified CIA documents expose a working relationship between Mexican PRI government officials beginning in 1947, with the creation of the Mexican Federal Security Directorate (DFS). This relationship evolved steadily over the coming years and in 1960, under the auspices of a CIA agent by the name of Winston Scott, the CIA began a program named LITEMPO. **(9)**

The LI in LITEMPO was the Mexico specific code created by the CIA. TEMPO was a code term created by Winston Scott to generate "a productive and effective relationship between the CIA and select top officials in Mexico." The program entailed the creation of an untraceable covert communication and co-ordination apparatus between the CIA and top Mexican officials including the Mexican president himself. **(10)**

LITEMPO included the 1968 President Gustavo Diaz Ordaz, his Secretary of the Interior Luis Echeverria Alvarez, the head of the DFS at the time Fernando Gutiérrez Barrios, and at least nine other high ranking government and military personnel as CIA agents, on the CIA payroll. Declassified documents also show that their payouts were deemed as excessive by some

CIA officials. The documents unveil the level of U.S. intelligence intervention in Mexico, with the full cooperation and blessing of official Mexican federal government authorities, without the knowledge of the Mexican people. **(11)**

Declassified Mexican Dirty War documents

In 2000, the PRI government lost the presidency for the very first time in 70 years to the former Coca Cola executive from the National Action Party (PAN), Vicente Fox. There was some hope of finding out the truth and perhaps finding justice, and Fox did declassify hundreds of thousands of documents related to the Tlatelolco Massacre and the Dirty War era.

The documents shed light on what truly took place, and an official investigation ensued, but was promptly shut down and never led to any charges. The PRI returned to power in 2012 under President Enrique Peña Nieto after two successive PAN presidencies under Fox and his successor Felipe Calderon. With the arrival of the PRI's Peña Nieto, the formerly declassified documents were once again designated as classified, and in classic PRI fashion, the truth was once again swept under the carpet. Currently the center-left leaning President Andres Manuel Lopez Obrador announced the declassification of the DFS documents, but they have yet to be made available to the public.

From Dirty War to Internal Defense to Paramilitarism

After the official Dirty War era, what we have seen taking place in Mexico are two specific evolving and ongoing strategies of internal defense. On the one hand, different versions of militarized police, the military itself, and or hybrids between the military and the police have been introduced and used as the primary public security forces. Though the constant justifications of this strategy of internal defense are threats of terrorism or organized crime, what has been evolving on the ground is strategic militarism with a particular focus on areas of economic and political interest. This has taken place where Indigenous communities are halting or hindering natural resource exploitation or slowing the construction of economic development corridors by engaging in grassroots liberation through community-based self-determination, self- defense, and autonomy. The second and much older strategy of internal defense has been the ongoing development and use of a wide variety of paramilitary organizations to carry out "deniable atrocities" with a particular focus on organized sectors of civil society and Indigenous communities.

Los Porros

In the late 1940s Mexico already had in place the beginnings of a counterintelligence program within higher education institutions in Mexico City. By the 1950s this conspicuous strategy of political control within higher education had spread throughout universities in Mexico City with a notable expansion in the National Autonomous University (UNAM), and the National Polytechnic Institute (IPN). **(12)** The strategy know as *porrismo* is still in place today.

A *porro* is a paid and protected student or non-student thug, who belongs to an organization much like a syndicate or union with other *porros*, functioning within a public education framework. They are paid and compensated in various ways for carrying out acts of violence against student organizers, particularly at student protests. They can generally be associated with right-wing conservative political alliances within Mexico's political parties, in particular the Institutional Revolutionary Party (PRI) and the National Action Party (PAN). These associations in addition to providing payment for services, also provide protection from prosecution or sanctions from the administration for said violent services rendered.

By the late 1960s, various *porro* organizations were active, specifically recruiting troubled young men and women throughout the university student body, but also marginalized youth from poor neighborhoods, as well as convicted violent criminals with prison sentences. Violent criminals had their charges commuted in order to be recruited into their organizations. Also in the 1960s *porros* began (and continue) to be associated with the football team Pumas at UNAM and its players. The word in Spanish for "cheer" is *porra*, hence the root of the name. *Porros* then and still today, are organized, paid, and protected violent cheerleaders for political, economic, and military interests within several higher education, high school and middle school institutions throughout Mexico. *Porros* are one of the historical roots of paramilitarism in Mexico, and certainly should be critically analyzed as a model of militarized counterintelligence and counterinsurgency, which continues to be applied against the general student body. Porros have functioned and continue to function with absolute impunity. **(13)**

Los Halcones

Also by the late 60s *porros* would begin to ascend into positions of power not just within university administrations but also as politicians and government administrators. This trend continues virtually unabated to this day. Others would be recruited among former police, military, and criminals to become *Halcones* or Hawks. The *Halcones* were a Black Operations Army shock troop created by the Federal Security Directorate (DFS) and the Central Intelligence Agency (CIA). The group was organized to violently repress protests and social movements such as the 1968 student movement. *Halcones* would carry out brutal attacks against student and community organizers throughout the Dirty War, including the June 10, 1971 massacre of over 100 people in what is today known as the Corpus Christi Massacre or the *Halconazo*.

The *Halconazo* took place with the compliance and cooperation of the police and the military, as neither intervened when the *Halcones* switched from using batons and sticks, to using high powered assault rifles to mow down defenseless students, allies, and bystanders. The *Halconazo* was irrefutably a U.S. backed, Mexican government sanctioned, paramilitary attack against unarmed civilians.

Paramilitary Forces

One could reasonably argue that the hyper militarized police we see around the world today are a form of paramilitarism. Within the Mexican context however, militarized police or the actual military carrying out police duties, has now pretty much become the norm. There is nothing new about militarized police forces, not just in Mexico or around the world, but throughout the United States as well. However, for the purposes of this book, paramilitarism as experienced in Mexico has specific functions, strategies, roots and intentions.

Paramilitary forces are armed civilians who receive training, support, and financing, or simply receive impunity from official entities such as a political party, a government administration, the police, or the military. A paramilitary organization may also be generated and supported by non-governmental institutions like corporations, banks, or individuals such as local land barons, or the political elite as well. Paramilitaries use violence to carry out social, political or economic objectives against a target civilian population that is either considered a disposable variable, a barrier, or a direct threat to a given political, economic, or military interest.

The primary purpose and function of paramilitarism is to generate and exploit what are known as deniable atrocities. That is to say, its purpose is to carry out atrocities such as extrajudicial executions, kidnappings, beatings, rape, and torture against a civilian population in such a way that governments, police, or the military can deny involvement in and/or responsibility for those atrocities once committed. These atrocities are used to dissuade social, political, or economic opposition.

A key calling card of paramilitarism is that the agents carry out their atrocities with total impunity. It is impunity of this nature that further delegitimizes governments and their justice systems altogether.

When a paramilitary group is generated from a local population to cause internal conflict in a target region, oftentimes ideological, political, religious, cultural, geographic, or social differences between opposing groups are exploited to generate violent confrontations.

A common end result of the "deniable atrocities" carried out by heavily armed paramilitaries around the world is the further official militarization, policing, and criminalization of the community, organization, group, or individual being targeted.

Disappearances

Disappearances have been carried out by unofficial paramilitary and official government forces from the Dirty War era up to now. During the Dirty War it was particularly political dissidents who were apprehended without any sort of judicial process, never to be seen again. Today it seems that anyone can disappear in Mexico for any number of reasons, many with no direct connection to any political or criminal activity whatsoever.

During the official Dirty War era throughout Latin America, some of the disappeared people ended up in secret prisons or concentration camps (sometimes for years on end) with absolutely no paperwork, no tracking system, no access to attorneys, and absolutely no way of being found by family members or friends. Others were permanently disappeared, with absolutely no trace of them, or their bodies ever again.

Disappearances are acts of terror not necessarily intended for the disappeared. Disappearances are acts of terror more specifically intended for those left behind, the family and friends of the disappeared. Disappearances are intended to terrorize entire communities if not entire countries into submission and silence. Disappearances are about controlling entire populations with fear.

Officially Mexico has reported 73,201 missing people from 1964 to 2020, over 40,000 of those since 2006 alone. The number is certainly higher due to underreporting, the lack of reporting of disappearances of undocumented immigrants from other countries, and the state-sponsored manipulation of statistics. Even so, official statistics indicate that at least seven people disappear every day in Mexico. These numbers have now far surpassed the number of disappearances during the official Dirty War Era, not just in Mexico, but in Argentina, Chile, and Guatemala as well. Though the majority of disappearances today have been related to organized crime activity, the lack of investigation and general impunity exposes at the very least the complacency, if not the outright involvement of the Mexican government.

The Federal Preventive Police (PFP)

On January 4, 1999, then PRI Mexican president Ernesto Zedillo introduced a new federal police force known as the Federal Preventive Police (PFP). According to an analysis by Dr. Graham H. Turbiville, then Director of the U.S. Army Foreign Military Studies Office (FMSO) based out of Fort Leavenworth, the PFP was described as follows:

> One of the most ambitious new law enforcement initiatives developed at the end of the century by the Mexican government is being implemented under President Ernesto Zedillo's "National Crusade Against Crime and Delinquency." Under this effort—after much contentious discussion—the Mexican Senate legislated the PFP on the 11th of December 1998, calling for a national law-enforcement body to combine the functions and many of the personnel of the Federal Highway Police (Policía Federal de Caminos), the Federal Fiscal Police (Policía Fiscal Federal) and the Federal Immigration Police (Policía Migratoria Federal). It was announced shortly thereafter that the resulting PFP would also include strong military and intelligence components.

> The PFP was made subordinate to the Interior Ministry— at the time under current presidential candidate Francisco Labastida Ochoa—and began to organize early in 1999. Its initial mission was to "safeguard the integrity and rights

of persons, prevent the commission of crimes, and pre-serve freedom, order and peace" nationally. Some 800 intelligence personnel were transferred from the Center for National Security Investigations (CISEN). (14)

According to Dr. Graham H. Turbiville of the FMSO, the PFP was created to:

- Combat organized crime and crimes that threaten national security through investigation and direct police actions.

- Prevent crime in/on federal facilities to include highways, railways, maritime ports, airports and other federal property.

- Carry out customs policing and investigation responsibilities.

- Maintain and restore public order.

- Wage a multifaceted struggle against drug trafficking.

- Police Mexican borders to control illegal immigration, smuggling and abuses against immigrants.

- Rescue hostages and kidnap victims, and seize facilities held by illegal groups.

- Police key federal natural resource areas.

- Collect and act on intelligence dealing with subversive groups and activities to include guerrillas, terrorists and other illegal paramilitary formations. (15)

The heart of the PFP counterinsurgency and counterterrorist operations lies with the CISEN components that were transferred to the new organization. This component actually formed in 1994 under CISEN as a response to the EZLN uprising in Chiapas. Initially designated the GAT— Gruppa Antiterrorista—it quickly helped integrate activities of the various security agencies. Weekly interagency meetings assessed strategic threats around the country, especially to key infrastructure targets from bombs and other attacks. As it grew and assumed new responsibilities, such as kidnappings, arms trafficking and organized crime, the GAT eventually became the Inter-Institutional Coordination Unit-GAT—or UCIDGAT as it became known in its Spanish acronym. That body transferred from the CISEN in 1999 and became the core of the PFP's subversive and criminal intelligence effort. (16)

Chapter 9

El Porrismo: National Autonomous University of Mexico – UNAM and Urban Paramilitarism

On April 20, 1999 at the UNAM, the University Student Assembly (AEU) became the General Strike Council (CGH), and the UNAM entered into a massive system-wide general strike. The 300,000 + student university system came to a grinding halt. The primary goal of the CGH was to stop a near 500% tuition increase at the institution. Among the list of demands by the CGH was also:

> The dismantling of the apparatus of repression and espionage created by university authorities as well as the ceasing of violent acts or sanctions against teachers, students, and workers who participate in the movement. (1)

In 1999, UNAM students were still dealing with *porros*. A *porro* is a paid and protected student and/or non-student thug, who belongs to an organization much like a syndicate or union with other *porros*, functioning within a public education framework. They are paid and compensated in various ways for carrying out acts of violence against student organizers in particular at student protests. The students at the 1999 UNAM strike had already dealt with them in their daily student life, before the strike. Therefore they would follow strict and disciplined protocols for engaging in civil disobedience. In 1999, school by school, the different university departments joined the general strike by voting unanimously and in person with student ID in hand so as to not be accused of being outside provocateurs. A large group of *porros* did, however, gather and lock down at the Law School, refusing to vote or leave the building. Students from across the campus mobilized and surrounded the *porros* and removed them peacefully from the campus with the threat of overwhelming force. The general student body had had enough, and inspired by the 1994 Zapatista uprising in Chiapas, students decided it was their turn to take back the university, which was being stripped from them by the austerity measures that the North American Free Trade Agreement - NAFTA and the neoliberal military-political economy were attempting to impose. (2)

Several high schools throughout Mexico City, which functioned within the UNAM system, joined the strike as well. Young people came together and organized a higher education system-wide strike, which garnered major international attention. The students were pushed up against a wall by the tuition hike. It is imperative to point out that many of these young people organizing the strike had parents and grandparents who had been through Tlatelolco, the *Halconazo* (*porros* and paramilitaries carrying out atrocities including a massacre), and almost 70 years of one-party rule under the Institutional Revolutionary Party (PRI). Young people and their families were simultaneously inspired by a history of student and popular rebellion, and then by the 1994 and ongoing Zapatista uprising. Entire families, not just the students in 1999, grew up with a fundamental awareness of political dissidence and government repression.

The 1999-2000 UNAM student strike became a topic of conversation across Mexican households. While many supported the strike, the mainstream media worked diligently to devalue the makeup of the contingent of strike organizers, claiming they were predominantly outside provocateurs and *porros* themselves. This and divisions within the General Strike Council generated complications in popular support and action. The strike however did have several victories. The primary victory was the fact that the tuition increase did not move forward as planned. The secondary victory was that though the students were under constant attack by *porros*, as well as other official and unofficial forces of repression, they were able to maintain the strike for 10 months. A third victory was that students not only talked about, but engaged in, and carried out strategies for self-determination, self-defense, and autonomy on the university campus during those 10 months. The creation of autonomous organizing and educational spaces throughout campuses during the strike was remarkable. This would be life changing to those who participated, and has continued to have repercussions to this very day. There are still several autonomous student-run spaces throughout the UNAM system including radio and cafeteria projects, autonomous meeting halls, and organizing spaces, which were fought for and kept long after the 1999 strike. **(3)**

On February 6, 2000, the Mexican Federal Preventive Police (PFP), which had been inaugurated three months earlier, unconstitutionally entered and occupied the National Autonomous University in Mexico City in order to end the 10 month long student strike. More than 700 students were arrested. The PFP did not leave completely from the UNAM campus until the 23rd of April.

According to an analysis by Dr. Graham H. Turbiville, then Director of the U.S. Army Foreign Military Studies Office (FMSO) based out of Fort Leavenworth, the PFP incursion into the UNAM campus during the student strike was described as follows:

> One of the most widely publicized PFP actions occurred early in February 2000 when Mexican authorities made the decision to retake portions of the campus at the Autonomous University of Mexico (UNAM) from strikers who had occupied campus buildings during the previous 10 months. The occupation of campus facilities began as a protest against a large tuition increase, but was soon accompanied by "plunder, theft, holding people captive, mutiny, injuring others and damaging university assets.

For students who participated in the General Strike, acts of "plunder, theft, holding people captive, mutiny, injuring others and damaging university assets" would only serve to delegitimize the student movement and justify repression. These acts were consistently committed by *porros* and not by student organizers. The PFP incursion into the UNAM campus and other striking schools was justified by actions carried out by paid and protected *porros*.

When faculty and students attempted to return to occupied campus areas late in January, members of the radical
General Strike Council (CGH) attacked and injured 37 strike
opponents.

There were several instances of teachers and younger students
asking to return to class, but they were never attacked by CGH
organizers and again the only violent attacks were carried out by
porros. If 37 strike opponents were injured, they were most likely *porros* who were injured after students defended themselves
from an attack.

On February 1, hundreds of PFP military riot police (from
the former 3rd Military Police Brigade) and explosives specialists broke through the barricades, evicted and arrested several hundred strikers, and seized homemade bombs
over a 10 hour period. Five days later the PFP, the PGR and
Federal Judicial Police cleared remaining UNAM campus
facilities at other locations and executed hundreds of arrest warrants in a remarkably well done and peaceful operation by 2,500 PFP personnel.

The PFP was not at all peaceful. Several students were beaten
and tortured during their arrests and detention.

Overall, the operations were supported by most Mexicans,
although some sharply criticized the government. The PFP
and other agencies sought to dispel widespread fear that
the strike had provided the opportunity for guerrillas such
as the Popular Revolutionary Army or Ejército Popular
Revolucionario (EPR) and the Ejército Revolucionario del
Pueblo Insurgente (ERPI) to establish a stronger urban
presence in Mexico City. However, recent guerrilla attacks
in the Mexican capital suggest that the EPR, ERPI and other
groups may have successfully transitioned from insurgencies based in remote southern states to urban presences

capable of at least nuisance attacks on military and police facilities. (4)

There is certainly no evidence that this supposed "widespread fear" of the presence of the EPR and ERPI was at all associated with the student strike.

If there was a guerrilla influence on the 1999 UNAM student strike it was the Zapatista National Liberation Army's 1994 uprising in Chiapas. I spoke with two former students who were present during the UNAM system wide student strike. One of the students, Emilia Gomita was in one of the UNAM high-schools named the School for Humanities and Sciences or CCH by its initials in Spanish, and Griselda Sánchez was a student at the UNAM itself. The following are excerpts from the interviews I conducted with them. (5)

Griselda:

> What was under discussion was an increase in fees for admission into the university. Up to that point the university had always been free. The cost was very symbolic. You basically paid cents to enroll. The fee was going to increase 500%, which would not have amounted to so much but it would have eliminated a huge amount of students. But what we would say is that it does not matter if the fee increase is less or more, but rather that education itself must be free.

> The history of activism at the university is huge. Since 1968 the students have maintained relationships with other struggles. So when 1994 came, several university activists went to Chiapas. There was an exchange of ideas which influenced the unanimous decision to start the student strike. It was older activists that would go to Zapatista territory then would return and share their experiences in political education circles.

Emilia:

For me the Zapatistas were key because they invited us several times to go and see how they lived. We would share with them how we were living and how we were organizing, and that is when we realized that we were part of a bigger plan.

Griselda:

We were being confronted by the same types of structural reforms, and the Zapatistas, in a certain sense, were able to communicate that we were the same. Not just as an Indigenous guerrilla in the Sierra of Chiapas, but rather that this was going to affect all of us the same way. One of the fundamental Zapatista demands has to do with education. So this idea of a fee increase was not random, but rather a key element of all of these structural reforms.

Emilia:

I was 17 when the UNAM system-wide student strike began and I was in one of the high schools in the UNAM system known as the CCH. So the decision to go on strike against the fee increase was made by the student body. Not all the high schools in the UNAM system made that decision as a majority or took over entire school campuses. We did. We were among the first high schools that decided we were going to join the student strike, and well, it is important to mention that our high school had 12,000 students at the time.

So, to begin with, imagine having control of a hectare of territory with all the necessary facilities to house 6000 people. Also imagine organizing to keep the space clean, active, fresh, and even prepare food. We made it edible. That was very impressive. So it was great because we

organized our meals with a cooking committee that organized a kitchen space. We organized a health commission
to take care of our health needs by taking over the school
clinic. We took over the printers and we started to broadcast radio. Suddenly we were building a small piece of autonomy. That was the interesting part about the strike, that
we had a territory under our control. It was our university.
The police did not come in. We did not allow anybody that
we did not want to come in. We decided how to handle that.
That was a big deal.

Los Porros

Emilia:

One of the reasons that we voted yes to the student strike
was that less than a month before the strike, a group of
porros occupied and took over the CCH high school. So they
started to scare female students, by threatening them, by
taking over classrooms with students in them. These were
big guys, and they were violent. So then some organized
young women from the afternoon class schedule invited
everyone to walk out of their classrooms with chants and
megaphones, and gather in the main campus area to kick
out the porros. So we kicked them out that day. They left
because they did not scare us and we did not leave; instead we all gathered in the main campus area. That was
my first experience with porros. The truth is that it made
us all excited.

Griselda:

The porros were at the student strike to stop any actions
carried out by the student strikers. They also participated
in what became known as the "extramural classes." After
months of the student strike, administrators started to call

for classes to be held outside of the university installations. The idea was to scare younger students into attending these "extramural classes" Because if not, the students "would lose a whole school year." At these extra mural classes, porros would be present as a sort of shock troop.

Emilia:

They began to organize counter protests outside of the schools, asking for the campuses to be returned to the authorities. Certainly there were actual students who just wanted to go back to school who attended these protests, but along with them there was a group of porros. So we would go to these counter protests and try to talk with the younger students who would be willing to listen but the porros would not allow those conversations to take place. They would get violent, and at least the younger students who just wanted to go back to school would see this violence and would begin to understand where we were coming from.

Griselda:

The most blatant and intense acts by the porros during the student strike was when they tried to take over one of the UNAM system high schools known as Prepa 3. In this case it was older people who came, even 50 year olds, who are clearly not high school students, and they attacked the high school students.

Emilia:

At the Prepa 3 High school there have always been more porros. So a bunch of us went from different schools to go help and when we arrived there were students who had been very badly beaten with metal pipes and things like that. I had not been afraid up until that point. Students had been beaten with metal pipes by grown men. We were kids between 15 and 25 years old. As we arrived the porros left, but then the police arrived and they surrounded us. They completely surrounded us. Several students were arrested, I and others were fortunate that the police buses filled up and several of us got help from reporters and bystanders who helped us escape into the crowd.

Griselda:

That whole situation was then used as the justification to call for the police to take over the schools. So those porro provocateurs at the Prepa 3 High School were like a Trojan Horse used to justify the use of the federal police.

The Federal Preventive Police (PFP)

Griselda:

It is important to note that among many legal stipulations with regards to the university's autonomy is that the police and the military are not allowed on campus. What the university administration does have, is its own private security guards known as "Auxilio UNAM." They too were kicked off campus during the strike. Security of the entire 700+ hectare university campus was taken over by student strikers with barricades and guard patrols.

We knew for months before that the PFP had been created. There was a big public announcement about the creation of a new federal police force. That announcement basically let us, the student strikers, know who it was that we would be confronted with. The PFP debuted on the student strike. I was at an assembly in the Che Guevara auditorium when someone screamed: "The police are already here!" The police had entered through all directions. It was a military incursion into a territory, they had everything very well planned out. They were soldiers pretending to be police. A Special Forces team of the PFP took the student strike leaders, who were clearly identified, directly to a prison known as the Reclusorio Norte. I was detained like many others who were not considered high priority and was released three days later, but not before being forced to sign a blank sheet of paper. We were put on lists. To this day we are all on lists.

There has always been a very strong element of espionage against students by university authorities since before and long after the 1999 student strike. For example in my department after the strike and during the return to classes, the person who was hired as our department head was Fernando Perez Correa who used to work for the CISEN, the Nation Security and Investigation Center (The Mexican CIA). So they placed him in one of the university departments which was considered a bastion of the whole university resistance movement, and supposedly one of the most dangerous. We used to say that they put a police officer on us. We never recognized his role as an academic director, rather that he was a police officer who was there trying to take apart the post-strike mobilizations for the freedom of political prisoners and to continue to pressure around additional demands.

Emilia:

If you know the history it is easy to imagine how far the nation-state will go, how little it cares about you, your health, or your well-being. When you know this history it becomes very easy to imagine thousands of possibilities. This is a symbolic violence, which can easily cause a level of fear, which can eventually paralyze you. We need to do things without worrying about there being spies or infiltrators. This was a tremendous lesson, which later I experienced in many other collectives, where situations can become so paranoid, because the reality is in fact that intense, but oh well. The paranoia about infiltrators, the cracks caused by who among us is good and who is bad etc., that breaks collectives apart more. That invisible threat breaks movements apart more than the actual threat. So you have to tell yourself: "Fine, they are watching us, but fuck them. They can hear us, but what we are fighting for is just for what is fair. When it comes to civil society, that fight can always be made in public.

Chapter 10
Oaxaca 2006 - A Laboratory of Repression

While Mexico saw an end to 70 years of one party rule under the Institutional Revolutionary Party (PRI) dictatorship with the election of Vicente Fox of the National Action Party (PAN) in 2000, the southern state of Oaxaca, Mexico would have the PRI in the governor's office for exactly 10 more years. In 2004, Oaxaca's incoming governor Ulises Ruiz Ortiz campaigned on the primary platform of putting an end to social protests in the city of Oaxaca. His justification was that social protests in the city were affecting the economic prosperity and growth brought about by the tourist industry. Within his first six months in office in 2005, URO, as Ulises Ruiz Ortiz came to be known as, would use police, paramilitaries, and *porros* to occupy and shut down a dissenting newspaper for an entire month, and would detain over 150 social activists and leaders of social organizations from throughout the state. The detentions were particularly treacherous because Ruiz would issue invitations for a dialogue with activists, and subsequently arrest them at the meeting points. By May of 2006 Ruiz would have created a general environment of state-sponsored political repression, which was absolutely undeniable by any standard. **(1)**

The state of Oaxaca is inhabited by 16 different Indigenous nations: Mixtecos or Ñuu sávi, Mazatecos or Ha shuta enima, Mixes or Ayuukjä'äy, Chinantecos or Tsa ju jmí', Chatinos or Kitse cha'tnio, Triquis (síí chihanj, sií xìyànj-an), Cuicatecos or Nduudu yu, Huaves or Ikoots, Chontales de Oaxaca or Slijuala xanuk, Amuzgos or Tzjon Non, Chochos or Chocholtecos or Runixa ngii-gua, Zoques de Oaxaca or Angpøn, Nahuas, Tacuates or Inyu, Ixcatecos or Mero ikooa, Zapotecos, as well as communities inhabited by Afromexicanos. Oaxaca is many nations within a state, which itself tends to act like a nation that is completely different from the rest of Mexico. Oaxaca has 570 municipalities, of which 418 are governed through some form of Indigenous traditional self-governance. Oaxaca is Native, and Oaxaca is rebellious.

Every year since 1980, the independent teachers' union known as Section 22, stages a permanent protest encampment in downtown Oaxaca City to demand above all, an increase in wages for Oaxacan rural teachers working predominantly in one of Oaxaca's Indigenous communities. This yearly protest was in fact seen as a nuisance by some Oaxacans, primarily among the business political class. Every year teachers from Section 22 block the downtown area, organize massive marches, and stage blockades throughout the city in order to pressure the government to hear their demands.

In May of 2006 the teachers installed their protest encampment in downtown Oaxaca, and Governor Ulises Ruiz Ortiz saw the protest as an opportunity to set the perfect example in his anti-protest political agenda. Nothing turned out to be further from the truth.

In Oaxaca, protest has been and continues to be a way of life. People in Oaxaca understand that the government is not there for them, and in order to be heard you have to make noise. One of the most common ways to make noise in Oaxaca City is to shut parts of the city down by blockading major intersections. On any given day, a huge variety of participants may decide to protest in this way. Average everyday citizens may engage in such a protest because of a hike in bus fares, health workers may protest over working conditions, or an Indigenous community may protest over access to their basic rights. This type of protest has become such an effective tool of popular political power in Mexico in general, but in Oaxaca in particular, that even the Institutional Revolutionary Party (PRI) has created massive membership organizations among their political base in farm-working communities and in the public transportation sector in particular. (2)

So in Oaxaca City sometimes you don't know who is protesting, or why, or whether or not their cause is just. Sometimes the protests orchestrated by these PRI organizations turn very violent as they act a lot more like gangland wars for territory.

This is particularly true in the transportation sector with buses, taxis, and cargo vehicles. A taxi protest among taxi services over territory can and has turned into a full blown shootout in the city of Oaxaca. (3)

At dawn, on June 14, 2006, Ulises Ruiz Ortiz held true to his campaign promise and sent state police to evict the teachers' protest encampment by force. Though evening security measures had been established, several protesters were caught off guard while sleeping in their tents. Amongst teargas, baton strikes, and screams, everyone in the encampment awoke and immediately fought back. At the time, the teachers had a community radio station known as Radio Plantón, (Radio Sit-In) at the Section 22 offices downtown, which had been transmitting updates on the teachers' protest. On the day of the eviction, the Section 22 offices were also raided, and the radio transmission was shut down. One of the last things said on the air before police broke into the building with tear gas was "We invite the people of Oaxaca to rise up against the government of Ulises Ruiz Ortiz!" Within hours, students at the Benito Juarez Autonomous University (UABJO) took control of the high powered university radio station in solidarity with the teachers' protest. (4)

Just as the tear gas spread throughout homes and businesses in downtown Oaxaca on that morning of June 14th, a totally unexpected popular rage spread throughout the city as well, and average everyday citizens not affiliated with the Section 22 teachers' union joined the teachers in the street, thereby giving birth to a massive popular urban uprising. By 9:30 am, the city's center was reclaimed by protesters, and the police retreated in defeat with eight police officers held hostage by the teachers' union. The police officers would be released to the Red Cross the following day. (5)

On June 16th the Section 22 Teachers' Union organized a Massive march in Oaxaca City. Average everyday citizens joined the march by the thousands. On the 17th of June a community-based general assembly was organized, and the Oaxacan People's Popular Assembly (APPO) was born. At the peak of its existence the APPO was composed of over 300 social organizations, community authorities, concerned individuals, and collectives. This was no longer a teachers' union strike; it was a broad-based, massive popular uprising. Neither the Ulises Ruiz Ortiz PRI state government, nor the Section 22 teachers' union could have imagined the radical popular turnout, solidarity, and militant actions.

The APPO, now functioning as a massive organization of organizations, and the Section 22 teachers' union, begin to function as a team. They unanimously agree to one primary demand above all others: Section 22's original demand that governor Ulises Ruiz Ortiz resign or that he be removed as governor of the state of Oaxaca. **(6)**

On July 22nd, the radio station occupied by the APPO at the Benito Juárez Autonomous University of Oaxaca (UABJO) in Oaxaca City was attacked by 50 paramilitaries. They opened fire on the station's radio cabin from the street as the DJ called for help. A large group of APPO supporters mobilized to the area and the paramilitary forces fled the scene. The station continued to transmit immediately after the attack. This is how the state government chose to dialogue with the protestors. **(7)**

On July 26th, the APPO and Section 22 installed permanent protest encampments surrounding the local offices of Congress, the Superior Tribunal of Justice, the State Attorney General's office, the Secretariat of Finance, the state police barracks, and the governor's home annex. Protest patrols were sent to prevent any government offices from opening or government vehicles from circulating in the city. The APPO and Section 22 had seriously begun to take Oaxaca City away from the official state government. **(8)**

Six days later on August 1st, a large group of women from the APPO organized a women's march and *cacerolazo* (banging of pots and pans) in Oaxaca City. At one point they decided to direct the march towards the installations of the state-run public TV and radio stations known as Canal 9 or CORTV. Once they arrived at the Canal 9 station, the women asked for a short time on the air to have their voices and demands heard. The security and administrators refused to provide a time slot, so the women entered and occupied the public radio and TV station and within hours were live on the air. **(9)**

On August 8th a group of *porros* at the UABJO set a trap to distract the DJs to leave the radio cabin long enough to sabotage the station by pouring acid over the transmitter. Radio University would go off the air, but the women who occupied the Channel 9 state-run TV and radio station were now transmitting on what they named *Radio Cacerola* (Radio Pots and Pans), as well as through the Canal 9 TV station. **(10)**

At dawn on the 21st of August an armed group of individuals attacked the APPO night guard watching over the state-run TV and Radio station's antennas on top of the Cerro del Fortin. The attackers then proceeded to shoot at the antennas themselves, destroying them. **(11)** Later that same morning, APPO activists occupied a major commercial radio station, and two major hubs for several different commercial radio stations, totaling over 12 major commercial radio stations occupied by the movement. That same evening a caravan of 30 pickup trucks with municipal, ministerial, and preventative police officers aboard began driving from protest encampment to protest encampments across the city of Oaxaca opening fire with assault rifles on protestors, civilians, and media alike. This "caravan of death" as it became known was spotted near the largest commercial radio station occupied by the APPO. On the air the DJ asked for reinforcements and, in solidarity, an individual by the name of Lorenzo Sampablo made his way there and was shot in the back by agents in the caravan of death. **(12)**

The next morning, on August 22nd, Oaxaca City arose with barricades erected by Oaxacans who blocked all transit throughout the city. Some barricades would exist day and night, while the majority were erected only after dark. The barricades and APPO security patrols would remain active until October 29th with the entrance of the Federal Preventive Police (PFP). **(13)** At the peak of the movement Oaxaca City had approximately 3000 barricades, and the APPO movement boasted 1.5 million participants across the state of 3 million inhabitants.

What took place over the six months of this massive popular urban uprising has been very well video documented in the film *Un Poquito de Tanta Verdad (A Little of So Much Truth)* by Corrugated Films, as well as historically chronicled by the author, journalist, and radio personality Fernando Lobo in his book about the 2006 APPO Uprising: *La Insurrección Transmitida (The Transmitted Insurrection)*. It has been 15 years since the APPO uprising and without the militant independent documentation such as in *Un Poquito de Tanta Verdad* and Lobo's book, it would be very difficult to tell any of the stories accurately, as the Mexican and international mainstream media either absolutely ignored or completely misrepresented the uprising. Lobo, years later, took on the task of cross referencing information to confirm dates and times in a way that is not only extremely informative, but is also critical to future generations in understanding the successes and failures of the movement as well as understanding the government's escalating repressive response.

I had the opportunity to interview Fernando Lobo and talk about specific aspects of the 2006 Oaxaca uprising which are most relevant to this book. The following are excerpts from that interview. **(14)**

> Ulises Ruiz Ortiz's government began with a repressive agenda ever since his electoral campaign. One of the political offers that Ruiz made as a candidate for governor was to eliminate or disappear public protests, arguing that these protests, which evidently are prolific in Oaxaca, stall the tourist industry. So that is how the scene was set. A governor who offers the elimination of marches and permanent sit-ins to his electorate, in essence dividing the society in two. On the one hand the protestors, on the other people who want traffic to circulate freely, and who consider that their right to free transit can justify a tremendous confrontation with riot police.

There was a small group, like a chamber of commerce among some, not all, restaurant and hotel owners downtown who had this demand. Ulises Ruiz then offers the neutralization, the regulation, and the elimination of public protests in his campaign. How? Well he had a very clear plan:

1. The creation of new riot police known as the Police Unit for Special Operations (UPOE).

2. Presentation to Congress of a series of initiatives intended to regulate public protests. In other words, establish the obligation of protestors to solicit a permit from the authorities.

3. The relocation of the primary state government offices in particular public service counters far away from downtown.

Ruiz is the governor who created "Administration City." All government services with public service counters are moved completely out of the city to an area between Oaxaca City and El Tule, to a big office complex for state government offices. The same thing happened with "Judicial City," which was located near Reyes Mantecon. The idea was that public protests would no longer be focused on the capitol building in downtown Oaxaca. These were Ruiz's aboveboard actions. Beneath the surface however, Ruiz was very active repressing social organizations. Ruiz began organizing a series of work meetings with leaders from the largest Oaxacan social organizations, and at those meetings he arrested several organizers.

So from the onset, Ruiz's government had a large number of political prisoners. Very early on, during his government administration Ruiz practiced the same politically repressive lines as his predecessors, the governors Jose Casab Murat, and Diódoro Carrasco Altamirano. They confronted these large groups of massive social movements by arresting leaders, coopting organizers by offering them government posts, offering money, or on the other hand, offering prison and torture. Those were the two options that were offered by the Oaxacan government in those cases. Since long before, there was a lot of experience and there was the formation of a base of porros, paramilitaries, and police officials who knew how to carry out repressive operations. They knew how to torture. They knew how to carry out coordinated attacks.

On the other hand, we have to say it, the social movement such as the Section 22 teachers' union and what came to be known as the APPO, the Oaxaca People's Popular Assembly, also had a tremendous organizational base that had already experienced arbitrary detentions, forced disappearances, torture, cooptations and sellouts etc. as well as several assassinations.

In a sense the 2006 Oaxacan uprising looked a lot like the 1968 student movement in Mexico City. The 1968 movement was not asking for democracy or social equality, or social development. No. What the 1968 student movement was looking for was a response to a series of demands focused upon an end to the federal government's repressive forces, freedom for political prisoners, and the dismantling of the riot police. This is how the 1968 movement started and then began to escalate from there. So in that sense the 2006 Oaxacan uprising started similarly, then both sides began to escalate. The government represses, and the movement grows. The government has to make a decision to increase repressive strategies, or to begin to negotiate terms. In the end, this is the game. Therefore I believe that at the core of the 2006 movement is the right to public protest.

After August, with the occupied radio stations, the barricades erected across the city, and the police completely
neutralized, we begin to see the appearance of well-known
porros (paid civilian thugs) and their followers. Sixteen
different incarcerated porros were liberated from Ixcotel
prison at this time and were put to work. You are set free,
here is a gun, and out you go. Their first mission was to
erect their own fake barricades, and to pretend to be part
of the APPO. They installed and controlled a large number
of barricades in the outskirts of the city so that if a driv-
er came through their barricade, the porros could pull out
a gun, and the next day the news could report that APPO
members have guns.

So at one point the commanding officers of active police
in Oaxaca during the 2006 uprising had under their command porros, state and municipal police, and shock troops
drawn from Institutional Revolutionary Party (PRI) based
farmworker and transportation cooperative organizations.
All of these satellite cooperative organizations of the PRI,
have shock troops. They joined forces with the porros and
police officers who were still willing to work clandestinely.
After August, there is no official police in Oaxaca, and everything is coordinated around the porros being infiltrated
as APPO members. The PRI organizations are brought in
to break apart APPO barricades. Well, these armed groups
grew and acquired a lot of clout during 2006. Where we do
see the presence of state police is in carrying out forced
disappearances, torturing detainees for one to two days,
and then presenting them in a prison.

On the 26th of August a new radio station appeared on the
turn-dial called "Radio Ciudadana" (Citizen Radio). The an-
nouncers talked about the APPO, saying "They are not from
here, they just want to destabilize." Those were just words,
until they started giving names and addresses of activists
on the air.

> By the end of the uprising every single repressive mechanism and tactic had been overcome until the arrival of the Federal Preventive Police (PFP). I personally saw the local porros join the PFP riot police lines. I saw them myself, step out between the riot shields, drugging themselves, and yelling chants like protestors. They were there because they had earned it, and it was clear that the PFP was ordered to tolerate them.

On the 28th of October the President of the Mexican Republic, Felipe Calderon Hinojosa of the National Action Party (PAN), gave the order to send the Federal Preventive Police (PFP) to Oaxaca to take the city back from the APPO and re-establish the rule of law. A counterinsurgency military directive known as DN-11 was enacted, and military personnel were mobilized to the area with checkpoints erected throughout the state of Oaxaca and thousands of soldiers mobilized to the outskirts of Oaxaca City. As many as 4000 PFP officers composed primarily of military personnel arrived in Oaxaca City. Their orders were to advance from two directions towards the city's downtown area, removing barricades along the way. On the morning of the 29th of October the PFP began its advance into the city with riot vehicles, tear gas, water cannons spraying an irritant, and PFP officers mostly armed with batons, shields, and "less-lethal" weapons, as well as several officers flanking the advance carrying AR-15 assault rifles. The battle for Oaxaca City would last from the 29th of October until the 25th of November, with a particularly notorious street battle between the PFP and the APPO taking place in front of the Oaxacan Benito Juárez Autonomous University (UABAJO) on November 2nd, the Day of the Dead, or All Saints Day. On this day the APPO was successful at defending the University's autonomy from the PFP incursion. **(15)**

By the end of the APPO uprising, an official death toll of 26, with many others disappeared, would traumatize and scar the social movement. The PFP detained over 400 APPO activists and airlifted them to the Western state of Nayarit near the nation's center. Several of the activists were tortured, and some were transported in helicopters, during which time they were threatened with being thrown alive from the helicopters, just like Augusto Pinochet's DINA officials did to activists during the Chilean military dictatorship. **(16)**

What happened in Oaxaca was one of the most important popular Indigenous urban uprisings of our time, as well as a cocktail of repression that included all official and unofficial means available to the state government. When we talk about weapons of state-sponsored repression in Mexico, what was lived and witnessed by the people of Oaxaca in 2006 was both unprecedented and orchestrated from counterinsurgency manuals and strategies developed over time by the military-political economy between the United States and Mexico.

Ulises Ruiz Ortiz would remain governor of Oaxaca until November, 2010. On the 31st of January, 2008 the commanding officer of the Auxiliary Banking, Industry, and Commercial Police (PABIC), Alejandro Barrita Ortiz, was assassinated in Oaxaca City. Barrita Ortiz's name would show up in several testimonies of torture during detention during the 2006 uprising. **(17)** On January 23, 2009, the ex-coordinator for Public Security during 2006, Aristeo López Martínez was also assassinated in Oaxaca City while driving one of his 14 luxury sports vehicles. López Martínez was a primary commanding officer carrying out operations against APPO activists during the uprising. **(18)** On October 23, 2010, a major leader of one of the paramilitary organizations utilized in 2006 in Oaxaca was assassinated, followed six days later by the assassination of one of the most notorious *porros* utilized during the counterinsurgency campaign against the 2006 APPO uprising. **(19)** These last two assassinations would take place in the final days of the Ulises Ruiz Ortiz administration. Though there is absolutely nothing concrete connecting governor Ruiz to the assassinations of these individuals, most APPO activists interpret the assassinations as a government attempt to leave no loose ends behind. The thought, regardless of evidence, is chilling.

Chapter 11
The Demarest Factor

On October 23, 2006, in Lawrence, Kansas, the *Lawrence Journal World,* a local newspaper, published an article which silently uncovered a funding scandal within Kansas University. In 2005, the university's Department of Geography received at least $500,000 in Department of Defense (DOD) funds to map communally held Indigenous lands in the states of San Luis Potosi, and Oaxaca in Mexico. **(1)**

Kansas University Geography professors, Peter Herlihy and Jerome Dobson received the DOD funding for their mapping project named the Bowman Expeditions. The Mexico based version of the project was named *Mexico Indigena,* which began mapping in 2005 in an Indigenous region known as *La Huasteca*, partially located in the state of San Luis Potosi. *Mexico Indigena* then moved its operation to the state of Oaxaca amidst the popular uprising of the Oaxacan People's Popular Assembly (APPO) in Oaxaca City in 2006. **(2)**

In early 2007 I was touring with workshops and documentary films and was invited to Kansas University (KU) to give a presentation. A graduate student organizer at KU showed me the *Lawrence Journal World* newspaper story about the DOD funding for mapping parts of San Luis Potosi and Oaxaca. The story was a huge red flag to me as well as to the KU graduate student and community members who came together to organize my presentation.

Collectively, everyone worked militantly to find out as much information about the mapping project as possible because KU already had a reputation of using social sciences for military and intelligence purposes. In fact it was Kansas University's own professor Felix Moos from the Anthropology Department who taught and developed Human Terrain Systems (HTS) in cultural competency for military operations. **(3)**

From February 2007 to September 2014 the U.S. Army ran the HTS program at the Training and Doctrine Command (TRADOC) in Newport News, Virginia. The HTS was a support program employing personnel from the social science disciplines – such as anthropology, sociology, political science, regional studies, and linguistics, among others, to provide military officials with scientific knowledge about the people and cultures they encountered in the field. **(4)** On October 31, 2007, The American Anthropological Association's Executive Board issued a statement on the U.S. Military's Human Terrain System project. The statement outlines the ways the HTS project violates the AAA Code of Ethics, which mandates that anthropologists do no harm to their research subjects. **(5)**

Student organizers from Haskell Indian Nations University who I met there in Lawrence, Kansas were key to my understanding of the historical significance and severity of the DOD funding project, but also made it clear that they were not surprised. Haskell was originally a so-called Indian boarding school with its own historical military list of white male Christian supremacist atrocities. These students helped bring much needed clarity to the mapping scandal within a historical framework.

The Foreign Military Studies Office (FMSO) is based out of Fort Leavenworth in Leavenworth, Kansas, just 40 miles from Haskell Indian Nations University. During the early 1800s and for 30 years, Fort Leavenworth was the command center of the Western Front during the U.S. expansion into Indigenous lands and the theft of these lands. It was also the epicenter of the U.S. Army War Department. During the U.S. intervention in Mexico in 1846, Fort Leavenworth was the outfitting post for the Army of the West. **(6)**

The FMSO is a research and analysis center under the U.S. Army's Training and Doctrine Command. It manages and operates the Joint Reserve Intelligence Center (JRIC) and conducts analytical programs focused on emerging and asymmetric threats, regional military and security developments, and other issues that define evolving operational environments around the world. Asymmetric threats are defined as terrorist organizations and guerrilla insurgent armies, while emerging threats are defined as social phenomena and in particular, social movements. (7) This was of deep concern as to FMSO intentions in funding the Bowman Expeditions in San Luis Potosi and Oaxaca.

The FMSO official assigned to the Bowman expeditions is Lieutenant Colonel Geoffrey B. Demarest. Demarest is an Ibero-American researcher at FMSO. During his military career, Dr. Demarest served in multiple assignments in Latin America. He served as the U.S. Military Attaché at the U.S. Embassy in Guatemala between 1988 and 1991, a time of heavily U.S. backed military repression against Indigenous communities in Guatemala including several high-profile cases of torture and murder involving graduates of the U.S. Army School of the Americas. Demarest is also a graduate of the U.S. Army School of the Americas himself. His areas of academic interest include emerging threats and responses, new strategic alignments, military history, and international law. Demarest holds a Ph.D. in International Studies from the Denver University Graduate School of International Studies, and a Juris Doctorate. He has practiced as a civil attorney, and has lectured on the legality of espionage. (8) He has written numerous declassified articles and essays dealing with internal conflict in so-called Latin America including the following:

"The Overlap of Military and Police Responsibilities in Latin America"

"Expeditionary Police Service"

"Tactical Intelligence in Low Intensity Conflict"

"The Strategic Implications of International Law"

"Mapping Colombia: The Correlation between Land Data and Strategy"

"Geopolitics and Urban Armed Conflict in Latin America" (9)

Dr. Demarest's first book published on September 1, 1998, titled *Geoproperty: Foreign Affairs, National Security and Property Rights*, considers private property ownership as an issue of national security and strategy. In it, he says:

> "Informally owned and unregulated land ownership favors illicit use and violence."

> "Places with informal property are doomed to violence. No formal property, no peace." (10)

Before his work on the *Mexico Indigena* project, Demarest was implementing his land data strategies in Colombia, at least until 2003. The March 2003 FMSO essay written by Demarest titled "Mapping Colombia: Land Data and Strategy," clearly states the ultimate purpose of geographic data to military strategy:

> The country cannot hope to establish the rule of law without extending effective, formal land ownership, which implies creation of the maps and registries attendant to that ownership.

> Incomplete mapping, beyond hamstringing military operations against guerrillas and illegal paramilitaries, puts Colombia's social, economic, and security objectives at risk. And to the extent that this is true for Colombia, it is all the more a reality in other countries of the hemisphere where property records are even less well-developed.

> While the forensic value of land ownership data is relatively obvious, not so obvious is the correlation between land data and military strategy, but this correlation precisely marks an essential attribute of successful counterinsurgency campaigns. (11)

In the same essay, Demarest expresses his analysis of power:

> Strategic power becomes the ability to keep and acquire

ownership rights around the world. National, sub-, supra- or transnational power can be measured accordingly. (12)

The topics of Demarest's essays extend beyond Indigenous lands, reverberating throughout all sectors of society, and in particular, the world's urban poor. In a spring 1995 FMSO essay titled "Geopolitics and Urban Armed Conflict in Latin America," Demarest criminalizes and warns against the potential of all of Latin America's urban poor:

> Moneyed interests in Latin America continue to isolate, physically and socially, the sprawling poor communities. The shantytowns become separately governed areas. They mark the physical dimensions of what in some ways are autonomous nations within nations. At some point their leadership may be seen as a national security threat as opposed to merely a public security threat. Therein lies their geopolitical importance. (13)

In a previous section of this same essay, Demarest lists anti-state actors who find a home among the world's poor:

> Distinctive features of the largest or so-called 'world cities,' of which Latin America has several, include marked economic and social polarization and intense spatial segregation. We also find what is probably an effect of these conditions: the complementary agendas and overlapping identities of a large array of anti-state actors. Anarchists, criminals, the dispossessed, foreign meddlers, cynical opportunists, lunatics, revolutionaries, labor leaders, ethnic nationals, real estate speculators and others can all form alliances of convenience. They can also commit acts of violence and handle ideas that provoke others. These ideas may be as specific as resisting a rise in bus fares, as immediate as an opportunity for looting following a mass celebration, or as broad as ethnic identity. (14)

A separate essay by the FMSO's Major José M. Madera of the United States Army Reserve titled "Civil Information Management in Support of Counterinsurgency Operations: A Case for the Use of Geospatial Information Systems in Colombia" describes with utmost specificity, the counterinsurgency and intelligence uses of open source GIS information, land data, for what the FMSO calls "Civil Information Management."

These FMSO essays, and Demarest's text book on the matter, expose a very particular and sinister military ethic, attitude, and strategy with regards to the control of large populations of poor people, Indigenous communities, and the disenfranchised in general.

> The coming center of gravity of armed political struggles in Latin America may be indigenous populations, youth gangs, drug cartels, foreign expatriates, or insurgents.
>
> Still, while sweeping generalities about potential armies of the dispossessed may be inaccurate, huge populations of poor and aspiring people in Latin American cities are a factor in the potential for organized violence. (15)

These specific attitudes include the systemic devaluation and criminalization of traditional Indigenous forms of grassroots liberation through community-based self-determination, self-defense, and autonomy as practiced throughout the so-called Americas. Cultural identity and Indigenous world views as a whole are regarded as an impediment to prosperity, progress, and security. In particular, traditional forms of communal land tenure, use, and rights, or in Demarest's words "informal land use," a core element of Indigenous self-determination, self-defense, and autonomy, are specifically cited as the primary impediment to progress, and security.

Together, the FMSO essays, Demarest's book GeoProperty, and his most recent book as of 2011, Winning Insurgent Wars,(16) speak to the intended segregation, marginalization, and criminalization of large portions of human society simply because they are poor. To Demarest it is imperative that territory and space occupied informally by the poor be privatized and regulated in order for progress and security to be assured.

In the face of this military-political and economic strategy, it is no wonder that millions of Indigenous and peasant farm workers, students, housewives, mothers, children, workers, and communities all over the world, are beginning to organize, train, and use a variety of different strategies and tactics for grassroots liberation through community-based self-determination, self-defense, and autonomy. The survival of Indigenous communities, in particular, depends on it.

Like communally held Indigenous land, unregulated shantytowns or barrios are considered precursors to crime and insurgency by Demarest. In the U.S. and in cities around the world, the privatization of poor communities through gentrification is a similar multi-faceted strategy of marginalization through devaluation, criminalization, and displacement. To be poor and organize your community to survive by its own means, to exercise community-based self-determination, self-defense, and autonomy whether you are Indigenous or not, according to the Demarest essays, is to be a threat to U.S. political, economic, and security interests domestically and abroad.

Chapter 12
Mexican Armed Forces Expand Influence and Power

In between the 1999 UNAM strike and the beginning of President Felipe Calderon's War on Drugs in 2006, the Federal Preventive Police - PFP reappeared several times.

The PFP was created by Ernesto Zedillo, the last of the PRI presidents during the political party's 71 years of one party rule. On June 2, 2000, the Mexican people ended that one party rule and elected Vicente Fox Quesada. Fox would be the first National Action Party (PAN) president ever. Fox also kept the Federal Preventive Police (PFP) exactly as it was.

Under President Vicente Fox, PFP agents were present at a protest against the World Economic Forum (WEF) in Cancun, Mexico, in 2001, and proceeded to literally crack skulls with their batons. **(1)**

In September of 2003, the PFP would again be massively mobilized back to Cancun by the Fox administration in order to provide security for the World Trade Organization (WTO) meeting there. The meeting attracted protestors from around the world with a wide variety of strategies on the one hand, and a lot of white privilege on the other. The PFP was kept tame for the most part, with the exception of a barricade checkpoint of several kilometers between the mainland and the island of Cancun. The PFP would coordinate directly with the Navy and Marines since Cancun is a major port of entry. The PFP intended to keep protestors out of the Island of Cancun, and it did keep most dark-skinned Mexican protestors out. White protestors or Mexican protestors with hotel card keys, nonetheless, were easily able to dress up as tourists and filter through the checkpoint, gain access to the island, and carry out a variety of protest actions. Several diverse direct actions did take place, including the suicide of the president of the Korean Farmworkers Union Lee

Kyung Hae. On September 9th, Lee Kyung Hae stabbed himself in the heart at the first PFP barricade between the mainland and Cancun Island. On the 13th of September the frontline PFP barricade/checkpoint was symbolically ripped open, an action that was coordinated and carried out only by women from Mexico and around the world. The PFP was certainly overwhelmed by the international make-up and diversity of protestors, but it is also clear that agents accomplished several intelligence objectives at the WTO protests, and PFP officials constantly filmed protestors. **(2)**

At the 3rd Economic Summit of Europe, Latin America, and the Caribbean in Guadalajara on the 28th and 29th of May of 2004 the PFP, again under Fox, reappeared and again brutally repressed protestors, prompting several declarations to be made about sexual assault at the hands of the police. **(3)**

In San Salvador Atenco in the state of Mexico, on May 2, 2006, a battle for communally owned farmland against the construction of a new airport to service Mexico City resulted in the brutal repression of community members, including several cases of sexual assault and torture, again at the hands of the PFP. Once again this occurred under Fox alongside the local and state police, under orders by then Governor of Mexico state Enrique Peña Nieto. In 2012 Peña Nieto would be granted the Mexican Presidency in a heavily contested election filled with evidence of mass fraud. **(4)**

Also in 2006, after a six month citywide protest shutdown in Oaxaca City, Mexico, by the Oaxacan Peoples Popular Assembly (APPO), the PFP was called in, once again under Fox. This time they arrived on October 29, 2006, and did not completely leave the city until January of 2007. The level of violence exercised by paramilitaries and *porros* during the six month uprising, coupled with PFP violence over a two and a half month long period, in particular on the 25th of November, has scarred the Oaxacan people to this very day. **(5)**

On December 11, 2006, just 10 days after taking office, Mexican President Felipe Calderon ordered thousands of Federal Preventive Police (PFP) to re-enforce military troops in the state of Michoacán in what would mark the beginning of the so-called Mexican Drug War. Oaxacans would watch with relief as the PFP left their state en masse. No one could have imagined the national bloodshed and mayhem in the war to come. **(6)**

As Calderon became more dependent on the Mexican military forces to fight his War on Drugs, the PFP was slowly devalued until its final dissolution in May of 2009. After over 10 years, the PFP was considered ineffective in its mission and was transformed into what was called the Federal Police, which would go on to fight the Drug War and carry out other operations previously assigned to the PFP. **(7)**

In June of 2010, President Felipe Calderon, made an urgent call for the creation of a national security strategy with a single command for police and military, known as the "Mando Unico." **(8)** The daily violence unleashed on Mexican streets by Calderon's War on Drugs was immediate, constant, and undeniable. It certainly contributed greatly to spiraling the country into the current national crisis of drug cartel violence. Yet on June 30, 2008, with congressional support, U.S. president George Bush Jr. activated the Merida Initiative, a security cooperation agreement between the United States, Mexico, and several Central American countries, which is ongoing. Assistance includes training, equipment, and intelligence but no direct funds to the Mexican government. As of March 2017, 1.6 billion USD in assistance had been granted to Mexico. This was in addition to ongoing weapons purchases made by the Mexican government through the U.S. government's Defense Security Cooperation Agency. With the bipartisan support of Congress, the Mérida Initiative is responsible for the majority of U.S. Foreign military aid to Mexico since 2008. **(9)**

Fast and Furious Gun Running

Between 2006 and 2010, the U.S. Bureau of Alcohol Tobacco and Firearms (ATF), carried out two operations in its Tucson and Phoenix field offices under the umbrella of Project Gunrunner. One was Operation Wide Receiver (2006-2007), and the other was Operation Fast and Furious (2009-2010), in which ATF officials under the auspices of the Department of State and Attorney General Eric Holder, allowed approximately 2000 firearms to be bought illegally by straw purchasers, (individuals purchasing on behalf of others) at Arizona gun shops, and then be illegally sold to Mexican drug cartels. The scandal came about amidst criticism from the Mexican federal government of the influx of weapons from the United States into Mexico. The guns, including 50 caliber assault rifles, showed up at crime scenes all across Mexico while no arrests of the intended target, high ranking organized crime members, have ever been made. The whole scandal was made public by the whistleblower and ATF agent in charge John Dodson, who spoke directly to CBS News. **(10)**

IMMUNITY

On March 19th 2009, a high ranking member of the Sinaloa organized crime cartel, Vicente Zambada Niebla AKA "El Vicentillo" was arrested in Mexico. He would be extradited to the U.S. in February 2010. In court, Zambada claimed to have immunity from prosecution. According to an April 10th, 2014 article by Patrick Radden Keefe, in the *New Yorker*:

> ...the case took a turn. Zambada's lawyers declared that he could not be prosecuted by the United States, because, they claimed, he had been secretly working as an informant for the Drug Enforcement Administration, even as he smuggled tons of cocaine across the border. In fact, according to his counsel, Zambada had been assured by his contacts at the D.E.A. that, in exchange for providing them with intelligence about the drug trade in Mexico, he would be guaranteed immunity against prosecution for his own role in the business. **(11)**

Zambada ended up entering a guilty plea for lesser charges, and at some point in 2020 he was silently released from prison in the

U.S.. It would seem that he did have immunity after all. **(12)** Though there has been no confirmation from U.S. officials, it is assumed that he has now entered a witness protection program. In order to secure his release he had to be vetted as a credible witness who offered credible intelligence to U.S. authorities. Among his many claims, Zamabada also testified that the Fast and Furious gun walking operation by the ATF was part of a deal to get weapons to the Sinaloa cartel.

The PRI Comes Back to Power

After a heavily contested presidential election with accusations of voter fraud, vote buying, and alliances made with cartels to assure voter suppression, the Institutional Revolutionary Party (PRI) came back to power under President Enrique Peña Nieto in December of 2012. **(13)**

Peña Nieto's presidential inauguration was met with massive protests throughout Mexico City in which the death of a protester resulted from a teargas canister shot to his head. Peña Nieto kept ex-president Calderon's Federal Police as it was, but also proposed the introduction of the Gendarmerie, a militarized police force planned to include 40,000 officers. The Gendarmerie was for all intents and purposes unsuccessful throughout his administration.

In 2013 Peña Nieto would use the Federal Police to heavily repress and eventually shut down a nationwide teachers' union protest in Mexico City with over 80,000 participants. The Federal Police and officers from the Secretariat of Public Security would also be filmed using heavy-handed tactics against protestors during the October 2, 2013 commemorative protests of the 1968 Tlatelolco Massacre. **(14)**

In 2013 and 2014 Mexican Federal Police were sent into the state of Michoacán to support and attempt to regain control over the armed "Comunitario" uprisings against the local organized crime cartel throughout the state. According to the Comunitarios, Federal police took heavy losses early on and lost the courage to act. In January of 2014, Peña Nieto attempted to deputize and legalize the Comunitarios themselves through his federal envoy Alfredo Castillo, only to replace him in December of 2014 with the U.S. Army School of the Americas graduate, General Pedro Felipe Gurrola Ramírez. **(15)** In 2014 Enrique Peña Nieto repeated former president Calderon's call for the need of a single command for military and police forces. **(16)**

On June 19, 2016, the Federal Police under Peña Nieto would open fire into a crowd at a road blockade in Nochixtlan, Oaxaca, killing at least eight protestors and injuring dozens of others. Footage of the Federal Police using live ammunition was filmed by a reporter from the *Guardian*. **(17)**

Kill Rate and Human Rights Abuses

According to a *New York Times* article dated May 26, 2016, while military forces under combat operations around the world have an average kill rate of one person killed per every four injured, the Mexican Army kills eight people for every one injured, and the Mexican Marines kill 30 people for every one injured. The vast majority of these executions are in fact extrajudicial, as they are very rarely, if ever, investigated. It would certainly seem that the Mexican military forces are most probably murdering innocent civilians and not just members of organized crime cartels. **(18)**

In 2016 Amnesty International released a video with information provided by 100 women who had been detained by security forces in Mexico. Of the 100 women, 97 were physically abused, 72 were sexually assaulted, and 33 were raped. **(19)** In 2016, Mexicans knew that security forces could do anything they wanted and never be punished.

Despite these attacks, by December 15, 2017 Peña Nieto was able to secure congressional support for a proposed new Law for Internal Security, which would grant the military the necessary legal framework to permanently engage in public security duties. **(20)** Peña Nieto pulled together all of his corrupt political cronies to hand public security duties to the military officially, but at the last minute the proposal was officially rejected by the Mexican Supreme Court. This is as close as the PRI ever came to legitimizing the use of the military for public security purposes.

Mexico's National Guard (Guardia Nacional)

On July 1, 2018 the Mexican people overwhelmingly elected Andres Manuel Lopez Obrador (AMLO) of his own MORENA political party, to be the President of Mexico. Obrador took office on December 1, 2018. According to an October 4th, 2018 article by Jorge Monroy of *El Economista*:

> (President Elect) Lopez Obrador confirmed that after the 1st of December when he was to be inaugurated, all of the police and military armed forces including the Marines, the Army, and the Federal Police, the State Police, and municipal police forces would be unified under a single command led by the armed forces. **(21)**

On March 26, 2019 AMLO created a new military police force known as the *Guardia Nacional (GN)*, or National Guard. The commanding officer, General Luis Rodríguez Bucio, is a graduate of the U.S. Army School of the Americas. **(22)**

According to an article published in *Small Wars Journal* by Patricia H. Escamilla-Hamm, titled "The Guardia Nacional (National Guard): Why a New Militarized Police in Mexico": **(23)**

> The GN is a gendarmerie-style force. Basically defined, gendarmeries or formed police are forces with police-military features, tactics and components... The GN became operational on 30 June 2019, so it is still in the process of construction, deployment, and training. Yet it already has around 100,000 forces with the goal of reaching a robust force of about 200,000 by 2024. So far, the GN is nearly three times (less than 38,000) the size of the Federal Police and the Gendarmerie together.
>
> The GN is a hybrid of civilian-military troops and leadership constituted by police from the extinct Policia Federal - Gendarmeria; the Policía Militar (Military Police-PM) transferred from the Secretaría de la Defensa Nacional

(Secretariat of the National Defense – SEDENA); Policía Naval (Naval Police – PN) from the Secretaría de la Marina (Secretariat of the Navy – SEMAR), and other military and civilian personnel. The following is a breakdown based on 91,161 GN forces as of 31 July 2020:

25,292 Police veterans from the Federal Police – Gendarmarie,

55,917 PM and active duty personnel temporarily commissioned from SEDENA,

9,952 PN and active duty elements temporarily assigned from SEMAR.

On May 11, 2020, AMLO issued an executive order that expanded and formalized the power of Mexico's armed forces to participate in public security tasks until 2024. **(24)** At the moment there is quite a bit of concern around the ambiguity about how exactly the Guardia Nacional will continue to function, and how permanent a single police military command will become.

What is certain is that up until now, efforts towards a national militarized police force under a single command, and the use of the armed forces for public security have amassed bodies, brutality, sexual assault, and disappearances. Meanwhile there has been absolute impunity for not just the criminal organizations, but for the police, the military, and the Mexican political and business elite. Because while average everyday Mexicans are being murdered, brutalized, tortured, kidnapped, sexually assaulted, and disappeared a select few from the business and political class are thriving upon all of this misery.

Public Corruption

On December 10, 2019, Genaro García Luna, the former director of the Mexican Federal Investigation Agency under PAN President Vicente Fox Quesada from 2002 to 2006 and the Secretary of

Public Security under PAN President Felipe Calderón Hinojosa from 2006 to 2012, was arrested in Dallas, Texas and charged by the New York District Attorney with conspiracy, accepting bribes from a major Cartel, and making false declarations. García Luna has pled not guilty, and is being held without bail while awaiting trial tentatively set for October 24, 2022. **(25)**

On October 15, 2020, Mexican General Salvador Cienfuegos Zepeda, the former Secretary of National Defense from 2012 to 2018 under PRI President Enrique Peña Nieto, was detained at the international airport in Los Angeles, California by the Drug Enforcement Administration (DEA). The same New York District Attorney's office that charged García Luna, was accusing Cienfuegos of links to an organized crime cartel in Mexico. Cienfuegos is the highest ranking Mexican official ever detained by the US government. **(26)**

On November 17, 2020, a joint statement was released by Attorney General of the United States William P. Barr and Attorney General of Mexico Alejandro Gertz Manero. **(27)** The statement read as follows:

> On Oct. 15, 2020, former Mexican Secretary of National Defense General Salvador Cienfuegos Zepeda was arrested in Los Angeles, California, on U.S. charges of conspiracy to manufacture, import, and distribute narcotics into the United States and money laundering.
>
> The Mexican Fiscalía General de la República, upon learning of the arrest and U.S. charges against General Cienfuegos, opened its own investigation.
>
> In recognition of the strong law enforcement partnership between Mexico and the United States, and in the interests of demonstrating our united front against all forms of criminality, the U.S. Department of Justice has made the decision to seek dismissal of the U.S. criminal charges against former Secretary Cienfuegos, so that he may be

investigated and, if appropriate, charged, under Mexican law.

At the request of the Fiscalía General de la República, the U.S. Department of Justice, under the Treaty that governs the sharing of evidence, has provided Mexico evidence in this case and commits to continued cooperation, within that framework, to support the investigation by Mexican authorities.

Our two countries remain committed to cooperation on this matter, as well as all our bilateral law enforcement cooperation. As the decision today reflects, we are stronger when we work together and respect the sovereignty of our nations and their institutions. This close partnership increases the security of the citizens of both our countries.

Acting U.S. Attorney Seth DuCharme asked Senior U.S. District Judge Carol Bagley Amon to dismiss charges against Cienfuegos affirming that the:

...United States has determined that sensitive and important foreign policy considerations outweigh the government's interest in pursuing the prosecution of the defendant, under the totality of the circumstances, and therefore require dismissal of the case... (28)

Cienfuegos was released and was returned to Mexico. On January 14, 2021, the Mexican Attorney General's office announced that there was no evidence that Cienfuegos had communications with any organized crime cartels, and he was exonerated. (29) The unwavering support of the Andres Manuel Lopez Obrador presidential administration for General Cienfuegos' release and subsequent exoneration has left political analysts questioning whether AMLO has simply aligned himself with the Army as a political move, or if the Army has used its power to impose itself on the AMLO presidency. What is clear thus far is that AMLO's extension of the military's continued carrying out of police duties until 2024, his creation of the National Guard under Army command, and his swift return and exoneration of general Cienfuegos from US prosecution, certainly demonstrate that AMLO has decided to make a team with the Army. The acting Deputy Director of Public Affairs for the Department of Justice, Nicole Navas Oxman, said:

> The United States reserves the right to recommence its prosecution of Cienfuegos if the government of Mexico fails to do so.... (30)

The Weapons

On August 4, 2021 the Mexican Federal Government filed a lawsuit against U.S. gun manufacturers Smith and Wesson, Barrett Firearms, Beretta U.S.A., Beretta Holdings, Century International Arms, Colt Manufacturing Company, Glock Inc., Sturm Ruger and Co., Witmer Public Safety Group, and D/B/A Interstate Arms Corp for not doing enough to stem the illegal proliferation of their firearms in Mexico. (31)

On September 27, 2021, the governments of Mexico and the United States announced the U.S.-Mexico Bicentennial Framework for Security, Public Health and Safe Communities. On December 14, 2021 both governments began actual work on the Bicentennial Framework, which they are calling an end to the Merida Initiative. So far, the Bicentennial Framework's first of three pillars is to: "Protect our communities." This was the 4th pillar of the Merida Initiative. (32) Only time will tell, but already with U.S. President Joe Biden giving the go-ahead for the continuation of a 5 million dollar weapons contract between U.S. based Sig Sauer and the Mexican Navy, there really doesn't seem to be anything changing at all. (33)

PART THREE: DRUGS

Chapter 13
Organized Crime

Though organized crime is driven primarily by two different factors in a society, protection or security, and the procurement of prohibited substances, it is imperative to relate organized crime to the social, political, and economic workings of everyday society. The Organized Crime Industrial Complex is literally like any other industrial complex. However it does encapsulate, both internally and externally, the functions of the State, transnational corporations, local small businesses, and even the philanthropic attributes of community organizations. (1)

Internally, criminal organizations are managed like governments and like businesses. They implement a political economic model that is favorable to their leaders, members, employees, and allies. Without this, there would exist no motivation to take the risks associated with engaging in organized crime.

Externally, organized crime functions primarily through corruption, which carries a tremendous amount of influence in official governance, politics, economics, transnational business, local business, banking, real estate, and again, even in charity work.

In order to critically analyze the true history of organized crime in the United States, it is indispensable to recognize the criminal nature of the founding of the U.S. nation-state to begin with. In addition to the pirates, criminals, and smugglers who first arrived from Europe to the Americas, the original gangstas in the U.S. as a nation-state were the so-called founding fathers. They were nothing but a band of hoodlums who gained power and wealth through legitimizing the criminal activities of theft, kidnapping, slavery, torture, murder, and genocide. The crimes committed in order to found the so-called United States, would today clearly be considered not only criminal at their core, but in fact would be designated as war crimes by modern nation-states. Despite current attempts to whitewash these historical facts, it is now common knowledge that the origins of the United States are fundamentally criminal.

As the nation gained economic and political power, it became more and more necessary to legitimize itself as a bastion of liberty, freedom, and independence, first and foremost, and then as a purveyor of democracy, justice, equality, and opportunity.

Though many criminal analysts and academics claim that organized crime arises primarily as a result of a weak state or government apparatus, as if criminal activity were solely the fault of under developed nation-states, or underrepresented ethnicities such as Mexicans or Indigenous people from Mexico, the truth is that the primary driving force behind organized criminal activity is the governmental prohibition of products and services. The secondary driving force behind organized criminal activity is public, political, business, and banking corruption. The third and final driving force behind organized crime is the illicit consumption habits of prohibited products and services. Forget liberty, freedom, independence, democracy, justice, and equality; the United States truly is the land of opportunity, in particular for organized crime.

The organized crime opportunities between Mexico and the United States are driven by the supply and demand generated through prohibition. Though the criminal organizations in both countries obviously carry a bulk of the blame, it is important to look at other factors and entities that are equally if not more responsible.

The omnipresence of organized crime in the life of average everyday citizens in both Mexico and the United States has led to the romanticization of organized crime in the entertainment media, with a simultaneous vilification in the mainstream news media. Criminal organizations dominate both media and what is not sufficiently present in either, is the role of government, transnational corporations, banking institutions, and business political elites.

It is not my belief that a strong nation-state or centralized government is the solution. Nor do I believe that any sort of governmental legislation or regulation of illicit products or services is necessarily an absolute solution either. However, in view of the point at which we have arrived in terms of addiction and violence, I do believe that the least of all evils with regards to illicit drugs and narcotics would be outright legalization, accompanied by a community-based public healthcare, education, and action campaign to address the core causes of addiction, which are all the possible contributors to trauma.

The dilemma lies in imagining a nation-state that is capable of carrying this out effectively, and herein resides yet another obfuscated truth about nation-states in and of themselves. They are corrupt and corruptible by nature. I have lost absolutely all faith in the ability of nation-states to set aside greed and corruptibility for the better good of communities. Simply put, the legitimizing relationship that the U.S. government has had historically and continues to have with Mexico, its political parties and leaders, and the Mexican armed forces is a relationship steeped in criminality and corruption, which has profited both nation-states consistently over nearly the last 100 years. With the state-sponsored subjugation of the Mexican people in order to grant the United States secure investments in natural resource extraction, there is enough criminality and corruption to go around; however, even more insidious is the continued sale of weapons by the U.S. government to the Mexican armed forces. This goes on despite overwhelming evidence of criminality, corruption, and a very long list of human rights abuses against Mexican citizens and international migrants in Mexico at the hands of the armed forces receiving the weapons. (2)

If we are to talk about organized crime with a critical lens, it is imperative to include the nation-state itself as an integral component of organized crime activity. It is the nation-state that creates the demand for organized crime through the prohibition of products and services, and it is the nation-state that perpetuates organized criminal activity through its inherent corruptibility. Finally it is the nation-state that has generated the violence in which we exist today by confronting this issue with the proliferation of for-profit weapons, militarism, and policing.

In the same vein, transnational businesses and the banking

industry must be included as pillars of organized crime activity. Transnational corporations facilitate the storage, transportation, and distribution of prohibited products and services. They also provide legitimizing businesses for investment by organized criminals. The banking industry has to be recognized as the final launderer of illicit profits made by organized crime activity. Despite the facade of legitimacy, billions of dollars of all this dirty money ends up in banks. (3)

The truth is that organized crime is directly connected to the daily lives of citizens through a network of corruption and corruptibility that even federal agents are unable to ignore. More important and incessant, however, is the relationship between organized crime and members of the elite class in societies. Organized crime is incapable of existing and persisting in a society without direct political and economic alliances with its elite class. This is as true of Mexico as it is of the United States, Europe, and the rest of the world. On the flip side of the same coin, organized crime is also incapable of existing and persisting without providing direct social aid and economic opportunities to a nation's poor or marginalized communities.

So in this sense, in Mexico the austerity measures of the neoliberal military-political economy certainly create the social political and economic vacuum through which organized crime is able to fill a void of basic needs being met. In fact one of the most common strategies of generating popular support for criminal organizations on the local level has included efforts such as the building of roads, schools, hospitals, clinics, churches as well as the provision of business loans, legitimate businesses, employment opportunities, and economic security for citizens who do not receive similar support from their governments, businesses, banks, or the elite class in their societies. The economic, political, social, and cultural importance of criminal organizations in both elite power circles and poor working class communities is irrefutable.

Governments of nation-states consistently attempt to create the illusion of justice, law enforcement, and incorruptibility in order to legitimize themselves and their functionality to their citizens and the world. One of the primary criminal rackets of the nation-state, in addition to land theft of course, is attempting to prove its own legitimacy through the illusion of democracy.

Public Corruption

Though there has been a steady decline in lawyers who hold political office in the United States, politicians with law degrees still dominate the political arena in U.S. politics. According to a study by the Harvard Law School Center on the Legal Profession published in the November/December 2015 issue of *The Practice*, in the section "Lawyers in Politics" titled "Declining Dominance: Lawyers in the U.S. Congress," we see a decline in the presence of lawyers in politics, though the legal profession consistently dominates other professions in the world of U.S. politics. Around the 1850s, approximately 80% of the members of Congress were lawyers. Though most recently that number has dropped to about 40%, there are still more members of Congress with Law degrees than any other educational background. **(4)**

In Mexico, in particular the National Autonomous University of Mexico (UNAM), student organizers always say the same thing: "Law school is where you go to learn how to break the law." In fact at UNAM, the Law School is one of the schools with the highest number of *porros*. A *porro* is a paid and protected student and/or non-student thug, who belongs to an organization much like a syndicate or union with other *porros*, functioning within a public education framework. *Porros* are paid and compensated in various ways for carrying out acts of violence against student organizers, particularly at student protests. **(5)**

When we think about the governments of nation-states as inherently corrupt and corruptible, the idea of lawyers dominating the political arena makes absolute sense. Though one might be inclined to consider the study of the law by politicians as a clear indicator that politicians have a vested interest in upholding the law, in fact, what we see in practice is quite the opposite. Lawyers are in politics in order to circumvent the law in order to gain the most wealth and power as possible. For the same reason, the second most dominant educational background in Congress is business. When you think about the law and lawyers, don't think about crime and justice, when you think about the law and lawyers think about political (public) corruption and the business of making money.

Two of the strategies U.S. politicians use to control the decision-making process based on a private property, for-profit, business agenda are 1. the ongoing voter suppression strategies of political parties and their administrators **(6)** and 2. the gerrymandering of voter districts. **(7)** However, to be clear, regardless of electoral politics, neither political party has ever fully represented the interests of communities over the interests of the private property, for-profit, business agenda.

Lobbying

According to Miriam Webster, lobbying means

> to conduct activities aimed at influencing public officials and especially members of a legislative body on legislation.

If lawyers and businesspersons become politicians, what do politicians become? Well, politicians become lobbyists. Although lobbying happens all over the world, U.S. lobbying is particularly notorious for being the least transparent and the most downright corrupt, racist, and slanted. **(8)** The way in which powerful political alliances, transnational corporations, financial institutions, and wealthy individuals are able to buy power and influence legally through a functioning system of legitimized corruption is laughable globally. Lobbyists are predominantly a mix of lawyers and ex-elected and administrative public officials. In the United States they work above all for the interests of private enterprise and business. According to a June 4, 2009 *Politico* article by Christine Mahoney titled: "Why Lobbying in America is Different"

In the U.S. 89% of corporations and 53% of trade associations succeed, while the majority of those fighting for the
broader good – 60% of citizen groups and 63% of foundations – fail in their lobbying goals. (9)

According to Mahoney's article, lobbying in the European Union
is in general much more balanced where either both sides of an
issue reach a compromise, or each side wins favorable legislation
an equal amount of times. In the United States, because of the
campaign based electoral process, politicians function in a fundraising system that is dominated and controlled by nothing other
than money.

In Mexico that exact same fundraising system exists within
electoral politics with even less transparency or regulation than
in the United States.

The Revolving Door

Perhaps the most incriminating aspect of the U.S. lobby is what
is known as the revolving door. The revolving door primarily
deals with how politicians go on to become lobbyists but also
the decisions of lobbyists to become politicians or work in an
administrative capacity in government. There are a number of
regulations for former politicians becoming lobbyists, such as
one to two year cooling off periods. More recently presidential
administrations have enacted stricter regulations for their staff,
but in the end, a former politician or administrative employee of
a government office can go on to work for a lobbying firm. Former government employees, depending on the cooling off period and place of employment, have access to their former place
of employment and often more importantly to the inner circle at
their former place of employment for life. (10) All that said, more
and more lobbyists in the United States are no longer registering
as lobbyists and are simply working for lawyer/lobbyist firms as
consultants, advisors, or specialists through a loophole known
as the Daschle Loophole, named after Tom Daschle who worked

as an unregistered lobbyist for years until registering just recently. They are shadow lobbyists. **(11)**

Regardless, the power of access to legislators and the legislative process due to sheer proximity, plus the power of influence in the inner circles of legislative bodies, makes U.S. American lobbyists the epitome of conspicuously concentrated wealth, power, influence, privilege, as well as legitimized corruption and corruptibility.

In Mexico lobbying is even less regulated. There is no cooling off period. Government officials and their family members are not allowed to lobby while in office. Lobbyists are supposed to register and report. There are no sanctions for a failure to do so. In Mexico there is also the omnipresence of organized crime in business, politics, and security, which in terms of conspicuously concentrated wealth, power, and influence, has given way to a completely new category of organized crime and public corruption known as Narco-Governance.

Chapter 14
The War on Drugs

Just as war and capitalist imperialism go hand and hand, the War on Drugs goes hand in hand with the neoliberal military-political economy. The outsourcing that takes place in the Organized Crime Industrial Complex not only has to do with raw materials, cheap farm and factory labor, and the cheap processing and manufacturing of synthetic illicit substances. In this international industrial complex, outsourcing also has to do with every single aspect of this war. The outsourcing of public corruption, the outsourcing of blame, and the outsourcing of a military response have been just some of the specific aspects of the War on Drugs that have been systematically transferred to countries like Mexico. The outsourcing of violence to poor neighborhoods and poor countries cannot be overlooked either. In the case of Mexico, it is not just the Mexican state that is expected to absorb the responsibility and take on the drug cartels; average everyday citizens in Mexico are far more exposed to organized crime violence than U.S. citizens ever were, even during the peak era of organized crime and mafia activity and dominance in the United States.

The transference of violence to the South has turned Mexico into an enormous mass grave in order to feed the drug consumption habits of U.S. citizens. It is true, however, that consumers are also victims of this drug war. U.S. federal government policies and programs towards consumption, abuse, and addiction have consistently been lacking in all senses. The result has been an insatiable demand for prohibited substances.

Behind the scenes however, organized crime in general, but the narcotics trade in particular, generates profits and power for a long list of individuals, businesses, institutions, and industries that either directly or indirectly benefit from the narcotics trade and the so-called war against it.

The U.S. (Bipartisan) War on Drugs

In 1969 U.S. President Richard Nixon of the Republican Party declared a "War on Drugs," which was focused on eradication, interdiction, and incarceration. In 1971, he declared that public enemy number one was "Drug Abuse." **(1)**

In 1994 John Ehrlichman, the former White House Domestic Affairs Advisor under President Nixon, made a statement about Nixon's "War on Drugs" in an interview with Dan Baum for a book titled *Smoke and Mirrors: The War on Drugs and the Politics of Failure,* saying the following:

> The Nixon campaign in 1968, and the Nixon White House after that, had two enemies: the antiwar left and Black people. You understand what I'm saying? We knew we couldn't make it illegal to be either against the war or Blacks, but by getting the public to associate the hippies with marijuana and Blacks with heroin, and then criminalizing both heavily, we could disrupt those communities. We could arrest their leaders, raid their homes, break up their meetings, and vilify them night after night on the evening news. Did we know we were lying about the drugs? Of course we did. (2)

The quote was not made public until 2016 in a *Harper's Magazine* article, and has been heavily contested by Ehrlichman's family. Regardless, it is clear today that Nixon was a racist who also despised the anti-war left. What is also clear however, is that it was Republican President Ronald Reagan who did in fact make the concrete policy changes that weaponized the so-called War on Drugs against racialized Americans and political dissidents. He classified marijuana as a Schedule 1 narcotic, and stiffened penalties for possessing it. He also led the U.S. Congress in making penalties for the possession of crack cocaine, predominantly consumed by the Black community, disproportionately harsher than the penalties for the possession of pure cocaine and methamphetamine, predominantly consumed by white Americans. Reagan's Drug War policies were also accompanied by a steep increase in the private prison industry, thereby turning incarceration in the United States into a major for-profit industry. (3)

Marijuana

The ongoing federal criminalization of marijuana, and classification of the plant as a Schedule 1 narcotic, although several U.S. states have now either decriminalized or outright legalized marijuana consumption for medical and recreational use, is just the beginning of the hypocrisy and intransigence of the U.S. federal government. As legal marijuana producers throughout the United States are both raking in the profits and generating tax based revenues for the states in which they are licensed to legally produce, Mexico is still unable to begin to contemplate entering the ever profitable global marijuana market due to the ongoing international criminalization of the plant.

To be clear, Mexico officially criminalized marijuana before the United States did, but because of lax enforcement and an increase in the importation of marijuana from Mexico to the United States, the U.S. government under President Richard Nixon began to apply political and economic pressure against Mexico to enforce its prohibition against marijuana more strictly. At one point through "Operation Gatekeeper" Nixon temporarily shut down the U.S. Mexico border with intensified searches of vehicles. (4)

Let us imagine for just a moment, what the economic, political, social, and cultural effects could have been for Mexico and the Mexican people if marijuana had never been prohibited and criminalized. The Mexican people would have never been pitted against one another as actors and bystanders in the illegal marijuana market. Mexicans could have been safe in developing a home grown product for recreational and medicinal use. Recreational use at this point is really only the very tip of the iceberg, given that the medical uses being explored, uncovered, and produced through legalization are multiplying. The effects on the local and international economy could have potentially been life changing for average everyday farmworkers and working class Mexicans.

Instead, the U.S. foreign policy of prohibition has created a supply vacuum, which propagated the birth of the narcotics cartels that are devastating the Mexican people today, just like the prohibition of alcohol gave birth to the mafias of that time period in the United States.

Bipartisan Blame

Though Nixon, Reagan, and then George Bush Sr. get most of the blame for the War on Drugs and its effects on Black, Indigenous, and other racialized communities, it is important to note that Democrat presidents Bill Clinton and Barack Obama did absolutely nothing to reverse the Drug War policies of their Republican predecessors. As a matter of fact, in order to garner support for their candidacies from conservative voters, both Clinton and Obama took "hard on crime" stances that continued to subjugate, criminalize, displace, and incarcerate Black and Indigenous communities at alarming rates. Former U.S. President Donald Trump's stance on drug abuse was so regressive that current President Joe Biden's pledge to bring things "back to normal" may seem like a relief on the surface, when in fact it is clearly the continuance of the same War on Drugs that it ever was. Though the Biden administration has declared an end to the Merida Initiative, and the Drug War itself, he has done nothing to halt the continuance of a $5 million dollar contract with SIG Sauer to continue to provide firearms for the different Mexican security forces with documented human rights abuses. (5)

Bodies and Impunity

What we are seeing today five decades later, as the dust settles, and the dead bodies continue to pile up with impunity, is that in Mexico the War on Drugs, has been and continues to function as a U.S. proxy war on the Mexican people. It is in the War on

Drugs where we can most clearly see the Mexican government, the Mexican armed forces, and the various military/police forces being used to carry out undeniable atrocities against their own population in accordance with the foreign policy of the U.S. government. In fact, the entire process of Mexican militarization and armament in the name of the so-called Drug War, has been a for-profit element of the United States' own Military Industrial Complex.

From December 1, 2006 to November 30, 2012, Mexico's president was Felipe Calderón Hinojosa of the National Action Party (PAN). Ten days after taking office, on December 11, 2006, Calderon declared an all-out war against several narcotics cartels in Mexico. This war is known as the Mexican War on Drugs and is commonly referred to as the "War against the Narco." **(6)** The most obvious difference between the Mexican and U.S. War on Drugs is that in Mexico, the nation's military was extra-legally unleashed against organized crime cartels. It became a full-blown military operation with direct assistance of over $1.6 billion in military aid from the U.S. federal government through the Merida Initiative from 2008 until 2021. **(7)** The aid included training, equipment, and intelligence but no direct funds to the Mexican government. This was in addition to ongoing weapons purchases made by the Mexican government through the U.S. government's Defense Security Cooperation Agency. **(8)**

During the period of Felipe Calderon's presidency from 2006-2012, the number of serious documented human rights violations committed by all security forces, and the military in particular, including arbitrary detentions, torture, sexual assault, death threats, coerced confessions, forced disappearances, extrajudicial executions, and absolute impunity and collusion from authorities such as investigators, prosecutors, and judges, has been shameless. **(9)** To make matters worse, the man chosen by President Calderon to lead his War on Drugs, his Secretary of Public Security Genaro García Luna, was arrested on December 9, 2019, and charged with taking millions in bribes from the Sinaloa Cartel. **(10)** Garcia Luna had a long intelligence, public security, and public service career through the presidencies of both Vicente Fox and

Felipe Calderon. Garcia Luna has a Master's Degree in Business Administration (MBA) from the University of Miami. Former President Calderon on the other hand, has a Master's in Public Administration from the John F. Kennedy School of Government at Harvard University, now known as the Harvard Kennedy School.

Calderon justified the unleashing of Mexico's military, which was an unconstitutional public security force, during his 2006 War against the Narco, and his successor, President Enrique Peña Nieto of the Institutional Revolutionary Party (PRI) did absolutely nothing to reverse this trend in militarized public security. In fact, it was Peña Nieto who was able to push through congressional approval for the military acting as the primary public security force with his "Law for Internal Security." One of Peña Nieto's greatest supporters for this law was the Secretary of National Defense General Joaquin Cienfuegos. Cienfuegos' argument was that it was too great a risk for his soldiers to carry out public security duties extra legally. On November 15, 2018, the Mexican Supreme Court invalidated the Law for Internal Security as unconstitutional. **(11)**

Under Mexico's current President Andres Manuel Lopez Obrador of his own MORENA Party, it certainly seems that with the introduction of the Guardia Nacional (GN) on March 26, 2019, and the executive order that expanded and formalized the power of Mexico's armed forces to participate in public security tasks until 2024, Mexico is becoming even more militarized within a legal framework today than ever before. **(12)**

Meanwhile in Mexico, violent deaths in general and human rights abuses by security forces in particular, continue to rise at alarming rates. In the United States the importation of fentanyl, a synthetic opioid, and methamphetamine has increased dramatically. According to a December 21, 2021 article by National Public Radio (NPR) titled "Mexican cartels are turning to meth and fentanyl production,"

...seizures of the synthetic opioid fentanyl soared 525% in the first three years of the current administration... Law enforcement seized 1,232 pounds (559 kilograms) of fentanyl in 2016-2018 and 7,710 pounds (3,497 kilograms) in 2019-2021.

Seizures of methamphetamines, meanwhile, more than doubled. Meth seizures rose from 120,100 pounds (54,521 kilograms) in 2016-2018 to almost 275,000 pounds (124,735 kilograms) in the last three years, an increase of 128%. (13)

Chapter 15
Narco-Governance, Narco-Business, and Narco-Paramilitarism

Among the multiple pieces of evidence linking local, state, and federal authorities in Mexico to organized crime, the most shameless is the impunity. To be more specific it is the number of dead bodies that are left completely uninvestigated, which is critically alarming.

According to the March 2021 International Narcotics Control Strategy Report (INCSR) of the U.S. Department of State's Bureau of International Narcotics and Law Enforcement Affairs, 90% of crime in Mexico goes unreported. **(1)** According to any Mexican newspaper, on any given day, only 5% of the murderers are ever charged. So in Mexico you have more than a 90% chance to get away with crime, and a 95% chance to get away with murder. **(2)** This is a tremendous incentive to use murder as a primary recourse by organized crime cartels, or by anyone hungry for money and power for that matter.

We understand that organized crime profits the most from the provision of prohibited items, but also from protection. Now protection is more complicated than it sounds. Of course there is the classic protection or, as the Italian mafia coined the term, *pizzo*, which can have several different literal meanings but comes down to the protection that is paid by an individual or business to organized crime. In essence what you are paying for is protection from potential violence from the very organized crime entity you are paying to protect you. In Mexico organized crime cartels sell the same type of protection under the name *derecho de piso*, which literally means your right to the floor. In different states, and to varying degrees from place to place, in Mexico the cartels charge for the floor you stand on.

When it comes to business and political elites, the relationship certainly has the potential to be more mutually beneficial as opposed to a top down arrangement. Protection paid for by these elites grants access to the brute power, wealth, and political strength of the criminal organization. People in positions of authority who are of interest to the criminal organizations pay protection with information and or impunity and are usually rewarded in cash bribes. Wealthy business owners pay in cash for protection but also gain access to the criminal organizations' political connections, as well as to the criminal organizations' paramilitary soldiers. For the business and political elite, having associations with organized crime in countries like Mexico has almost become fashionable.

What an Uprising Can Expose

Between 2008 and 2015 in Mexico, thanks to several community-based armed uprisings by Indigenous and non-Indigenous people throughout the state of Michoacán against the local dominant cartel, we learned in excruciating detail just how deep the charging of *piso* could go in Mexico, and just how deep narco-governance and narco business ran.

During the peak of this cartel's activity in Michoacán, everyone had to pay *piso*. Tortilla makers had to charge more for tortillas to make their quota. Avocado pickers had to voluntarily give a day's pay once a week. Any business with a storefront or any agricultural or industrial activity had to pay. (3) Higher up on the social ladder as the amounts of *piso* grew larger, however, then what in fact was purchased was not just protection from the cartel, but access to the cartel as a tool of repression against the competition, against striking workers, against protestors, and against the government itself. At one point in Michoacán, the entire avocado industry, the entire mining industry, and the entire lumber industry were protected by organized crime. They were protected from the government for operating without the proper licensing. They were protected from labor that was organizing their workers. They were protected from communities that resisted the exploitation of their natural resources and the desecration of Mother Earth. The cartel had diversified into any and all profitable activity, including the for-profit activities of transnational corporations. If you ate an avocado between 2009 and 2015, you probably ate a transnational corporation / cartel avocado. (4)

There is yet another level to the protection scheme, which has to do with official public corruption. The cartel must protect itself, its employees, its associates, and its entire supply chain from criminal prosecution. This protection is only available at a price, through bribes given to public officials, the police, and the military.

So what happens in an environment where public officials already have a hunger for power and money, and an electoral system that functions solely on the premise of money, power, corruption, and fraud? What happens when you have an entire business class that is also hungry for power and money, and faces barriers that the government is unable or unwilling to address legally? What happens when you also have a national financial system that primarily serves to launder illicit earnings? Well, all of these elements in conjunction create an environment that is ripe for 1. narco-governance, the convergence of official government entities and organized crime cartels, 2. narco-business, the convergence of business/finance and organized crime cartels, and 3. narco-paramilitarism, the use of the organized crime cartel paramilitary soldiers for social, political, or economic interests in a given region.

In the state of Michoacán throughout 2008 to the present date, average everyday folks have seen it all. In different states throughout Mexico, neoliberalism has become a narco-paramilitary political economy, where criminal organizations have simply become microcosms of the United States' own military political economy. The system of money and power itself has generated organizations that are blurring the lines of criminality and legitimacy by incentivizing money, power, and control above all else. Today it has become significantly more difficult to know with any amount of certainty who exactly is in control, who exactly has the most power, and who has the most money: political parties, business and political elites, or organized crime cartels. The response certainly varies from region to region, but it would be safe to say that power, money, and control is at the very least shared among these three sub groups.

With regards to narco-paramilitarism, the phenomenon has all the characteristics of classic paramilitarism, with the added incentive of organized crime profits, and a tremendous veil of protection generated through rampant public corruption.

Paramilitary forces use violence to carry out social, political or economic objectives against a target civilian population that is either considered a disposable variable, a barrier, or a direct threat to a given political, economic, or military interest.

A key calling card of paramilitarism is that the paramilitary forces carry out their atrocities with total impunity. It is impunity of this nature that further delegitimizes governments and their justice systems altogether.

Clearly not all narco-violence can be attributed to a state sponsored strategy of narco-paramilitarism, and certainly levels of narco-governance vary between nations, governmental administrations, and regions. Narco-business, narco-governance, and narco-paramilitarism are much more complicated than that.

With a simple historical overview of the use of low intensity warfare and deniable atrocities as strategies for political, economic, and social control, however, the idea that a substantial number of the business and political elite, public security forces, authorities, financial institutions, and transnational corporations rely on criminal organizations in order to secure certain political and economic interests makes absolutely perfect sense.

At this point the nation is inundated by guns for hire, because there is a demand for guns for hire. In almost every case of state sponsored deniable atrocities against political dissidents in Mexico historically and to date, the use of hired thugs, criminals, and narcotics users to carry out said atrocities has been a recurring strategy.

As a result, the use of paramilitary violence to secure political and economic interests has also become a norm. In addition, the potential for massive narco-paramilitary violence is greater, because even though the government itself has shown little respect for basic human and community rights, the organized crime cartels spark greater fear in the general population. Again, 90% of all crime committed in Mexico goes unreported, and 95% of the murders go un-prosecuted. It is fear that has become the ultimate tool for social, political, and economic control of the Mexican people in general, and of Indigenous communities in particular, along with control of their labor, their natural resources, and their territories.

There is quite a bit more to say about narco-governance, narco-business, and narco-paramilitarism in Mexico. It would seem that these are the most shameless, grotesque, corrupt, and disgraceful aspects of the neoliberal narco-paramilitary political economy. They are certainly shocking enough to warrant an endless list of movies and TV series, most of which are not too far removed from the truth. Today you can literally watch a telenovela style (soap opera) series about drug trafficking, and then you can google dates and names to check and corroborate facts. At this point there is no need to write about that which has been overexploited for entertainment purposes by the mainstream media. The question is when are we going to see a Netflix series on the real drug dealers --the global pharmaceutical and healthcare industry otherwise known as the Pharmafia-- or the real gangstas --the banks and international financial institutions also known as the Original Bankstas?

Chapter 16
The Real Drug Dealers: The Pharmafia

Opium

The opium trade has its roots in transnational free trade, which was literally imposed on China by the British despite China's desire to ban the importation and sale of opium in its territory. The First Opium War from September 4, 1839 to August 29, 1842 began when Chinese officials seized British opium stocks, and threatened opium merchants with the death penalty. China was concerned with the economic impact of the opium trade, as well as with the growing number of opium addicts in its territory. The British won the First Opium War with a superior naval advantage and as a result, claimed Hong Kong as a colony of the British Empire. The Second Opium War from October 8, 1856 to October 24, 1860 simply expanded European influence over international trade with China, now including access to additional ports of trade in China for France and the Russian Empire. **(1)**

In terms of the United States, the international opium trade greatly benefitted powerful and wealthy families, and was a primary factor in generating the wealth to build some major U.S. cities such as Baltimore, Philadelphia, and Boston. The United States' first multi-millionaire was John Jacob Astor, an opium smuggler. Warren Delano Jr., maternal grandfather of the 32nd U.S. President, Franklin Delano Roosevelt, made a large fortune as an illegal smuggler of opium to China during the period of opium prohibition. Another famous U.S. opium smuggler during both Opium Wars was Francis Blackwell Forbes, who also amassed a tremendous amount of wealth for his family. **(2)** Forbes was the great grandfather of former U.S. presidential candidate, John Kerry. The Forbes family is one of the Boston Brahmins, a classification given to families among Boston's political and business elite. (3) In addition, these families are also associated with Anglicanism, which is just another way of saying white male Christian supremacy. It is no wonder that even though members of this elite political and economic circle were directly responsible for the illegal opium trade to China, over the course of time the script has been conveniently transformed to place blame on the Chinese themselves for the global opium trade.

Historically, as long as opium made Europeans and U.S. Americans wealthy, the adverse effects on others who did not share the Anglican identity were attributed to their own self undoing, and not to the profits made by smugglers and criminals from the proliferation of the highly addictive narcotic. Over time opium would be cultivated in China, and with mass migration from China to the Americas, dens for opium consumption began to pop up in San Francisco in particular. Due to anti-Chinese racism coupled with white male Christian supremacy, opium dens in San Francisco were legally banned in 1875 under the pretense that white Americans were beginning to frequent them. For the white male Christian business political elite, the consumption and subsequent addiction to opium by non-whites was not seen as a problem. As white consumption and addiction increased, however, so did concerns over the narcotic's effect on society. (4)

The History of Some Pharmaceutical Opioids

In 1804, the German pharmacist Friedrich Wilhelm Adam Sertürner isolated the morphine alkaloid from the opium poppy, and in 1817 he would publish his findings after dangerously experimenting on himself and three young boys. Morphine made it much easier to control dosages for patients, and in 1827, sales by Heinrich Emanuel Merck began. This greatly aided the creation of the transnational German science and technology corporation the Merck Group, which today includes approximately 250 companies in 66 countries with around 57,000 employees.

In 1897, Felix Hoffmann pursued the synthesizing of heroin, the first semi-synthetic opioid, for the Bayer pharmaceutical company in Elberfeld, Germany. Heroin was first marketed as a safe morphine substitute for children. In 2020, Bayer reported having 117,046 billion euros in assets, and 99,538 employees worldwide. Oxycodone, an opioid medication, was first introduced by Bayer in 1916.

Fentanyl was first produced by the Belgian physician Paul Adriaan Jan, Baron Janssen, in 1960. He founded Janssen Pharmaceutica, which today employs 20,000 people and is now a subsidiary of Johnson & Johnson along with approximately 250 subsidiary companies in 60 countries. The transnational corporation Johnson & Johnson sells products in over 175 countries around the world and in 2020, reported $82.6 billion in sales.

As an aside, to understand the economic impact and strategic importance of opium and the opium trade, in a September 16, 1993 article in the *Seattle Times* by Gardiner Harris titled "Fort Knox Vaults Harbor Millions In Opium, Morphine -- Stockpile Held For Emergencies." Harris tells us that at two of the primary gold bullion depositories in the United States, Fort Knox in the state of Kentucky, and the U.S. Mint at West Point, NY, in addition to the strategic gold reserves held, 68,269 pounds of black opium and white morphine are also strategically stored. **(5)** That is enough of these narcotics to supply the entire nation for a year, and enough to destroy the pharmaceutical opioid market if the narcotics were ever released as a commercial commodity. Since then the U.S. government has spent millions in preserving the narcotics and converting the opium into morphine. According to a Public Affairs Questions/Answers and Fact Sheet from the U.S. Mint obtained through FOIA Request #2017-09-205, the morphine is no longer stored at the depository. All of this raises several interesting questions, such as where did all that opium and morphine come from, how was it acquired, and where did all the morphine go? **(6)**

Opioid Epidemics in the USA

It is clear that peaks in opium and opioid addiction throughout history correlate significantly to acts of war in which soldiers have suffered painful injuries, therefore requiring strong pain medications. The American Civil War, World Wars I and II, the Vietnam War and the Afghanistan War all produced waves of opium or opioid addiction. This in turn has proven to be disgustingly profitable to major transnational pharmaceutical corporations, while being absolutely devastating to a substantial number of the working poor communities that send their sons and daughters off to war.

The first major recognized opioid epidemic was the heroin epidemic immediately after the Vietnam War, as U.S. veterans of the war returned home and left the military. Although several studies have shown that U.S. soldiers overwhelmingly became addicted in Vietnam, and received treatment before going home, statistics reveal that returning soldiers were no longer addicted because they were showing negative opioid test results while enlisted. However once out of military service, veterans' addiction to heroin and other opioids increased substantially. (7) This in turn affected Black and Indigenous veterans disproportionately because of the racist stigma and stereotypes about Black and Indigenous addicts.

The current opioid crisis began in the 90s and was absolutely exacerbated by opioid producing pharmaceutical corporations that deliberately deceived government regulators and the general public about the addictiveness of prescription opioids. According to the National Institute on Drug Abuse website drugabuse.gov :

> In the late 1990s, pharmaceutical companies reassured the medical community that patients would not become addicted to prescription opioid pain relievers, and health-care providers began to prescribe them at greater rates. This subsequently led to widespread diversion and misuse of these medications before it became clear that these medications could indeed be highly addictive. Opioid overdose rates began to increase. In 2017, more than 47,000 Americans died as a result of an opioid overdose, including prescription opioids, heroin, and illicitly manufactured fentanyl, a powerful synthetic opioid. That same year, an

estimated 1.7 million people in the United States suffered from substance use disorders related to prescription opioid pain relievers, and 652,000 suffered from a heroin use disorder (not mutually exclusive).

-Roughly 21 to 29 percent of patients who have been prescribed opioids for chronic pain misuse them.

-Between 8 and 12 percent of people using an opioid for chronic pain develop an opioid use disorder.

-An estimated 4 to 6 percent who misuse prescription opioids transition to heroin.

-About 80 percent of people who use heroin first misused prescription opioids. (8)

Pharmaceutical Lobby and Legislation

In terms of power, wealth, and influence today, the Pharmaceutical and Health Products Industry has surpassed all other industries in terms of lobbying expenses every single year since 1999. According to data collected by the lobbying watchdog website opensecrets.org the Pharmaceutical and Health Products Industry spent a total of $4,990,257,367 from 1998 through 2021 on lobbying. This is twice as much money spent by the Oil and Gas Industry ($2,489,418,498), and four times as much money spent by the Defense and Aerospace Industry ($1,232,991,613) during the same time period. In 2021 the Pharmaceutical and Health Products Industry spent $266,846,347 on lobbying, employing 1,616 registered lobbyists, 59.47% of whom were former government employees. The Pharmaceutical and Health Products Industry hired 961 former government employees to work as registered lobbyists. (9)

It is important to keep in mind, however, that there is a growing trend of unregistered lobbyists working for lawyer/lobbyist firms as consultants, advisors, or specialists through a loophole known as the Daschle Loophole, named after Tom

Daschle, who worked as an unregistered lobbyist for years until registering just recently. They are known as "shadow lobbyists."

To make matters worse, the Pharmaceutical and Health Products Industry has been spending hundreds of millions of dollars on lobbying through "Dark Money" groups. **(10)** Basically, such groups are registered non-profit and social welfare organizations, unions, and trade associations that are under no legal obligation to disclose any of their donors; therefore, these organizations can receive an unlimited number of donations from corporations, individuals, and unions. This deliberately creates a situation where voters have no recourse to the exact identification of those donating to their politicians and public officials. Again, from 1999 through 2021, the Pharmaceutical and Health Products Industry has outspent all other industries on lobbying. With the substantial presence of shadow lobbyists and dark money, the level of clandestine political influence and power exercised by this industry is unprecedented, but more importantly it makes the issue of the corruptibility of public officials through their actions against the public's interest, simply irrefutable.

Drug Enforcement Administration (DEA) Investigators Turned Pharma Lobbyists

According to a collaborative investigation for the *Washington Post* on December 22, 2016, by journalists and researchers Scott Higham, Lenny Bernstein, Steven Rich and Alice Crites, titled "Drug industry hired dozens of officials from the DEA as the agency tried to curb opioid abuse":

> Pharmaceutical companies that manufacture or distribute highly addictive pain pills have hired dozens of officials from the top levels of the Drug Enforcement Administration during the past decade, according to a Washington Post investigation.

The hires came after the DEA launched an aggressive campaign to curb a rising opioid epidemic that has resulted in thousands of overdose deaths each year. In 2005, the DEA began to crack down on companies that were distributing inordinate numbers of pills such as oxycodone to pain-management clinics and pharmacies around the country.

Since then, the pharmaceutical companies and law firms that represent them have hired at least 42 officials from the DEA — 31 of them directly from the division responsible for regulating the industry according to work histories compiled by The Post and interviews with current and former agency officials.

....While The Post did not find evidence that the officials violated conflict-of-interest regulations, the number of hires from one key division shows how an industry can potentially blunt a government agency's aggressive attempts at enforcement.

"It's obvious that they targeted the office," said Joseph T. Rannazzisi, who ran the diversion division for a decade before he was removed from his position and retired in 2015. 'If you want to understand how we were doing our investigations, the best way to do it is to take our people who are doing the investigations and put them in place in your company. It's not difficult to understand why you would take these guys. They know the law."

The DEA diversion officials who have gone to the industry since 2005 include two executive assistants who managed day-to-day operations; the deputy director of the division; the deputy chief of operations; two chiefs of policy; a deputy chief of policy; the chief of investigations; and two associate chief counsels in charge of legal affairs and enforcement actions against pharmaceutical companies. (11)

According to a follow-up article on October 15, 2017 in the *Washington Post* by Scott Higham and Lenny Bernstein titled "The Drug Industries Triumph over the DEA":

> A handful of members of Congress, allied with the nation's major drug distributors, prevailed upon the DEA and the Justice Department to agree to a more industry-friendly law, undermining efforts to stanch the flow of pain pills, according to an investigation by The Washington Post and "60 Minutes." The DEA had opposed the effort for years.
>
> The law was the crowning achievement of a multifaceted campaign by the drug industry to weaken aggressive DEA enforcement efforts against drug distribution companies that were supplying corrupt doctors and pharmacists who peddled narcotics to the black market. The industry worked behind the scenes with lobbyists and key members of Congress, pouring more than a million dollars into their election campaigns. (12)

In an interview on October 17, 2017 for the nationally syndicated TV news program "60 Minutes" conducted by Bill Whitaker, with DEA Investigator Joseph Rannazzisi, the following exchange takes place:

> BILL WHITAKER: You know the implication of what you're saying, that these big companies knew that they were pumping drugs into American communities that were killing people.
>
> JOE RANNAZZISI: That's not an implication, that's a fact. That's exactly what they did. In the late 1990s, opioids like oxycodone and hydrocodone became a routine medical treatment for chronic pain. Drug companies assured doctors and congressional investigators... that the pain medications were effective and safe. (13)

Prescription opioid producing pharmaceutical corporations hired 42 former DEA officials, including 31 from the division responsible for regulating the pharmaceutical industry, and lobbied legislators to approve a law in 2017 that would ease proposed restrictions on the flow of opioids.

According to the Centers for Disease Control and Prevention:

> Nearly 841,000 people have died since 1999 from a drug overdose. Over 70% of drug overdose deaths in 2019 involved an opioid...

> Overdose deaths involving opioids, including prescription opioids, heroin, and synthetic opioids (like fentanyl), have increased over six times since 1999. Overdoses involving opioids killed nearly 50,000 people in 2019, and nearly 73% of those deaths involved synthetic opioids. (14)

Legal Settlements with Pharmaceuticals

At this point, enough white people have died from opioid overdoses to warrant a declaration by bi-partisan government officials of an opioid epidemic, even though both Indigenous and Black communities have been dealing with undiagnosed and untreated substance abuse disorders for decades because of the stigma associated with being a Black or Indigenous addict. Proportionately opioids still kill Indigenous community members at higher rates today than other groups, and while opioid deaths among whites have begun to decrease, overdoses in both Indigenous communities and the Black community continue to climb. (15) Also, lawsuits against opioid manufacturers by Indigenous tribes and their sovereign governments have been disproportionately unsuccessful compared to local, state, and federal litigation. (16)

The national opioid epidemic has now forced government officials to begin to target pharmaceutical opioid producers, marketers, and distributors in several criminal cases. However to date there has been no mention of litigation against opioid lobbyists, legislators who received donations from pharmaceutical lobbyists to push forward lenient legislation, or the 42 former DEA agents who left the Agency to join pharmaceutical lobbyists. Neither do there seem to be any official probes to date into pharmaceutical lobbying through dark money or pharmaceutical shadow lobbyists.

So far, on January 23, 2020, the executive John Kapoor, founder and former CEO of Insys Therapeutics, producer of the opioid Subsys, was charged, convicted and sentenced to five and a half years in prison. According to a report on January 23, 2020 by National Public Radio (NPR) journalists Gabrielle Emanuel and Vanessa Romo titled "Pharmaceutical Executive John Kapoor Sentenced to 66 Months in Prison in Opioid Trial":

> Kapoor and four other executives were found guilty last year of orchestrating a criminal conspiracy to bribe doctors to prescribe the company's medication, including to patients who didn't need it. They then lied to insurance companies to make sure the costly oral fentanyl spray was covered.
>
> The painkiller, which was intended for cancer patients, could cost as much as $19,000 a month.
>
> Two other executives pleaded guilty and became cooperating witnesses.
>
> The other executives received sentences ranging from one year to 33 months, significantly less than many of the prison terms recommended by the federal prosecutors.
>
> Earlier on Thursday, Insys sales chief Alec Burlakoff was sentenced to 26 months in prison for his role in the bribery and fraud scheme.
>
> "This was an offense of greed," Burroughs said before sentencing Burlakoff.

> The sales executive hired <an exotic dancer> as a Subsys sales representative to help persuade doctors to boost prescriptions. The woman... eventually was promoted to oversee a third of the company's sales force. (17)

Perhaps most readers have never heard of Insys, but there is no doubt that household names like Johnson & Johnson, CVS pharmacies, Walgreens, and Walmart, all resonate with anyone living in the United States. These are some of the major opioid retailers and just one manufacturer facing opioid litigation today, and they are joined by manufacturers Purdue, Teva, and Endo as well as distributors McKesson, Amerisource-Bergen and Cardinal Health.

All of these manufacturers, distributors, and retailers, are part of a proposed global settlement deal, which is being monitored by a global settlement tracker at opioidsettlementtracker. com. These are only the big names; the level of litigation against doctors, pain clinics, and small time manufacturers, distributors, and retailers is overwhelming. The problem is that the evidence demonstrates beyond a shadow of a doubt that there is a parallel epidemic of crime and corruption surrounding the prescription opioid industry that implicates not only the manufacturers, distributors and retailers, but also legislators, government officials, and regulators, as well as former narcotic agents from the DEA.

On October 21, 2020, the U.S. Justice Department announced a global resolution of criminal and civil investigations with opioid manufacturer Purdue Pharma and a civil settlement with Purdue's owners, who are members of the multi-billion dollar Sackler family. In the original deal the Sackler Family and Purdue agreed to pay billions and would file for bankruptcy relinquishing ownership of the opioid manufacturer in exchange for immunity from further prosecution. **(18)** The settlement deal was opposed by 24 states, and on December 16, 2021, a federal judge ruled that the bankruptcy judge did not have authority to give the Sacklers immunity in civil liability cases. **(19)**

According to a report on September 14, 2019 by Brian Mann of National Public Radio (NPR):

New York's Attorney General Letitia James says the Sackler family used wire transfers, Swiss bank accounts and real estate deals to hide a billion dollars in profits from the sale of their opioid medication OxyContin. (20)

Among the Swiss banks used to hide Sackler money from opioid litigation is the Swiss branch of HSBC Bank. (21)

PART FOUR
MONEY

Chapter 17
HSBC – The Original Bankstas

On March 3, 1865 a Scotsman by the name of Thomas Sutherland founded the Hongkong and Shanghai Bank in the then colony of British Hong Kong. The bank then opened offices in Shanghai, China a month later. The Hongkong and Shanghai Banking Corporation incorporated in Hong Kong on August 14, 1866. **(1)**

This Financial Institution's Roots are Empire and Opium.

The British won the First Opium War against China on August 29, 1842 with a superior naval advantage, and as a result claimed Hong Kong as a colony of the British Empire and physically imposed the opium trade from India to China, and then throughout the world. The Second Opium War from October 8, 1856 to October 24, 1860 simply expanded European influence over international trade with China, most of which consisted of the opium trade.

Thomas Sutherland worked for the steamship business of the Peninsular and Oriental Steam Navigation Company (P&O), building new wharves on shipping docks. Sutherland became the Hong Kong superintendent of P&O as well as the first chairman of Hong Kong and Whampoa Dock in 1863. By the end of the Opium Wars, opium made up 70% of the trade coming to China's ports and Sutherland saw a unique opportunity to create a bank for the lucrative international narcotics trade. **(2)** According to a February 2012 article in *Le Monde Diplomatique* by Jean-Louis Conne:

> Sutherland understood that the time was right for a commercial bank. In 1865 he and a few others founded the Hong Kong and Shanghai Banking Corporation now known as HSBC. The board was chaired by Francis Chomley, and included the remarkable Thomas Dent, founder of Dent &

Co. In 1839 a senior Chinese government official, Lin Zexu, known for his competence and moral standing, issued a warrant for Dent's arrest in an attempt to close his warehouses, which infringed the Chinese ban on opium. That helped trigger the First Opium War, which ended in August 1842 with the unequal treaty of Nanking. **(3)**

In 1987 HSBC acquired full ownership of U.S.-based Marine Midland Bank, and in 1999 HSBC purchased U.S.-based Republic National Bank of New York for $10.3 billion. Today HSBC Holdings plc is a British multinational investment bank and financial services holding company with a total equity of $204.995 billion and assets of $2.984 trillion as of December 2020. HSBC has over 200,000 employees, with offices in 64 countries and territories across the world, serving around 40 million customers. HSBC is one of the most powerful banks in the world. In 2020 HSBC ranked 7th largest bank in the world in terms of total assets.

The following information was taken directly from the Statement of Facts attachment of a Deferred Prosecution Agreement (DPA) between the United States Department of Justice, Criminal Division, Asset Forfeiture and Money Laundering Section; the United States Attorney's Office for the Eastern District of New York and the United States Attorney's Office for the Northern District of West Virginia (collectively, the Department) and HSBC Bank USA, N.A. (HSBC Bank USA); and HSBC Holdings plc (HSBC Holdings) made public on December 11, 2012. **(4)**

(The order of the paragraphs has been reorganized for chronological and narrative continuity. No edits have been made to the wording and content of each paragraph, with the exception of explanations of terms.)

HSBC Mexico

In 2002, HSBC Group acquired *Grupo Financiero Bital (Bital)*. Bital was the fifth-largest bank in Mexico with approximately 1,400 branches and six million customers. In early 2004, Bital became HSBC Mexico. HSBC Mexico offered accounts denominated in Mexican pesos or U.S. dollars. From at least 2004 through 2008, physical U.S. dollars deposited at HSBC Mexico branches that were not needed for daily operations were sold to HSBC Bank USA through Banknotes. *(Banknotes are what HSBC calls its business of wholesale buying and selling of bulk cash.)* At the time of the acquisition, HSBC Group's Head of Compliance acknowledged there was "no recognizable compliance or money laundering function in Bital at present." HSBC Group Compliance believed it would take from one to four years to achieve its required *Anti-Money Laundering (AML)* standards at HSBC Mexico. Until at least 2010, however, HSBC Mexico's AML program was not fully up to HSBC Group's required AML standards for HSBC Group Affiliates. As described below, before 2009, many of the AML problems at HSBC Mexico involved U.S. dollar accounts, which ultimately affected HSBC Bank USA.

HSBC Mexico Did Not Maintain Sufficient Know Your Customer (KYC) Information on U.S. Dollar Customers

From 2002 until at least 2009, HSBC Mexico did not maintain sufficient *KYC* information on many of its customers, including those with U.S. dollar accounts. A financial institution's KYC information should include customer information such as address, the reason for maintaining the account, expected activity, and the source of U.S. dollars. The lack of sufficient KYC information at HSBC Mexico was repeatedly raised in internal audits and by HSBC Mexico's regulator, the *Comisión Nacional Bancaria y Valores (CNBV)*. These concerns were raised with the CEOs of HSBC Mexico and HSBC Group.

One area in which KYC was particularly poor was HSBC Mexico's Cayman Island U.S. dollar accounts. Mexican law prohibited most individuals from maintaining U.S. dollar denominated deposit accounts in Mexico unless they lived near the U.S.- Mexico border or were a corporation.

However, Mexican law permitted almost any Mexican citizen to maintain offshore U.S. dollar accounts. These HSBC Mexico accounts were based in the Cayman Islands, but were essentially offshore in name only, because HSBC Mexico had no physical presence in the Cayman Islands and provided the front and back office services for these accounts at its branches in Mexico. Customers holding these accounts did all of their banking, including depositing physical U.S. dollars, at branches in Mexico. Nevertheless, the accounts were legal under Mexican and Cayman law.

In January 2006, HSBC Mexico conducted an internal audit of the Cayman Islands U.S. dollar accounts. At that time, there were only approximately 1,500 such accounts. Over 50% of the audited accounts lacked the proper KYC information, while 15% of audited accounts did not contain any KYC documentation. Over the next two years, nothing was done to address the KYC issues with these accounts. By 2008, there were 35,000 Cayman Island U.S. dollar accounts. At least 2,200 of these accounts were designated "high risk" due to suspicious activity within the accounts and/or negative information regarding the account owners. In July 2008, the total outstanding balance of these high risk Cayman accounts was approximately $205 million. Without adequate KYC information, HSBC Mexico knew very little about who these high risk customers were or why they had such large amounts of U.S. dollars. However, even without the benefit of adequate KYC information, the risks were obvious. Indeed, one HSBC Mexico compliance officer noted "the massive misuse of [the HSBC Mexico Cayman Islands U.S. dollar accounts] by organized crime." One example, identified by HSBC Group's Head of Compliance in July 2008, involved "significant USD [U.S. dollar] remittances being made by a number of [HSBC Mexico's Cayman Islands U.S. dollar] customers to a US company alleged to be involved in the supply of aircraft to drug cartels."

HSBC Mexico Failed to Terminate
Suspicious Accounts

When suspicious activity was identified, HSBC Mexico re-peatedly failed to take action to close the accounts. Senior business executives at HSBC Mexico repeatedly over-ruled recommendations from its own AML Committee to close accounts with documented suspicious activity. In July 2007, a senior compliance officer at HSBC Group told HSBC Mexico's Chief Compliance Officer that "[t]he AML Committee just can't keep rubber-stamping unac-ceptable risks merely because someone on the business side writes a nice letter. It needs to take a firmer stand. It needs some cojones. We have seen this movie before, and it ends badly."

Even when HSBC Mexico determined that a relationship should be terminated, it often took years for the account to actually be closed. In December 2008, there were approxi-mately 675 accounts pending closure based on suspicions of money laundering activity. Closure had been approved for 16 of those accounts in 2005, 130 in 2006, 172 in 2007, and 309 in 2008. All 675 of these accounts remained open into at least 2009, with transactions being actively con-ducted through them despite facing pending closure based on suspicion of money laundering activity.

HSBC Mexico's High Volume of U.S. Dollar Exports

Between 2004 and 2007, HSBC Mexico exported over $3 billion U.S. dollars per year to the United States through Banknotes. (Banknotes are what HSBC calls its business of the wholesale buying and selling of bulk cash.)

In November 2007, Banco de Mexico, the central bank of Mexico, expressed concerns about the volume of U.S. dol-lars exported by HSBC Mexico back to the United States. Specifically, Banco de Mexico wanted an explanation as to why HSBC Mexico's U.S. dollar exports were significantly larger than its market share would suggest.

In February 2008, HSBC Mexico's CEO met with the head of the CNBV and the head of Mexico's financial intelligence unit, *Unidad de Inteligencia Financiera (UIF)*. Again, the volume of HSBC Mexico's U.S. dollar exports was raised as a concern. Specifically, HSBC Mexico's CEO was told that law enforcement in Mexico and the United States were seriously concerned that the U.S. dollars being deposited at HSBC Mexico might represent drug trafficking proceeds. HSBC Mexico's CEO was also told that Mexican law enforcement possessed a recording of a Mexican drug lord saying that HSBC Mexico was the place to launder money. HSBC Mexico's CEO immediately raised these issues with HSBC Group's CEO, Head of Legal, Head of Audit, and Head of Compliance.

An HSBC Mexico internal investigation following the February 2008 meeting with the CNBV and UIF revealed that a very small number of customers accounted for a very large percentage of physical U.S. dollar deposits. For example, in January 2008, 312 customers accounted for approximately 32% of total physical U.S. dollar deposits.

Moreover, a significant amount of the physical U.S. dollar exports came from Culiacan, in the Mexican state of Sinaloa. Culiacan is home to the Sinaloa drug cartel. HSBC Group and HSBC Mexico were both aware of the money laundering risks in doing U.S. dollar business in Sinaloa state. In 2007, HSBC Group learned of what was referred to in its employees' emails as a "massive money-laundering scheme" executed by HSBC Mexico employees and managers at multiple branches in Sinaloa state. HSBC Mexico closed all of the accounts involved in this scheme and terminated employees. However, HSBC Mexico branches continued to accept U.S. dollar deposits in Sinaloa state. From 2006 to 2008, HSBC Mexico exported over $1.1 billion in physical U.S. dollars from Sinaloa state to HSBC Bank USA.

Despite the warnings from Mexican officials in late 2007 and early 2008, HSBC Mexico exported more physical U.S. dollars in 2008 than in any previous year, over $4.1 billion. Finally, after the CNBV raised concerns directly with the HSBC Group's CEO in November 2008, HSBC Mexico stopped accepting physical U.S. dollar deposits at its branches. HSBC Mexico was the first bank in Mexico to adopt such a measure, after which Mexican regulators issued new regulations consistent with this practice.

HSBC Bank USA

HSBC Bank USA, headquartered in McLean, Virginia, with its principal office in New York City, operates throughout the United States and has customers and offers services to customers around the world. It offers customers a full range of commercial and consumer banking products and related financial services. Its customers include individuals, small businesses, corporations, financial institutions and foreign governments. Some of the products HSBC Bank USA offered during the period in question are considered high risk by the financial services industry and require stringent AML monitoring and oversight. In addition, HSBC Group Affiliates conducted business in many high risk international locations, including regions of the world presenting a high vulnerability to the laundering of drug trafficking proceeds.

HSBC Bank USA Failed to Conduct Due Diligence on HSBC Group Affiliates

One of HSBC Bank USA's high risk products was its correspondent banking practices and services accounts. Correspondent accounts are established at banks to receive deposits from, make payments on behalf of, or handle other financial transactions for foreign financial institutions.

In essence, correspondent banking involves the facilitation of wire transfers between foreign financial institutions and their customers, and other financial institutions with which the foreign financial institution does not have a direct relationship. Such correspondent accounts are generally considered high risk because the U.S. bank does not have a direct relationship with, and therefore has no diligence information on, the foreign financial institution's customers who initiated the wire transfers. To mitigate this risk, the *Banking Secrecy Act (BSA)* requires financial institutions to conduct due diligence on all non-U.S. entities (i.e. foreign financial institutions) for which it maintains correspondent accounts. There is no exception for foreign financial institutions with the same parent company.

HSBC Bank USA maintained correspondent accounts for a number of foreign financial institutions, including HSBC Group Affiliates, within its *Payments and Cash Management (PCM)* business. HSBC Bank USA was required under the BSA to conduct due diligence on all foreign financial institutions with correspondent accounts, including HSBC Group Affiliates.

Despite this requirement, from at least 2006 to 2010, HSBC Bank USA did not conduct due diligence on HSBC Group Affiliates for which it maintained correspondent accounts, including HSBC Mexico. The decision not to conduct due diligence was guided by a formal policy memorialized in HSBC Bank USA's AML Procedures Manuals.

HSBC Bank USA Failed to Adequately Monitor Wire Transfers

Another way for financial institutions to mitigate the risks associated with correspondent banking is monitoring the wire transfers to and from these accounts. From 2006 to 2009, HSBC Bank USA monitored wire transfers using an automated system called the *Customer Account Monitoring Program (CAMP)*. The CAMP system would detect suspicious wire transfers based on parameters set by HSBC Bank USA. Under the CAMP system, various factors triggered review, in particular, the amount of the transaction and the type and location of the customer. During this period, HSBC Bank USA assigned each customer a risk category based primarily on the country in which it was located. Countries were placed into one of four categories based on the perceived AML risk of doing business in that country (from lowest to highest risk): standard, medium, cautionary, and high. Transactions that met the thresholds for review and the parameters for suspicious activity were flagged for additional review by HSBC Bank USA's AML Department. These were referred to as "alerts."

From 2006 to 2009, HSBC Bank USA knowingly set the thresholds in CAMP so that wire transfers by customers located in countries categorized as standard or medium risk, including foreign financial institutions with correspondent accounts, would not be subject to automated monitoring unless the customers were otherwise classified as high risk. During this period, HSBC Bank USA processed over 100 million wire transfers totaling over $300 trillion. Over two-thirds of these transactions involved customers in standard or medium risk countries. Therefore, in this four-year period alone, over $200 trillion in wire transfers were not reviewed in CAMP.

Between 2000 and 2009, HSBC Bank USA, and its executives and officers, were aware of numerous publicly available and industry-wide advisories about the money laundering risks inherent to Mexican financial institutions. All of these advisories or events were known to numerous HSBC Bank USA AML officers and business executives at or near the time they occurred.

Despite this evidence of the serious money laundering risks associated with doing business in Mexico, from at least 2006 to 2009, HSBC Bank USA rated Mexico as "standard risk," its lowest AML risk category. As a result, wire transfers originating in Mexico, including transactions from HSBC Mexico, were generally not reviewed in the CAMP system. From 2006 until May 2009, when HSBC Bank USA raised Mexico's risk rating to high, over 316,000 transactions worth over $670 billion from HSBC Mexico alone were excluded from monitoring in the CAMP system.

HSBC Bank USA Failed to Monitor Banknotes Transactions with HSBC Group Affiliates

HSBC Bank USA's Banknotes business involved the wholesale buying and selling of physical currencies (i.e., bulk cash) throughout the world. The business was based in New York with operations centers in London, Hong Kong and Singapore. These operations centers reported to the Head of Global Banknotes in New York. Banknotes was the largest volume trader of physical currency in the world, controlling approximately 60% of the global market. Banknotes customers included central banks, global financial institutions and non-bank entities such as *Casas De Cambio (CDCs)* and other money services businesses. Banknotes sold customers physical currency to be utilized in daily operations and/or purchased excess physical currency the customers did not need to have on hand. Banknotes' largest volume currency was the U.S. dollar. Purchased U.S. dollars were transported by Banknotes into the United States and deposited with the Federal Reserve. Banknotes derived its revenue from commissions earned in connection with trading, transporting, and storing the physical currency.

Banknotes was a high risk business because of the high risk of money laundering associated with transactions involving physical currency and the high risk of money laundering in countries where some of its customers were located. In an attempt to mitigate these risks, Banknotes' AML Compliance monitored customer transactions. The purpose of transaction monitoring was to identify the volume of currency going to or coming from each customer and to determine whether there was a legitimate business explanation for buying or selling that amount of physical currency.

Despite the high risk of money laundering associated with the Banknotes business, from 2006 to 2009, Banknotes' AML compliance consisted of one, or at times two, compliance officers. Unlike the CAMP system for wire transfers, Banknotes did not have an automated monitoring system. As a result, there were times when one, or at times two, Banknotes' compliance officers were responsible for personally reviewing the transactions of approximately 500 to 600 Banknotes customers.

On April 28, 2006, *the U.S. Department of Treasury Financial Crimes, Enforcement Network (FinCEN)* issued Advisory FIN-2006-A003, "Guidance to Financial Institutions on the Repatriation of Currency Smuggled into Mexico from the United States," which reported:

U.S. law enforcement has observed a dramatic increase in the smuggling of bulk cash proceeds from the sale of narcotics and other criminal activities from the United States into Mexico. Once the U.S. currency is in Mexico, numerous layered transactions may be used to disguise its origins, after which it may be returned directly to the United States or further transshipped to or through other jurisdictions.

The Advisory was circulated to all Banknotes personnel involved with Mexico and to those responsible for AML compliance within HSBC Bank USA.

Despite the Advisory from FinCEN issued several weeks earlier, Banknotes stopped regular monthly monitoring of transactions for HSBC Group Affiliates, including HSBC Mexico, in July 2006, leaving only targeted and quarterly reviews of HSBC Group Affiliates' Banknotes volumes that did not trigger automatic monitoring. As a result, discrepancies and suspicious activity in HSBC Group Affiliates' transactions were not monitored and/or reported from July 2006 to July 2009. At the time this decision was made, Banknotes purchased approximately $7 billion in U.S. currency from Mexico each year, with nearly half of that amount supplied by HSBC Mexico. From July 2006 to December 2008, Banknotes purchased over $9.4 billion in physical U.S. dollars from HSBC Mexico, including over $4.1 billion in 2008 alone.

HSBC Bank USA Failed to Provide Adequate Staffing and Other Resources to Maintain an Effective AML Program

In the face of known AML deficiencies and high risk lines of business, HSBC Bank USA further reduced the resources available to its AML program in order to cut costs and increase its profits. By 2007, only a year after the written agreement had been lifted, HSBC Bank USA had fewer AML employees than required by its own internal plans. Moreover, beginning in 2007, senior business executives instructed the AML program to "freeze" staffing levels as part of a bank-wide initiative to cut costs and increase the bank's return on equity. This goal was accomplished by not replacing departing employees, combining the functions of multiple positions into one, and not creating new positions.

Even senior compliance officers were not replaced after they left HSBC Bank USA. In 2007, HSBC Bank USA's AML Director, the bank's top AML officer in the United States, left the bank and was not replaced. Instead, HSBC Bank USA's

Head of Compliance assumed the role while maintaining all of her other responsibilities. A short time later, HSBC North America's Regional Compliance Officer, the top compliance officer in North America who oversaw Compliance and AML at HSBC Bank USA, left and was not replaced. Instead, over objections from HSBC Group's Head of Compliance, HSBC North America's CEO and HSBC Group's Head of Legal asked HSBC North America's General Counsel to assume the role of top compliance officer, in addition to all of her other responsibilities. HSBC Group's Head of Legal and HSBC Group's Head of Compliance have confirmed that the desire to save costs was the primary justification for merging the two roles.

In March 2008, HSBC Bank USA's Chief Operating Officer for Compliance conducted an internal review of the Bank's AML program. The March 2008 AML Review, which was presented to senior business executives and compliance officers, found that the AML program in PCM was "behind the times" and needed to be fundamentally changed to meet regulators' expectations and to achieve parity with other banks. Specifically, the March 2008 AML Review noted that AML monitoring in PCM was significantly under-resourced. At the time, only four employees reviewed the 13,000 to 15,000 suspicious wire alerts generated per month. In contrast, following remedial measures undertaken by HSBC, HSBC Bank USA currently has approximately 430 employees reviewing suspicious wire alerts.

Despite the findings in the March 2008 AML Review, HSBC Bank USA failed to address the lack of AML resources. In April 2008, an AML employee told a senior executive in Compliance, "[HSBC Bank USA] Compliance was in the midst of a staffing crisis." During this time, a number of AML employees noted that requests for additional resources were discouraged and, ultimately, these employees stopped making staffing requests.

By October 2009, a senior executive in Compliance re-
marked, "AML has gone down the hole in the past 18
months." HSBC Bank USA did not begin to address the resource problem until late 2009.

Drug Trafficking Proceeds Laundered
Through HSBC Bank USA

HSBC Bank USA's AML violations resulted in at least $881
million being laundered through the U.S. financial system. A
significant amount of the laundered funds were drug trafficking proceeds involved in the *Black Market Peso Exchange
(BMPE)*. The BMPE is a complex trade-based money laundering system that is designed to move the proceeds from
the sale of illegal drugs in the United States to the drug cartels outside of the United States, often in Colombia, often
through the use of bank accounts. As set forth below, the
use of HSBC Bank USA for BMPE transactions was discovered through a narcotics and money laundering investigation
conducted by U.S. Immigration and Customs Enforcement's
Homeland Security Investigations (HSI) El Dorado Task
Force in New York, in conjunction with the U.S. Attorney's
Office for the Eastern District of New York.

The cartels, many of which operate in Colombia, need to
convert U.S. dollars to Colombian pesos. There are two major obstacles to the conversion of bulk U.S. currency into
Colombian pesos: (1) Because of U.S. AML laws and regulations, it is difficult to deposit large volumes of bulk cash
at banks in the United States, and (2) Colombia has very
strict currency controls and tax laws making it difficult and
expensive to convert U.S. dollars to Colombian pesos in
Colombia.

To solve the first problem, Colombian drug cartels smug-
gle U.S. currency across the U.S. border into Mexico. The
U.S. currency is smuggled out of the United States because

drug traffickers perceive that Mexico had less stringent AML laws, making it easier for the cartels to deposit large amounts of physical U.S. dollars in Mexican banks and CDCs.

To solve the second problem, Colombia's strict currency controls and tax laws, the Colombian cartels use the BMPE. In the BMPE, middlemen, often referred to as "peso brokers," transform bulk cash from the sale of illegal drugs into revenue from the sale of legitimate goods. In this process, the peso brokers purchase bulk cash in United States dollars from drug cartels at a discounted rate, in return for Colombian pesos that belong to Colombian businessmen. The peso brokers then use the U.S. dollars to purchase legitimate goods from businesses in the United States and other foreign countries, on behalf of the Colombian businessmen. These goods are then sent to the Colombian businessmen, who sell the goods for Colombian pesos to recoup their original investment. In the end, the Colombian businessmen obtain U.S. dollars at a lower exchange rate than otherwise available in Colombia, the Colombian cartel leaders receive Colombian pesos while avoiding the costs associated with depositing U.S. dollars directly into Colombian financial institutions, and the peso brokers receive fees for their services as middlemen.

The Department alleges, and HSBC Bank USA and HSBC Holdings do not contest the allegation that, beginning in 2008, an investigation conducted by HSI's El Dorado Task Force, in conjunction with the U.S. Attorney's Office for the Eastern District of New York, identified multiple HSBC Mexico accounts associated with BMPE activity. The investigation further revealed that drug traffickers were depositing hundreds of thousands of dollars in bulk U.S. currency each day into HSBC Mexico accounts. In order to efficiently move this volume of cash through the teller windows at HSBC Mexico branches, drug traffickers designed specially shaped boxes that fit the precise dimensions of the teller windows. The drug traffickers would send numerous boxes filled with cash through the teller windows for deposit into HSBC Mexico accounts. After the cash was deposited in the accounts, peso brokers then wire transferred the U.S. dollars to various exporters located in New York City and other locations throughout the United States to purchase goods for Colombian businesses. The U.S. exporters then sent the goods directly to the businesses in Colombia.

The Department alleges, and HSBC Bank USA and HSBC Holdings do not contest the allegation that accounts at HSBC Mexico were identified by tracking wire transfers originating from HSBC Mexico into HSI undercover accounts in the United States and through seizures and analysis of U.S. based business accounts that were funded by wire transfers from accounts targeted for illegal BMPE activity. Since 2009, the investigation has resulted in the arrest, extradition, and conviction in the United States District Court for the Eastern District of New York of numerous individuals illegally using HSBC Mexico accounts in furtherance of BMPE activity. The investigation further revealed that, because of its lax AML controls, HSBC Mexico was the preferred financial institution for drug cartels and money launderers. The drug trafficking proceeds (in physical U.S. dollars) deposited at HSBC Mexico as part of the BMPE were sold to HSBC Bank USA through Banknotes. In addition, many of the BMPE wire transfers to exporters in the United States passed through HSBC Mexico's correspondent account with HSBC Bank USA. As discussed above, from 2006 to 2009, HSBC Bank USA did not monitor Banknotes transactions or wire transfers from HSBC Mexico and did not detect the drug trafficking proceeds as they flowed into the United States.

On December 11, 2012, the U.S. Department of Justice announced the Deferred Prosecution Agreement with HSBC, levying a record-breaking 1.9 billion dollar fine on the international banking institution. HSBC had to pay a $1.256 billion forfeiture as part of the Deferred Prosecution Agreement as well as an additional $665 million in civil penalties. The fine of $1.9 billion was equivalent to five weeks' worth of HSBC's earnings at the time. In addition to the fine, HSBC also had to agree to undergo five years of independent monitoring by a monitor of their choosing, who would be approved by the Department of Justice. Though HSBC admitted guilt to several criminal counts, through the Deferred Prosecution Agreement the bank remained immune from criminal prosecution despite overwhelming evidence that it not only consistently failed to implement controls against money-laundering, but also that HSBC had a culture and politics of deliberately ignoring computer generated money laundering alerts. **(5)**

In view of the fact that HSBC got a $1.9 billion fine and five years probation for laundering cartel money. Assistant Attorney General Lanny Breuer said:

> "Had the US authorities decided to press criminal charges, HSBC would almost certainly have lost its banking license in the United States, the future of the institution would have been under threat, and the entire banking system would have been destabilized." (6)

The entire banking system would have been destabilized.

The U.S. Attorney General at the time, Eric Holder, echoed Breuer's remark with a statement made at a Senate Subcommittee Hearing. Though Holder clarified that it would be inappropriate to make that statement about HSBC, this was his response when questioned about Breuer's declaration on the HSBC's money laundering Deferred Prosecution Agreement.

> I am concerned that the size of some of these institutions becomes so large, that it does become difficult for us to

> prosecute them when we are hit with indications that if you
> do prosecute, if you do bring a criminal charge, it will have
> a negative impact on the national economy, perhaps even
> the world economy, and I think that is a function of the fact
> that some of these institutions have become too large.
>
> I think it has an inhibiting influence, an impact on our ability
> to bring resolutions that I think would be more appropriate,
> and I think that is something that we, that you all need to
> consider. (7)

Before working at the U.S. Department of Justice both Assistant Attorney General Lanny Breuer and Attorney General Eric Holder worked at the law firm Covington & Burling. Covington and Burling is known for defending major transnational corporations and private banks against cases brought by the Department of Justice. Just one month after the December 2012 announcement of the Deferred Prosecution Agreement between the Department of Justice and HSBC, Assistant Attorney General Lanny Breuer announced he would be leaving office. He officially left his office in early March, and on March 28, 2013 he announced he would be going back to work for his former employer as the Vice Chair of Covington & Burling. In an interview at Covington's Washington office, across the street from Justice Department headquarters on Pennsylvania Avenue, published on March 28, 2013 via Reuters by Aruna Viswanatha, Breuer said of his future prospects at Covington & Burling:

> "I think money-laundering will continue to be very big ...
> for four years we built up a pretty big infrastructure and
> recruited great lawyers to work on it...," (8)

Though by law, Breuer would have to wait two years to have direct contact with the Department of Justice on ongoing cases, he could consult on new cases involving the DOJ immediately. Eric Holder resigned as Attorney General on September 25, 2014, and he rejoined Covington & Burling in July of 2015, just three years into the independent monitoring of HSBC's Deferred Prosecution Agreement. In January of 2018 both Breuer and Holder along with three other Covington attorneys were depicted on the cover of *The American Lawyer* magazine in recognition of Covington as "Finalist for White Collar/Regulatory Litigation Department of the Year" by C. Ryan Barber. Two clarifying statements from the article were:

> The Regulator Whisperers: Covington uses its knowledge of—and respect for—the DOJ to win big for clients.

> Covington's understanding of the workings of the Justice Department was put to work to score favorable resolutions for clients. (9)

There exists no better evidence that the "revolving door" is clearly wide open at the U.S. Department of Justice.

On February 18, 2015, Swiss authorities raided the Geneva, Switzerland offices of HSBC. According to a February 18, 2015 article by Jill Treanor of *The Guardian*:

> Investigation into suspected 'aggravated money laundering' comes after Belgium and France begin scrutinizing tax affairs of Europe's biggest bank.

> Prosecutors said the investigation into "suspected aggravated money laundering" was prompted by "the recent published revelations" about the private bank. The revelations, by The Guardian, the BBC, Le Monde and other media outlets, showed that HSBC's Swiss banking arm turned a blind eye to illegal activities of arms dealers and helped wealthy people evade taxes.

> A search was being led by Prosecutor General, Olivier Jornot, and First Prosecutor Yves Bertossa. The inquiry could later be extended to people suspected of committing or participating in money laundering, prosecutors said. (10)

In April of 2015 HSBC entered an agreement with Swiss authorities to avoid prosecution or the publication of the Swiss authorities' findings by paying a compensation of 40 million Swiss Francs, approximately $42,951,360 dollars. **(11)**

On May 27, 2016, Jennifer Shasky Calvery officially resigned as the director of the Treasury Department's Financial Crimes Enforcement Network (FinCEN), a position she held from September 22, 2012 until May 27, 2016, and took a position as the Global Head of Financial Crime Threat Mitigation at HSBC. **(12)**

The 2012 HSBC Deferred Prosecution Agreement Independent Monitor

On March 31, 2017 the U.S. Department of Justice submitted a report to U.S. District Judge Ann M. Donnelly, who was responsible for following up on the monitoring of HSBC through the 2012 Deferred Prosecution Agreement. After offering several examples of advances and changes in HSBC's conduct with regards to Anti-Money Laundering the report goes on to say about the independent monitor Michael Cherkasky's concerns:

> ...the Report finds that the bank's Anti-Money Laundering (AML) and sanctions compliance program still struggles. The Monitor notes several areas of concern including: a) the quality of the data that the bank relies upon to detect money laundering and sanctions risks; b) the transaction monitoring systems that the bank relies upon to flag risky transactions; c) the implementation of sanctions controls at the country level; d) the adjudication of alerts; e) the risk assessment tools used across the Group; and f) the maturity and sufficiency of the compliance program both from a resources and an organizational perspective.
>
> For example, the Report states that the Group's AML transaction monitoring system lacks sufficient AML typologies and is hampered by persistent rules that automatically

suppress transaction-monitoring alerts. The Report expresses concern that, even after the rollout of several
planned remediation projects, the bank will still not control
for all AML red flags.

Additionally, although HSBC is the world's leading trade finance bank, and despite a poor review of the bank's trade
finance business by the Monitor in 2015, the Report finds
that financial crime compliance controls for trade finance
transactions are lacking. Similarly, significant financial
crime risks remain inherent in the correspondent banking
business line. Finally, systemic programmatic issues continue to put the bank at risk of potential financial crime.

As a result of the Monitor's foregoing concerns and others, he remains unable to certify that the bank's compliance program is reasonably designed and implemented to
detect and prevent violations of AML and sanctions laws.
Nor can the Monitor currently certify that HSBC has implemented and adhered to all of the remedial measures
outlined in paragraph 81 of Attachment A of the DPA. (13)

On December 11, 2017 HSBC proudly announced it had ended its 5 year Deferred Prosecution Agreement with the U.S.
Department of Justice, which in turn also announced that all the
charges against HSBC had been dropped. (14)

On December 10th, 2019 the U.S. Department of Justice announced another Deferred Prosecution Agreement this time with
HSBC's Swiss Arm HSBC Private Bank (Suisse) SA. wherein the
bank admitted to helping U.S. taxpayers conceal income and assets
from the Internal Revenue Service (IRS), agreed to pay a $192.35
million penalty, and once again avoided prosecution. (15)

The final 1000 page report on HSBC by the independent monitor Michael Cherkasky has never been released to the public.
Both HSBC and the Department of Justice argue that the report
would make HSBC and other financial institutions vulnerable to
the weaknesses exposed in the bank's Anti-Money Laundering

policies and strategies. On August 7, 2020, Assistant U.S. Attorney for the Eastern District of New York David K. Kessler rejected a Freedom of Information Act (FOIA) request submitted by BuzzFeed's Jason Leopold for the release of Cherkasky's full report. **(16)**

HSBC laundered billions and wire transferred over 200 trillion, and not a single individual went to prison, yet according to a November 16, 2021 News Release Summary from the Department of Justice U.S. Attorney's Office for the Southern District of California:

> An indictment was partially unsealed yesterday in federal court charging 29 alleged members of an international money laundering organization that is tied to the Sinaloa Cartel and the Jalisco New Generation Cartel in Mexico.
>
> During the past week, federal, state, and local law enforcement officials have arrested 21 defendants throughout San Diego, Calexico, and Bakersfield, California, who were allegedly involved in a sophisticated international money laundering scheme.
>
> According to the indictment and other public records, this Imperial Valley-based *Money Laundering Organization (MLO)* laundered in excess of *$32 million* in drug proceeds from the United States to Mexico. The money laundering organization secured contracts with drug trafficking organizations in Mexico to pick up drug proceeds in cities throughout the United States, including Baltimore, Detroit, Los Angeles, Philadelphia, Boston, Denver, Chicago, New York City and numerous others.
>
> "This complex financial investigation is a perfect example of the unrelenting focus shown by Homeland Security Investigations (HSI) and its partners in the Costa Pacifico Money Laundering Task Force to stop criminal organizations attempting to launder illicit narco dollars," said HSI

San Diego Special Agent in Charge Chad Plantz. "The key to dismantling Drug Trafficking Organizations is disrupting the flow of illicit funds and attacking the money laundering element of the organizations. HSI will continue to work with its fellow law enforcement partners to protect U.S. financial infrastructure and use our comprehensive investigative authorities to stop criminal organizations engaged in drug trafficking and money laundering."

An indictment is not evidence of guilt. The defendants are presumed innocent and entitled to a fair trial at which the government has the burden of proving guilt beyond a reasonable doubt.

SUMMARY OF CHARGES

Conspiracy to Launder Monetary Instruments (18 U.S.C. §§ 1956(a)(1) and (h))

Maximum Penalties: Twenty years in prison, $500,000 fine or twice the value of the monetary instrument or funds involved. (17)

"The key to dismantling Drug Trafficking Organizations is disrupting the flow of illicit funds and attacking the money laundering element of the organizations." - HSI San Diego Special Agent in Charge Chad Plantz

There is a significantly higher possibility that a small-time money laundering organization - MLO, or a local Mexican branch manager of an international banking institution is working under the very real and demonstrated threat of physical violence by organized crime cartels. However in the case of the HSBC USA and HSBC holdings executives, the power is absolutely in their hands. The decision to ignore and or hide anti-money laundering (AML) alerts and Suspicious Activity Alerts (SARs), and continue to do business with criminal organizations is made from a position of extreme wealth, power, and privilege.

According to a September 21, 2020 investigative article by Anthony Cormier, Jason Leopold, Tom Warren, Scott Pham, John Templeton, Jeremy Singer-Vine, Richard Holmes, Michael Sallah, Tanya Kozyreva, and Emma Loop for *BuzzFeed*, in collaboration with the International Consortium of Investigative Journalists, HSBC executives joked that:

> "You wouldn't want something to happen to Buffalo, would you?"
>
> This was the joke — which sounded a lot like a threat — that compliance officials at the bank's New York City office would make when American law enforcement or regulators talked about punishing the bank for its behavior, according to two people who heard it. With thousands of employees in that Rust Belt city, the bank could upend the economy there if it picked up stakes. "It would be a nuclear bomb," one bank official told BuzzFeed News.
>
> The bank wielded that worst-case outcome as a weapon, two sources said, to make sure politicians and regulators didn't come down too hard. (18)

The HSBC money laundering scandal alone is enough of an indictment of not just the commercial banking industry, but also of the entire criminal justice system. However HSBC is not the first, nor will it be the last bank to receive a Deferred Prosecution Agreement from the U.S. Department of Justice to avoid criminal charges for federal crimes including money laundering. In 2010, the U.S.-based Wachovia Bank received a similar Deferred Prosecution Agreement from the Department of Justice for laundering money generated from illegal transactions, again, with Mexican Casas de Cambio (CDCs). Wachovia was ordered to pay a total of $160 million: $110 million in civil forfeitures related to money laundering and a $50 million fine. Wells Fargo Bank purchased Wachovia in 2008 and ended the bank's relationship with the CDCs. No Wachovia executive was ever prosecuted or charged with any crimes. **(19)**

According to BuzzFeed as part of its investigation into criminal activity by banks:

> BuzzFeed News has identified 17 other financial institutions that received the same type of deal — a deferred prosecution for anti-money laundering or sanctions violations — that HSBC has made since 2010. At least four of them went on to break the law again and get fined. (20)

According to a September 20, 2020 article by the International Consortium of Investigative Journalists titled "Global banks defy U.S. crackdowns by serving oligarchs, criminals and terrorists":

> Secret U.S. government documents (known as the FinCEN files) reveal that JPMorgan Chase, HSBC, and other big banks have defied money laundering crackdowns by moving staggering sums of illicit cash for shadowy characters and criminal networks that have spread chaos and undermined democracy around the world.
>
> The records show that five global banks — JPMorgan, HSBC, Standard Chartered Bank, Deutsche Bank and Bank of New York Mellon — kept profiting from powerful and dangerous players even after U.S. authorities fined these financial institutions for earlier failures to stem flows of dirty money.
>
> U.S. agencies responsible for enforcing money laundering laws rarely prosecute megabanks that break the law, and the actions authorities do take barely ripple the flood of plundered money that washes through the international financial system.
>
> In some cases the banks kept moving illicit funds even after U.S. officials warned them they'd face criminal prosecutions if they didn't stop doing business with mobsters, fraudsters or corrupt regimes. (21)

Chapter 18
A Roadmap to U.S. Capitalist Imperialism:
World Reserve Currency and International
Financial Institutions

Gold, Silver, and Other Precious Metals

Before we talk about currency, money, or even wealth, it is important to talk about the origin of precious natural mineral resources such as gold and silver. For colonizing European countries and the United States in particular, the extraction of mineral resources has consistently come upon the backs, sweat, and blood of Black and Indigenous people across the globe. The massive quantities of silver and gold extracted from the Indigenous territory of Mexico, and the gold extracted from throughout the Indigenous territory of the United States is once again only legally justified through the Doctrine of Discovery; this is a systemic white male Christian supremacist belief that Europeans and white U.S. Americans have a divine right to the land and her resources despite the presence of the land's original Indigenous inhabitants. Gold and silver, which were among the original currencies, have a history of colonial violence, theft, racism, and genocide, which absolutely cannot be ignored in this discussion.

Currency

Currency today is basically just money. Formally it is a "recognized unit of exchange," but when we say currency, we basically mean money. Today there are new types of money or currency such as digital currency, frequent flier miles, and corporate bucks, etc. For purposes of this discussion, more than anything I want you to think about money in terms of bills, like a dollar bill, or a 20 peso bill. Nationally, money works because the government of a country and the people of that country basically agree that a valueless piece of paper, does indeed have an actual value.

Unless your 20 peso bill or your dollar bill looks very shady, the chances of a person in Mexico or the United States challenging the worth of your bill is almost unheard of.

Internationally things get very interesting and very revealing, as well. One country's money is not worth as much as another country's money, and how that is decided basically comes down to an imposed series of agreements around how much everybody's money is worth. A currency's value is decided in comparison to other currencies' value. The factors that go into deciding how one nation's money is considered more valuable than another nation's money is exactly what we will talk about in this chapter.

Central Banks

Under the current dominant Global Financial System, in order for a currency or money to work nationally and internationally, each country has to have what is known as a central bank. These are banks for the government itself and for commercial banks. They are also responsible for regulating commercial banks, printing money, and making monetary policy. In the United States there is a particularly unique central bank known as the Federal Reserve or "the Fed." In Mexico the central bank is Banco de Mexico. Finally, in order for central banks to do business or engage in currency exchange, the central bank from one country communicates and comes to agreements with the central bank of another country through what are known as International Financial Institutions.

International Financial Institutions (IFIs)

An International Financial Institution (IFI) is basically a bank that works between two or more countries and is regulated by international law. All of the major IFIs functioning today were created and are boarded by the central banks of multiple countries. Under the current dominant global economic system these IFIs are deemed necessary for global currency exchange (money exchange), monetary policy, and the international trade of goods and services. International Financial Institutions have also presented themselves as the primary responders to the economic needs of poor and developing countries. As revealed by their ongoing practices and tendencies, the reality is quite the opposite.

The Bank for International Settlements (BIS)

The oldest International Financial Institution still functioning is the little- known, and quite secretive Bank for International Settlements (BIS), which was established in 1930 by Germany, Belgium, France, the United Kingdom, Italy, Japan, the United States, and Switzerland. It was originally created to manage reparations imposed on Germany after the First World War. The bank opened in Basel, Switzerland on May 17, 1930.

By 1932 however, the German war reparations had been abolished altogether, and the BIS shifted completely to its secondary focus of facilitating cooperation between the central banks of its member nations.

During World War II, the BIS claimed neutrality and though it postponed its yearly Board of Director's meetings until after the conflict was resolved, it continued to operate as a bank for its member nations including Nazi Germany.

According to a brief on U.S. military documents related to the BIS and Nazi collaboration, on the U.S. National Archives website *]* **s://www.archives.gov** Holocaust-Related Records at the National Archives, Holocaust-Era Assets, Military Agency Records:

> During World War II the president of the bank was an American Thomas H. McKittrick. The general manager was a Frenchman, Roger Auboin; and the assistant general manager was Paul Hechler, a German and Nazi Party member. Among its board of directors were Hermann Schmitz, head of I.G. Farben; Baron Kurt von Schroder, head of the J. H. Stein Bank of Cologne (and leading officer and financier of the Gestapo); Walter Funk, the Reichsbank president; and Emil Puhl, Reichsbank vice-president. At the Bretton

Woods Conference in 1944 the Allies called, in Resolution V, for the elimination of the BIS, in part because it was seen as a money-laundering entity for the Germans. In 1948 the BIS handed over $4 million in looted gold to the Allies. The BIS still exists, located in Basel, Switzerland. (1)

It is important to note that as mentioned above, the President of the BIS from January 1940 to June 1946 was a Harvard educated U.S. banker named Thomas Harrington McKittrick. World War II did not end until September 2, 1945. Though McKittrick and the BIS were complicit in laundering looted Nazi gold, and though eventually the BIS paid restitution for some of the transactions, McKittrick went on to work as the Senior Vice President and Director of the Chase National Bank from 1946 to 1954. Chase Bank kept open offices in Nazi occupied France for the duration of World War II. In 1998 Chase Bank acknowledged seizing about 100 accounts belonging to Jewish residents of France during the Vichy regime in Nazi occupied France. (2)

The Bank for International Settlements (BIS) today

According to the BIS's own website:

> Sixty-three central banks and monetary authorities are currently members of the BIS and have rights of voting and representation at General Meetings. (3)

According to an August 1, 2013 article by Adam LeBor in the *Sydney Morning Herald*, titled "How bankers helped the Nazis":

> From the 1950s to the 1990s the BIS hosted much of the planning and technical preparation for the introduction of the euro. Without the BIS the euro would probably not exist. In 1994, Alexander Lamfalussy, the former BIS manager, set up the European Monetary Institute, now known as the European Central Bank.
>
> The BIS remains very profitable. It has only about 140

customers (it refuses to say how many) but made a tax-free profit of about 900 million pounds last year. Every other month it hosts the Global Economy Meetings, where 60 of the most powerful central bankers... meet.

No details of meetings are released, even though the attendees are public servants, charged with managing national economies. (4)

According to a July 2, 2013 article on Harvard University's Edmond J. Safra Center for Ethics by Gregg Fields:

One fact is undeniable: From the beginning, the BIS achieved immunity from essentially all banking regulation and international laws. Although it functioned as a central bank, it wasn't actually connected to a government. It was virtually self-governing. Located in neutral Switzerland, it gained another layer of protection by not being subject to even the notoriously secretive Swiss banking laws. For years it didn't bother to put a sign on its door. That autonomy continues. (5)

The current president of the BIS is the Mexican economist Agustin Carstens, who has a Master's and Doctoral degree in Economics from the University of Chicago. (6)

World War II

As the Second World War drew closer to an end, the United States was in a unique position of military, political, and most importantly of all, economic power. The nation had suffered almost no military attacks on its territory with the exception of the Japanese attack on the U.S. military base at Pearl Harbor on the Hawaiian Island of Oahu on December 7, 1941. While the vast majority of Europe was in shambles, the United States stood tall, strong, and intact, as well as militarily, politically, and economically powerful.

Bretton Woods Conference

From the 1st to the 22nd of July 1944, representatives from all 44 allied nations met and deliberated at the Mount Washington Hotel in Bretton Woods, New Hampshire. The result of this meeting was the creation of a global monetary system in which eventually and over time, all of these countries and others agreed to set their national currencies to the U.S. dollar at a certain exchange rate, and the U.S. dollar would be set to actual gold at $35 USD per ounce of gold. Regardless of the U.S. dollar being set to gold, what was primarily established at the Bretton Woods Conference was that the U.S. dollar would now be the primary World Reserve Currency.

A World Reserve Currency is a foreign currency held in the central bank of a nation, in theory to have a backup currency to stabilize its own national currency, and in order to have a foreign currency with which to engage in the international trade of commodities.

While the United States had the largest gold reserves in the world, the other countries in the Bretton Woods agreement were basically forced to hold U.S. dollars in their central bank reserves instead of gold. This was particularly true for England, which prior to the Second World War, was the primary global economic empire. Through the Bretton Woods agreement and the establishment of the U.S. dollar as the World Reserve Currency, England would begrudgingly relinquish the throne of global economic empire, and hand it over to the United States. (7)

It is true that the Bretton Woods System did establish, organize, and facilitate the creation of an international currency exchange system that continues to be fundamental to the dominant global economic system of international trade, foreign currency exchange markets, commerce, and banking. What is absolutely not true is that the process was, or that the system itself has ever been democratic or optional for that matter. To begin with, it was a clearly slanted endeavor, in which the decision about the worth of multiple nations' currencies was made in the wake of a devastating world war. This decision was clearly made from a position of power by the United States and gave absolutely no alternative to the other participating nations. **(8)**

From a political and economic perspective it is significantly easier to perceive the implementation of the Bretton Woods System by the United States in 1944 as a strategic kick to the head, as opposed to an offer to lend a helping hand to European nations that metaphorically were already on the floor.

The Bretton Woods System officially came to an end in 1971 with what is known as "the Nixon shock," in which U.S. President Richard Nixon unilaterally canceled the international convertibility of the U.S. dollar to gold. **(9)** Though the end of the Bretton Woods System gave way to the current global economic system of freely floating fiat currencies, the Bretton Woods institutions, the International Monetary Fund and the World Bank, remain very much intact, and the U.S. dollar is still the dominant World Reserve Currency. More countries hold more U.S. dollars than any other foreign currency held in their central banks. It is also the currency upon which the prices of major international trade commodities such as gold and oil are set. The purchase of gold and oil internationally through central banks is done in dollars.

The Bretton Woods Institutions Today

Another key element of the Bretton Woods System was the creation of two major International Financial Institutions: the International Monetary Fund (IMF) and the World Bank. Though their initial primary purposes have shifted through history, and in particular after the Nixon Shock, the current role of the IMF and the World Bank is still to ensure primarily U.S. domination over the Global Financial System, Foreign Currency Exchange, and international trade.

The International Monetary Fund (IMF)

According to *Investopedia*:

> Composed of 189 member countries including the United States, the International Monetary Fund has a primary

mission to ensure monetary stability around the world. Member countries work together to foster global monetary cooperation, secure financial stability, facilitate international trade, and promote employment and economic growth. It also aims to reduce poverty around the world.

The IMF maintains its mission in three ways. First, it keeps track of the global economy and those of its member countries. The group employs a number of economists who monitor member countries' economic health. Each year, the IMF provides each country with an economic assessment.

Secondly, it gives practical assistance to members by providing policymakers to help plan fiscal policies, coming up with tax and fiscal legislation, along with overseeing the economy through analysis. Finally, the IMF lends money to countries with balance of payments difficulties. It provides this financial assistance as long as the borrowing country implements initiatives suggested by the IMF.

The group's loan program doesn't come without criticism, however. Some countries cannot obtain traditional financing sufficient to meet their international obligations. By providing loans, the IMF helps countries develop policy programs that solve the balance of payments problem.

But these loans are loaded with conditions. A loan provided by the IMF as a form of rescue for countries in serious debt ultimately only stabilizes international trade and eventually results in the country repaying the loan at rather hefty interest rates. (10)

World Bank

According to *Investopedia* the World Bank's purpose

> is to aid long-term economic development and reduce poverty in economically developing nations. It accomplishes

this by making technical and financial support available. The bank initially focused on rebuilding infrastructure in Western Europe following World War II and then turned its operational focus to underdeveloped countries.

World Bank support helps countries reform inefficient economic sectors and implement specific projects, such as building health centers and schools or making clean water and electricity more widely available.

The World Bank is composed of two separate International Financial Institutions: The International Bank for Reconstruction and Development (IBRD) offers loans to middle-income and "creditworthy" low-income governments and The International Development Association (IDA) offers interest-free loans and grants to the world's poorest countries. Today there are 189 members of the International Bank for Reconstruction and Development (IBRD). (11)

The World Bank itself is part of what is known as the World Bank Group which includes a total of five International Financial Institutions including the World Bank's International Bank for Reconstruction and Development (IBRD), and the International Development Association (IDA). The other three IFIs within the World Bank Group are the International Finance Corporation (IFC), the Multilateral Investment Guarantee Agency (MIGA) and the International Center for Settlement of Investment Disputes (ICSID).

The International Finance Corporation (IFC) finances investment, capital mobilization, and gives advisory services to businesses and governments in economically developing nations. The Multilateral Investment Guarantee Agency (MIGA) promotes foreign direct investment in economically developing nations. The International Center for Settlement of Investment Disputes (ICSID) provides investment dispute conciliation and arbitration.

Structures for Global Imperialism

First and foremost it is important to critically analyze just how democratic the Bretton Woods Institutions are in order to understand the underlying argument that these institutions are structures for economic imperialism.

The International Monetary Fund's most powerful position is that of the Managing Director. Every single one of the 12 Managing Directors of the IMF have been white people from European countries. The first ten were all white men. The last two have been white women. The Managing Director is assisted by the Deputy Managing Director. Every single one of them has been a U.S. citizen, with the exception of Stanley Fischer, an Israeli-American. One has been an American of Asian descent and two have been women. The most recent Deputy Managing Director is the Indian-American Gita Gopinath. Out of 12 Chief Economists for the IMF, all with the exception of Gita Gopinath have been men. Of the 11 men, 10 have been white men. 6 of the 12 have been from the U.S., 2 French, 1 British, 1 Canadian, 1 Dutch, 1 Israeli, and 1 Indian.

Voting power at the International Monetary Fund is based on a quota system. Each member country is assigned a quota based upon the country's relative size in the global economy. Each country's quota determines its voting power. How much money a country gives to the IMF decides how much voting power that country has. It is also important to point out that the IMF is made of two types of member countries. On the one hand are countries that are economically powerful enough to pay quotas which provide the economic resources that the IMF then offers as loans. On the other hand are the countries that receive the loans. The countries that receive the loans are powerless, and the countries that fund the IMF loans are in the only positions of power, with European countries and the United States dominating both positions of authority and voting power absolutely. The United States holds approximately 17.46% of the total vote. These countries follow the United States in order of voting power: Japan (6.48%), China (6.41%), Germany (5.60%), France

(4.24%), United Kingdom (4.24%), Italy (3.17%), India (2.76%) and on down. The United States has unique veto power over major policy decisions.

All but one of the 13 World Bank presidents have been men, all but one have been white, and all but one have been U.S. citizens. 9 out of the 15 chief economists for the World Bank have been U.S. citizens. Today the United States holds approximately 15.85% of the total vote among the World Bank members. These countries follow the United States in order of voting power: Japan (6.84%), China (4.42%), Germany (4.00%), the United Kingdom (3.75%), France (3.75%), India (2.91%), Russia (2.77%), Saudi Arabia (2.77%), and Italy (2.64%), and on down. The United States has unique veto power over major policy decisions.

The IMF and the World Bank literally present themselves as global economic saviors. If you go to these institutions' websites they would have you believe that they are the superheroes of the story, saving the world's poor. Indeed they are truly the only major lending institutions that take the so-called "economic risk" of lending money to poor and developing nations around the world. They make a big deal about many of the loans being very low-interest loans, which honestly is not always true.

To begin with, loans, assistance, and support from the IMF and the World Bank are directly tied to fomenting foreign private investment in the borrowing nations. This is done by literally forcing the borrowing nations to carry out what are known as structural reforms, which include but are not limited to the following: (12, 13, 14)

- Austerity measures that force governments to raise taxes (for the poor and working classes, not the wealthy) and cut government spending above all for social programs.

- The devaluation of the borrowing nation's currency in order to make its exports cheaper and more marketable.

- Restructuring foreign debts, which usually includes higher interest rates or more conditions.

- Eliminating food subsidies.

- Raising the price of public services.

- Cutting wages

- Offering less domestic credit.

- Liberalization of markets to guarantee a price mechanism and open up the nation to free trade.

- Privatization, of all or part of state-owned enterprises such as telecommunications, transportation, oil, healthcare, and education.

- Enhancing the rights of foreign investors by literally changing national laws to protect their rights and investments. These could be environmental, labor, social, or Indigenous rights laws intended to protect the land and communities from the effects of foreign investment.

- Focusing the national economic output on direct exports and natural resource extraction. (At this point the extraction of precious metals such as gold far exceeds the extraction that took place during colonial conquest of the global south. This economic strategy has perpetuated and exacerbated corporate colonialism for mineral resources that have been looted time and time again.)

- Increasing the stability of investment (by allowing the participation of foreign investors) with the opening of companies.

- Reducing government expenditures as a whole

In essence what these structural reforms do is create an environment where foreign investors and their political and economic interests are prioritized over national sovereignty and the interests of the general population, in particular the interests of workers, students, farmworkers, and women, but above all the interests of Indigenous people. Why? Because within any national framework, Indigenous peoples' territories have been and continue to be the most environmentally protected through community-based strategies for self-determination, self-defense, and autonomy. Therefore these territories have most of the earth's true wealth, which consists of natural resources such as water and biologically diverse rainforests, as well as the coveted resources of economic interest to the Global Financial System such as precious minerals and fossil fuels. In the end, the IMF and World Bank loans and projects have systematically displaced Indigenous peoples in favor of foreign investment in economic developments or even for-profit enterprises. When these International Financial Institutions show results in economic development, the majority of the economic benefits are either for foreign investors, including transnational corporations, or the borrowing country's own business and political elite. The poor, and in particular Indigenous people, are systematically treated as disposable variables in these International Financial Institutions' economic equations. As a result, the structural reforms encouraged by the IMF and the World Bank also generate civil, popular, and ethnic conflicts over territory, resources, and the well-being of communities, which are then systemically met with state sponsored violence and brute force. Mexico as a borrowing nation is no exception.

So to be clear, the Global Financial System is run by blatantly undemocratic International Financial Institutions in order to impose the U.S. dollar as the World Reserve Currency, and in order to facilitate the looting of poor country's natural wealth in exchange for loans filled with conditions that target a nation's poor and, in particular, Indigenous communities. Once a country is hooked on debt and follows through with imposed structural reforms, it is also locked into a vicious cycle in which foreigners are able to loot multiple nations' wealth without firing a single bullet. This is "low intensity colonialism". The IMF and World Bank are not saviors, they are debt dealers and facilitators of a scheme that benefits financial institutions, transnational corporations and the business political elite of borrowing nations.

This is one of the fundamental reasons why the Mexican peso exchange rate for U.S. dollars is 20 to 1.

In an environment where the Global Financial System works in this way with such a lack of morals, ethics, and human decency, it is no wonder that organized crime narcotics cartels have flourished in this world of economic globalization. They have done so by following the exact same economic model that benefits from natural resource extraction, foreign currency exchange, international trade, and good old supply and demand. Meanwhile small Indigenous communities in Mexico are confronted with social, political, and economic devaluation by not only the Global Financial System, but also by their own government, which is a legitimized member of all the major International Financial Institutions.

The absence of cultural awareness, a sense of community, empathy, and humanity in this Global Financial System honestly leaves little hope for the well-being of Indigenous people. In Mexico the situation is compounded with the social political environment of a full-blown drug war, rampant corruption, and tendencies towards narco-governance, which makes odds of community-based liberation nearly inconceivable.

PART FIVE
LIBERATION

Chapter 19
Cherán

On April 15, 2011, the Indigenous P'urhépecha municipality of Cherán, Michoacán rose up against an organized crime cartel, and perhaps much more importantly, rose up against the entirety of institutional government in the 25,000 person municipality. Their uprising and ongoing social movement is against what they call "narco-governance." (1)

In Cherán, the stories of banking institutions such as HSBC (2012) and Wachovia (2011) paying nominal fines and receiving deferred prosecutions from criminal charges for laundering cartel money, was news, but it came as no surprise. Organized crime had been prevalent in the Indigenous P'urhépecha municipality since the year 2000. After a 2008 mayoral race that left the community very divided, an Institutional Revolutionary Party (PRI) candidate won the election. Immediately after the 2008 mayoral race, illicit activity increased substantially in the community, which began experiencing the devastating effects of dog-eat-dog capitalist imperialism, in which organized crime is just another dog.

Neighboring communities with unlicensed illegal logging contracts began to ravage the community's most precious forests, which have been traditionally respected as a spiritual connection to the earth by the Indigenous P'urhépecha people. The logging began to look a lot more like pillaging, and when community members began to attempt to defend their forests, they were met with a real life nightmare: the loggers were not only aided and protected by government agencies and local police, but the entire logging operation was also being coordinated by members of a major organized crime cartel. What began to happen in Cherán was a confluence of organized crime, institutional corruption, and transnational resource extraction. (2)

The first community members who attempted to defend their forest were quickly assassinated. From 2008 to 2011 the situation only became worse. Over the course of those four years, loggers took 20,000 of the 27,000 hectares of forest that Cherán had in its territory. Criminals charged protection money known as "piso" for anyone to run even a small business in the community of Cherán. The forest was ravaged and terror reigned as people felt that they were at risk at any given time. The city would become a ghost town by sunset. During this time, between 2007 and 2011, Cherán lost over 50 community members. Some were murdered and others simply disappeared, never to be seen again. **(3)**

Several community members have stated, while continuing to ask for anonymity, that at the peak of the cartel activity in Cherán, when cartel members came through town to take someone, kill someone, charge protection money, or transport something through town, all of the cell phone service would be shut off completely. All available cell phone services in the community --the entire cell phone network-- would shut down. As cartel members and illegal loggers rode through town to and from the forest they began to threaten community members saying things like "When we are done with the forest, we are coming for the women next." Then in 2011, word got back to the community that the loggers and criminals had begun to log near several key natural springs that were primary water sources not just for Cherán, but also for 40 small communities throughout the region. **(4)**

The murders, disappearances, kidnappings, threats, criminal amounts of illegal logging, charging of protection money, reign of terror, and now the threat to the community's primary water source had to come to an end. A group of women had begun quietly organizing an action to bring the terrorizing of their community to a halt. When they heard about the water springs, they accelerated their action, and at dawn on the morning of April 15, 2011, a small group of women began to ring the church bells, as is often done during a town emergency. With children and youth at their side, more women joined the spontaneous uprising and immediately attempted to block loggers who would travel through town on their way to the forest during the early hours of the morning. When one of the loggers tried to run over some of the women, the community reacted as a whole. With sticks, rocks, and bottle rockets, people confronted the loggers and began burning their vehicles. Then they began detaining the loggers themselves. **(5)**

It is at this point that conclusive evidence of the ongoing complicity of the local police with the criminals was exposed: Local police officers themselves guided organized crime thugs to the place where the loggers were being held in an attempt to violently release them by force. The community was able to fend off this initial retaliatory attack and proceeded to erect 300 campfire barricades known as *"fogatas"* at intersections throughout the entire town in order to prevent loggers or cartel members from traveling through town and committing acts of violence. An additional five checkpoints were established at the entry roadways to the community. **(6)**

The local mayor, his cabinet, and all the local police fled the community, leaving community members to fend for themselves. As the police fled Cherán, they also left their weapons, uniforms, and vehicles at the police headquarters. Community members immediately seized all of these weapons, vehicles, and uniforms in order to defend themselves during the uprising. If nobody would defend Cherán, then the people of Cherán would have to defend themselves. At this point all cell phone service was shut down again and furthermore, TV and radio signals were jammed. Cherán was completely cut off from the world. This and many other details that would come to light during the first months of the uprising further exposed the collusion of local politicians, the police, and even communications businesses with the organized crime cartel and the very violent and illicit logging activity. Within days of the uprising, the community collectively decided that it no longer trusted the government, politicians from any political party, the mainstream media, or any of the police. **(7)**

It was during this time that one of the most absolutely astonishing aspects of the uprising came to function in the spontaneously initiated *fogatas* or campfire barricades. Again, 300 of these barricades were erected throughout the community for security purposes, but they also became core meeting points, and eventually would become the basis for the collective decision making process that Cherán established at that time and continues to practice today. **(8)**

Each of the 300 *fogatas* belongs to one of four neighborhoods or *barrios* in Cherán: 1st *Barrio* or Karhákua, 2nd *Barrio* or Jarhukutini, 3rd *Barrio* or Ketsikua and 4th *Barrio* or Paríkutini, also jokingly known as Paris. The *fogatas* met every night during the uprising. Each *fogata* began to send proposals and a representative to neighborhood assemblies and then to larger community general assemblies. **(9)**

At the *fogatas* it was Cherán's elders who reminded younger inexperienced community members that 40 years earlier, before institutional forms of government and political parties had arrived in Cherán, the community practiced its traditional form of community-based self-governance known as *"Usos y Costumbres,"* or practices and customs. **(10)**

Through the organizing structure of the *fogatas*, the neighborhood assemblies, and the general assemblies, the community of Cherán came to a consensus about returning to its traditional form of self-governance. The consensus process was almost two months long. During the final stages, every community member who was 18 years old or older, was obliged to participate in the General Assembly. During that time the weapons that the community had seized from the police were handed over to adolescent community members, who were tasked with protecting the five community entry points. **(11)**

On April 27, 2011, youth from throughout the community organized a group called "Youth United for Cherán". In addition to printing and handing out information about the uprising at the community checkpoints, the youth took workshops, purchased a radio transmitter, and created the community radio station named *"Radio Fogata."* The youth themselves state that the local commercial radio station and the general mainstream media distorted the truth about what was happening in Cherán, and tried to discredit the uprising. Radio Fogata was key to sharing the truth and a tool for keeping the community informed and alert throughout the uprising. **(12)**

During the uprising, the youth in Cherán were a militant, disciplined, and organized element that was key to the entire process.

Community members simply say that during the initial consensus process, they referred to their history and elders in order to return to the way the community was organized before political parties, police, and organized crime existed. They began to organize for self-determination and self-defense and chose to return to their traditional P'urhépecha forms of self-governance as they began the long walk towards autonomy. A general council of twelve community elders was chosen and a system of several operational councils was formed in order to carry out the community's daily logistical, social, economic, and political needs. **(13)**

The community originally had three demands: safety, justice, and the reforestation of their territory. Members have at this point absolutely and effectively reforested the entire region. This aspect of their struggle has been taken very seriously by them; protecting the forest is both a traditional and a spiritual obligation. Cherán does not believe that anybody will ever be able to bring justice for their dead, disappeared, or displaced people as a result of the conflict, nor do community members expect anyone in power to understand the justice they seek for the forest. They understand that justice is something that they will have to obtain on their own from now on. **(14)**

When it comes to safety and security, historically, Cherán had been "policed" or defended by members of the community. In a voluntary rotation members from each of the four "barrios" or neighborhoods would patrol the community for self-defense in a body known as the *"Community Ronda."* After the uprising the General Council made a call out for volunteers to participate in the *Ronda*, or community guard. Community members maintain that police are imposed by the government, but the *Ronda* is a traditional way in which community members protect themselves and their community. Today the *Ronda* is separated into two parts: The *"Ronda Comunitaria,"* which is responsible for patrolling and protecting the community within its borders, and the *"Guardabosques"* or Forest Defenders, which patrol the outskirts of town and go deep into the forests in order to protect community members living in those more rural areas and to protect the forest itself. **(15)**

Today, ten years after beginning to walk towards autonomy, community members say that officially there are over 100 members of the *Ronda* and *Guardabosques*, however in reality the *Ronda* is every single community member and person from the outside who stands in solidarity with Cherán They say: "We are all the *Ronda*." **(16)**

Cherán is not the first community in Mexico to return to its traditional means of community self-defense, nor is it the first place in the state of Michoacán, nor in the Indigenous P'urhépecha region. Other communities have engaged in similar practices of self-governance and self-defense, and little by little more and more communities are seeing traditional self-governance and self-defense as a viable alternative to corrupt politics and submission to organized crime. Cherán is, however, the only federally recognized autonomous Indigenous municipality in the state of Michoacán. This recognition came about from their uprising, and not from the good will of the government.

Cherán's community-based government councils change every three years and in May of 2021, new members were once again rotated into the different governing councils for the fourth time since the uprising. Cherán is one of the safest municipalities in Mexico, if not the world. Its example has inspired multiple uprisings against narco-governance throughout the state of Michoacán and throughout Mexico.

On August 16, 2013, the Security Council of Cherán released this statement to the nation:

> It is with great concern that we view the state and federal governments simulating attention to the problems of our Michoacán and our nation. Through their actions they are discrediting our nation's three branches of government --Executive, Legislative and Judicial -- by perpetrating cover-ups, nepotism, corruption, and even treason to the homeland in the interests of the transnational corporations and the mean interests of other countries. We now see the effects of huge neoliberal interests that foster the wearing down of social organization; the inducement of confrontation between brothers and sisters of the same blood; and the loss of consciousness in its purest sense, that of identity -- all in order to achieve their purpose: the super-exploitation of our natural and human resources.
>
> In view of the above, we urge our brothers and sisters in our state and our country to collectively reflect on all this from the space in which you find yourselves, and furthermore, to develop strategies for re-defining our social condition, taking into account the adversities now imposed on us. The struggle must be undertaken from our own trenches, collectively and without power plays.
>
> **Respectfully yours, Security Council of the Indigenous Community of Cherán K'eri (17)**

Chapter 20
Liberation

In the United States, particularly among the political class of U.S. voters, there is for the most part an extremely distorted perspective on power, wealth, democracy and the actual history of the country itself, as well as the role it has played in the history of the world in general. The concepts of freedom, independence, liberty, justice and democracy have consistently been distorted and slanted by white male Christian supremacy, and the corrupt, criminal forces of capitalist imperialism. The underlying selfishness, greed, and brute violence during U. S. history and the present have been consistent and conspicuously evident.

In this country, freedom means the absolute preservation and defense of individual independence. Independence means the absolute preservation and defense of private property. Liberty means the absolute preservation and defense of capitalist imperialism. Justice means the absolute preservation and defense of a system of white male Christian wealth, power, and control. Democracy, or more specifically democratization, means the absolute preservation and defense of U.S. political, economic, and military interests. Around the world, and throughout the nation state's entire history, U.S. democratization has consistently meant impositions through political, economic, and military ultimatums and the violence to back them up.

Liberation on the other hand, and grassroots community-based liberation in particular, is first and foremost about collective liberation, and not individual independence. It is about communal and collective ownership, responsibility, discipline, and governance, and not private property and centralized forms of power. It is about mutual aid and solidarity, and not capitalist imperialism. It is about reciprocity and restoration and not white male Christian wealth, power, and control. It is about consensus-based decision making processes and collective obligations, and not about impositions and political, economic, and military ultimatums and violence.

The word freedom itself has been so tainted by the U.S. war propaganda machine that it even sounds more like an imposition than an agreement. Individual independence, private property, capitalist imperialism and democratization are not a formula for liberation. Liberation can only be achieved collectively and horizontally. None of us can be free if any of us are not free. My liberation depends on your liberation. Your liberation depends on my liberation. If we are not trying to liberate one another, then we are not trying to be free at all.

Grassroots Community-Based Liberation

In order to talk about grassroots community-based liberation, we have to unpack our ideas about power itself, and not just political, economic, or military power, which are concepts that come from the oppressors. What about other concepts of power that come from below, from poor people, from workers, from students, from communities, from Indigenous peoples? In this sense, we must ask ourselves several questions. What is power? Where does power come from? Who has which power? Who has no power? Does someone or a small group have all the power? Can power be reclaimed? Can power be created or generated? What kind of power leads to grassroots community-based liberation? We can easily perceive that the power of the oppressors is vertical like a skyscraper or a pyramid scheme. We can just as easily perceive power that comes from below, from poor people, from workers, from students, from communities, from Indigenous peoples as horizontal, like a large crowd of people or a machete making a path.

Grassroots community-based liberation is organized through horizontal power structures. An effective horizontal power structure is able to successfully confront a vertical power structure; however, the goal of horizontal power structures is not just to prevent the exploitation of the earth and her people, and the hoarding of power, wealth, and resources by vertical power structures. Those are immediate needs, but their long-term, ongoing goal is to build the type of world in which those participating want to live, or what the Zapatista National Liberation Army refers to as "a world in which we all can fit."

In each and every one of the examples presented in this book, horizontal power structures simply refer to people organized collectively and in unity for a common objective and/or against a common threat or enemy. The level of collectivity and unity is what has made these examples either stronger or weaker over time. In each example, be it one of Indigenous communities, students, teachers, workers, or an entire city, there already were varying degrees of collectivism; however, being pushed into a corner by a common threat or enemy, brought people together and encouraged them to use what existed or create altogether new horizontal power structures through militant unity and collectivism. Without a doubt, the examples of grassroots liberation presented in this book by Indigenous peoples are the examples with the most success, longevity, and permanence.

The Zapatistas

"Enough is enough"

The Zapatista National Liberation Army, known as the EZLN, began as an insurgent army in 1994, and by the group's own definition of an army, the organization was vertical. However, the decision to create and cede decision-making power to this organization had first been made by consensus with members from six different Indigenous nations. Almost a decade later, a strategic decision was made to achieve the goal of horizontality and autonomy. In 2003, the EZLN stepped down from its decision-making role and facilitated the process and the creation of civilian community-based organizing structures known as *Caracoles* (conch shells), and horizontal, rotating civilian self-governing councils known as *Juntas de Buen Gobierno*

(Good Governance Councils). Today the Zapatista Indigenous liberation movement is 300,000 members strong and has contributed to the creation of autonomous communities throughout over half of Mexico's southeastern state of Chiapas.

UNAM

"...education itself must be free."

The strike at the National Autonomous University of Mexico (UNAM) in 1999 began through a group of proposals made in a collective, consensus-based decision-making process within a student wide general assembly, which then went on to hold a unanimous, documented, in-person, public vote in assemblies throughout the campus to create the assembly-based General Strike Council. Though the Council became divided, and over time lost cohesion, the primary goal of preventing a University entrance fee hike was achieved. The 1999 student strike also gave future student generations very important lessons about urban strategies for the reclamation of public space, and grassroots community-based self-determination, self-defense, and autonomy.

OAXACA

"I never knew my neighbors, until I met them at the barricade."

In the Oaxaca City 2006 popular uprising, although the Section 22 Teacher's Union leadership functioned through a mixed bag of both vertical and horizontal power structures, and the Oaxacan People's Popular Assembly (APPO) suffered its own internal power struggles as an organizing structure, the thousands upon thousands of average everyday Oaxacans who at one point erected 3000 barricades in community-based self-defense, showed the world that a city of 800,000 can in fact defend and organize itself spontaneously.

Cherán

"We are not from the left or the right. We are from the bottom, and we are coming for those on top."

In Cherán's 2011 uprising against narco-governance, the 300 improvised campfire barricades that, block by block, were spontaneously erected in the municipality of 25,000 people became spaces for collective meeting, organizing, and decision making, all the while serving as militant community-based tactics for self-defense. The campfire barricades then fed directly into the community's return to a traditional P'urhépecha form of self-governance as the smallest expression of community assemblies. Today, though the fires have been put out and the community has returned to peace, the people of the campfire barricades still meet and send representatives with a group consensus to the neighborhood assembly; then the entire community is invited to the General Assembly, Cherán's top authority. In other words, the whole community is the top authority.

In each situation mentioned in this book, a unified group of people facing tremendous odds was able to effectively mount a horizontal power struggle against the vertical power structures of a university, a transnational corporation, a public authority, the police, the military, a paramilitary organization, the government itself, a cartel, or narco- governance.

Principles of Unity and Resistance

Grassroots community-based liberation is a conceptual strategy for the ultimate goal of autonomy. Some concrete immediate short-term tactics to achieve this are direct action and self-defense, while the long-term concrete tactics are community-based self-determination, and the reclamation of public space and territory, more specifically Native land. The guiding principles for these strategies and tactics can obviously vary from place to place, community to community, and culture to culture, yet should be based on collective forms of clarity, communication, consent, consensus, and then action.

Though the Zapatistas made a list of principles of unity and resistance more famous by establishing several of them as guiding principles for their 1994 uprising, the truth is that these principles come particularly from Indigenous communities throughout so-called Mesoamerica. Many of the key principles shared by the Zapatistas have also been upheld by Indigenous-based social and political movements throughout Mexico. Though these principles are specific to a geography and set of Indigenous communities and world-views, they are also a perfect guide for both Indigenous and non-Indigenous communities and for activists in solidarity with, community-based struggles for liberation. How we walk on this earth and organize with her people is key to the success of these types of movements and oftentimes, the best of intentions do not bring the best results.

The first principles listed below, when separated from the rest, can have a very romantic and utopian tone and feel to them. This is not at all a criticism of the use of these principles, but rather a criticism of their misuse by outsiders who tend to separate them from the rest of the principles, effectively making them toothless. When included, however, with the remainder of the principles, there is an unequivocal clarity about just who is included, and who is excluded from horizontal movements for grassroots community liberation. **(1)**

One No, Many Yeses

One no, many yeses is about the welcoming acceptance of a diversity of tactics and strategies when engaging in struggles for community-based liberation. One resounding No to empire, to the powerful, to corruption, to political, economic, and military impositions, and many Yeses to the different tactics and strategies we employ to struggle, resist, and confront that which is oppressing our communities as we build the alternative that we want.

One World In Which Many Worlds May Fit

This principle continues to celebrate the possible diversity of not just social movements but of communities and our world as a whole. The Zapatistas in particular took note of how they, as Indigenous peoples within the nation state of Mexico, have never been treated as though they fit into the context of the nation state. The Zapatistas have never declared a desire for sovereignty apart from the Mexican state, but instead a desire to be included with peace, justice, and dignity while also having their Indigenous autonomy respected.

We Are All the Same Because We Are All Different

This principle again celebrates the inclusion of a diversity of identities, and worldviews in a broader social movement for grassroots community-based liberation.

Respect Not Displace

This principle is rooted in respect for people and communities with different opinions and worldviews, as long as these are not rooted in the oppression of the earth and other people. The idea is that you cannot simply displace or exclude people who do not think exactly like you; on the contrary, you have to try to find commonalities and build with respect.

The next four principles have to do with basic guidelines for how to go about organizing in a community, be it our own or not.

Walk By Asking

The idea behind this principle is that the only way to move forward with a community is to begin by asking the community itself about its immediate and long-term needs and goals. Many outsiders and returning community members have a lot of great ideas about how to support communities in their struggles and movements. These ideas, however, may or may not have to do with what the community is actually confronting immediately or what the community wants for itself long term. In an urban setting, walking by asking literally means going door to door in order to get community input before any proposal is ever acted upon.

Teach By Learning

The best way to teach anything, is to do so first by learning. There are plenty of examples for exercising this principle, but let's imagine that a community member leaves the community to get a formal education, then wishes to return to the community with ideas and proposals for change and improvements. To come back to the community thinking that a formal education is enough to make necessary changes is both arrogant and inappropriate. This attitude creates a power dynamic between those with a formal education and those without. A person may very well have specialized knowledge, which can indeed help a community improve its general well-being, but sharing, proposing, and implementing that knowledge is best done by first learning what community members, young and old, have to contribute from their lived experience and knowledge of community-specific situations.

Propose Not Impose

This principle from a Zapatista perspective seems to stand in direct opposition to those of some of the classic armed insurgencies with rigid vertical power structures throughout so-called Latin American history. These insurgencies imposed, above all, Eurocentric political ideologies without taking into account Indigenous strategies for community-based liberation. Though the Zapatistas declare no one specific political ideology, the movement partially draws from communist and anarchist political theory. More importantly, however, it is clear that through a long and complicated processes of community-based consensus, a broad- based Indigenous perspective on community-based liberation is at the core of the rebel movement. Specific Zapatista stances include radical Indigenous feminism, support and solidarity with the LGBTQ+ community and struggles, acceptance of various religious beliefs, and an openness in their communities and their movement to the world in general. These stand out and substantially set the Zapatista movement apart from past movements with classic vertical power structures. These specific stances also illustrate how the Zapatistas have never been afraid to take into consideration perspectives from outside their own reality.

Build Not Destroy

This principle basically makes it clear that it is more important to build the world that we want to live in than to destroy the world in which we do not want to live. Often social movements, particularly armed rebellions, may have a tendency to focus on the destruction of an eminent threat or enemy, and can lose sight of the more important aspect of building the alternative. Today in 2022, 28 years after the 1994 Zapatista uprising, and 40 years after the Zapatistas intentionally began to Walk by Asking in 1982, despite the constant, ongoing state- sponsored violence against the group, there are a total of 47 autonomously self-governed Zapatista centers or municipalities within the 12 *Caracoles*, with approximately 300,000 Zapatistas holding almost half of the state of Chiapas.

Though these principles are about building horizontal grassroots community-based liberation, this does not mean that there is no structure, authority, or leadership. Different situations require different types, according to a community's worldview. The following six principles reflect how a chosen leader or authorities should act with responsibility and obedience to the community.

From Below and Not From Above

How does one lead from below and not from above? In the dominant western worldview of leadership there is always a vertical relationship between leaders and their "subjects"; it is usually a top down endeavor shaped like a pyramid. However, you literally have to turn that pyramid upside down in order to understand leadership and movements that come From Below and Not From Above. This principle in particular would exclude anyone who would wish to impose anything on the community from above, or from a position of power.

Represent, Not Replace

When chosen to lead, or to speak on behalf of a community or a movement, it is absolutely imperative to represent the community and its consensus, and not replace it with one's own beliefs, desires, or opinions. When we lead, it is because the community has chosen us to represent its will, not replace it. This principle in particular excludes anyone who would try to replace the will of the community with his or her own will, without consensus.

Serve Others, Not Oneself

This principle is a direct critique of the classic corrupt politicians who take advantage of their positions of power to serve themselves and not others. In Cherán, Michoacán every three years a new council of 12 elders is chosen to represent the community's will in all matters. The idea is that the 12 elders carry out the decisions made in general assemblies by community members, and not that they make decisions or take actions on their own. Every three years, they are reminded to Serve Others, Not Oneself. This principle in particular excludes the corrupt, the corruptible, and systems built upon corruption.

Everything for Everyone, Nothing for Ourselves

The rumor here is that the Mexican government initially offered the Zapatistas land and a Volkswagen Beetle to settle their dispute. The Zapatistas, however, responded with "Everything for Everyone, Nothing for Ourselves." Regardless of whether or not this is true, it is clear that the Zapatista struggle has been about a broad grassroots community-based struggle for collective liberation and not for personal gain. Unfortunately many movements that gain traction and power, then also gain negotiating power with their oppressors and can become corrupted and isolated from other movements by accepting assistance or support for themselves as individuals or smaller groups isolated from a broader movement with similar needs. This principle in particular excludes individuals or groups of individuals who would negotiate and hoard wealth and resources for themselves, or their families and cohorts, before ensuring that everyone has their most basic needs.

Command or Lead by Obeying

Once in a position of leadership as chosen by the community, one is given the authority to Lead or Command by Obeying. By obeying what? The community, the will of the community, and the consensus-based decisions made by the community. In this scenario, for example in Cherán, the General Assembly decides, and the Council of Elders and other community authorities carry the decisions out. They are not empowered to make decisions, but rather to carry out decisions made by the group. This principle excludes positions of authority or power that are based upon making decisions and carrying them out without consensus.

Exercise Power, Not Take Power

This principle takes us back to the root of grassroots community-based liberation which is an absolute alternative perspective and critique on power itself. The idea here is that social movements should never be about taking positions of power from the powerful, and replacing them with people of their own, but rather that those positions of power themselves do not contribute to community-based liberation at all. The type of power that is required for liberation is exercised collectively and does not seek the acceptance of the authorities or official positions of authority. This principle in particular does clarify who should be excluded from community-based struggles for grassroots liberation: the powerful and those who seek and desire power over others and over Mother Earth herself.

Ya Basta - Enough is Enough

Enough is Enough is the point at which these principles transform from a worldview or way of life, into specific steps for resistance, rebellion, and fundamental change towards grassroots community-based liberation. Enough is Enough is the point at which a community can be pushed no further, and is left with no choice except to engage in self-defense, self-determination, and building its own autonomy.

Goals, Strategies, Tactics

A first step towards engaging in grassroots community-based liberation in this sense would be to stop believing that we are incapable of governing ourselves. We have to use our historical memory to understand that the greatest threat to this white male Christian supremacist military-political economy has never been communism, terrorism, or organized crime, but rather the greatest threat to all incarnations of capitalist imperialism has always been and continues to be grassroots community-based liberation for self-determination, self-defense, and autonomy. This is the threat posed by the 1968 student movement in Mexico, the 1994 Zapatista uprising, the 1999 UNAM student strike, the 2006 APPO uprising in Oaxaca, the 2011 popular uprising against narco-governance in Cherán, Michoacán, and the struggle of any anti-fascist, anti-racist or organized group of people of color, farmworkers, women, territorial defenders, workers, or any community or neighborhood for their own self-determination.

We can no longer depend on the governments of nation states to take care of us and our communities. We have to figure out how to take care of ourselves, how to organize ourselves, how to govern ourselves, and how to defend ourselves.

Direct Action

**"Dreams and reality are opposites.
Action synthesizes them."**

— Assata Shakur, Assata: An Autobiography (2)

Direct actions really do get the goods. Consistently throughout the history of the world in general, and in particular the history of so-called Mexico, the working class, and Black, Indigenous and People of Color (BIPOC) communities in the so-called United States, the only way poor people ever got what was rightfully theirs, has been accomplished through direct actions. Whether they be protests, marches, blockades, lockdowns, barricades, strikes, non-violent civil disobedience or struggles for armed self-defense, direct actions have been primarily responsible for fundamental social, political, and economic change in both countries. Any rights granted to a society's most disenfranchised citizens, have primarily been accomplished in this way. After 40 years of confronting neoliberalism and centuries of worldwide colonialism and capitalist imperialism, the only true political power that communities have is that of thousands of people willing to risk their lives, their liberty and their physical well-being, while simultaneously building the alternatives they seek.

The Zapatista principle of *Ya Basta*, is a call to direct action, and in this case in particular has been a call to the armed self-defense of Indigenous territories throughout the Mexican state of Chiapas. The *Ya Basta* is also a call to the entire world to engage in decentralized autonomous direct action for collective liberation. It is critically important to note, however, that the principle of *Ya Basta* is the last principle on the list. In other words, the decision to engage in large-scale direct action requires an entire process of clarity, communication, consent, consensus, and community building long beforehand.

Decentralized autonomous direct actions carried out by smaller groups can be very effective as long as they do not put others in danger or at risk of persecution without their consent. However massive and community-based direct actions that have gone through a process of clarity, communication, consent, and consensus have a much higher possibility of not just drawing attention to issues and demanding change, but of effectively accomplishing the desired change. The types of direct actions depend on the situation, but community consent and support is what makes the difference.

Community-Based Self Defense

"Only a fool lets somebody else
tell him who his enemy is."

— Assata Shakur, Assata: An Autobiography (3)

If you are not contributing to white male Christian wealth and power, and to the neoliberal military political economy, then you are considered disposable. If you are creating real alternatives or challenges to white male Christian wealth and power, in particular through exercising community-based self-determination, self-defense, and autonomy, then you are considered a threat. Communities that engage in strategies, tactics, and practices for grassroots community-based liberation expose themselves to repression, and state sponsored violence. Most BIPOC communities in the world are struggling for self-determination and autonomy on a daily basis, and therefore they have always been exposed to violence and have always been considered a threat.

These communities are treated as enemy combatants in a war of social, economic, political, and military control based on white, male, and Christian supremacy. Therefore a logical step towards building and maintaining community-based self-determination anywhere, is community-based self-defense. Communities that organize for self-determination and autonomy better damn well be ready, willing, and able to engage in community-based self-defense.

Yes, self-defense does include physical training and preparation, this should go without saying. However there are many other elements that must also be considered:

- Community-based education and a living memory of our diverse community-based struggles is part of self-defense. This involves building educational alternatives for our young people with a core foundation in critical thought and analysis, decolonized historical and social narratives, and the inclusion of all local and historical struggles relevant to the student community. It can be as simple as building and sharing the necessary curriculum, to building an alternative learning space or school, to reclaiming an existing space for this purpose, to demanding this type of education for our youth from existing educational spaces. If the ultimate goal is grassroots community-based autonomy, however, then building or reclaiming an existing space and turning it into a completely different educational project will have a much greater success, than asking for a change in the existing public education framework.

- Teaching, learning, and practicing camaraderie, cooperation, de-escalation, conflict resolution, humility, respect, responsibility, discipline, and dignity are all part of self-defense. Huge barriers to building community-based liberation are in-fighting and inter-community violence. It is important to note that divide

and conquer tactics have always been employed by
white male Christian supremacists throughout history
against BIPOC communities. And whether or not most
community violence is part of a strategy of divide and
conquer, the effect is the same regardless. There is
a tremendous amount of trauma, pain and displaced
anger in our communities that will require spaces and
an environment of healing.

• Teaching, learning, and practicing anti-fascism, anti-
patriarchy, anti-homophobia, anti-transphobia, anti-
sexism, anti-racism are part of self-defense. In the face
of ongoing economic disparity, the politically extreme
right has gained a tremendous amount of traction
with working- class white people around the world. It is
becoming clear that more and more poor working-class
white people are seeking a struggle for community-
based liberation in right-wing spaces that tend to be
fascist, patriarchal, homophobic, transphobic, sexist,
and racist. Though these spaces have gained numbers
and legitimacy, they lead to the systemic oppression
of entire sectors of society and need to be actively
challenged. It is not, and has never been enough to
simply not consider yourself a fascist, a patriarch, a
homophobe, a transphobe, a sexist or a racist. You have
to actively practice anti-fascism, anti-patriarchy, anti-
homophobia, anti-transphobia, anti-sexism, anti-racism
in your own family and immediate social circles as well
as in your daily life in order to build community- based
self-defense, self-determination and autonomy.

• Ultimately unlearning and refusing to propose,
colonialism while teaching, learning, and practicing
decolonization has to be a constant process for each

and every one of us. This would include challenging and dismantling all white male Christian supremacist structures of politics, economics, society, education, and governance within a community, and then deferring to local Indigenous communities whenever possible to do so, and if not to local BIPOC, community members in order to build the alternatives.

All of these things in conjunction with preparation and training for physical self-defense can begin to guarantee a possibility for building real community-based self-determination and autonomy. When push comes to shove, as it has for a very long time now, the right of communities to organize their own strategies and tactics for self-defense must be respected and supported.

One of the greatest barriers to community-based self-defense has been a very powerful shift towards pacifism and non-violence as a primary means of political expression in Europe and the United States. We should all be open to a diversity of tactics, (One No, Many Yeses) and we cannot expect everybody to show up in the same way as everybody else. Not everybody has the same willingness or possibilities to take the same risks as everyone else. Non-violent direct action is a valid form of political resistance. However, the dilemma comes about when proponents of non-violence and pacifism criticize, prohibit, and criminalize community-based self-defense as violent. We must understand that non-violence comes from a position of privilege wherein its practitioners have a choice in the matter, while so many other people on the planet exist in choice-less situations of constant violence wherein non-violence could and does very well mean death. Pacifists who put their lives and liberty on the line for their community deserve respect, but we have to recognize the differences between pacifism and resistance and passivity and complacency. We must begin to understand that self-defense is non-violent. Self-defense is a valid and key element of self-determination. It is a tool for survival, not for violence.

Community-Based Self-Determination

> "The schools we go to are reflections of the society that created them. Nobody is going to give you the education you need to overthrow them. Nobody is going to teach you your true history, teach you your true heroes, if they know that that knowledge will help set you free."

— Assata Shakur, Assata: An Autobiography (4)

There is no way to gain community-based autonomy without building the infrastructure and organizing mechanisms to first and foremost talk and meet with one another, come to a consensus about community needs, and begin to figure out ways to meet those needs. This would be a self-defense tactic in the immediate short-term; over time, however, the more basic needs are met collectively the more self-determination and eventual autonomy are built. We absolutely have to stop believing that we are incapable of governing ourselves, meeting our own needs, taking care of, and defending ourselves. We are absolutely capable of building real alternatives to electoral politics and institutionalized governance, and we can also build the necessary community-based structures or mechanisms for self-governance.

Meeting and coming to consensus with a diverse group of people within a community is no easy task anywhere. It becomes more complicated the more disconnected the community is from itself. In many Indigenous communities both in the United States and Mexico there are traditional or community-based meeting and organizing spaces and strategies. In urban centers throughout the United States in particular, however, outside of churches, mosques and other religious gathering spaces, there are very few spaces or even efforts towards gathering the community, facilitating discussions, and developing consensus-based decision making processes. In a sense, the community has to want to learn and teach itself how to meet and organize. Unfortunately these meeting spaces do arise spontaneously, yet temporarily, when a community has been faced with an atrocity, such as on-going police or gang violence. In order to prevent atrocities and practice community-based self-determination and self-defense, it is critical to have pre-existing and ongoing meeting and organizing spaces, and mechanisms for community-based decision making, or alternately to take advantage of spontaneous moments of unity and resistance to reclaim and establish physical space for the purposes of meeting and organizing.

The reclamation or expropriation of spaces is a common theme and tactic in each and every single one of the examples presented in this book. The UNAM student strikes occupied the 300,000 student university campus and several associated schools throughout Mexico City for over 10 months, The Zapatista uprising literally took land back and distributed it among its Indigenous support base. Today the organization has a presence in half the state of Chiapas. The 2006 Oaxacan People's Popular Assembly (APPO) uprising occupied the entire city of Oaxaca with a particular focus on all government offices and establishments throughout the city for six months. The 2011 P'urhépecha uprising in Cherán, Michoacán led to the recuperation of their entire 25,000 person municipality, including its surrounding forests, from the clutches of not just an organized crime cartel, but the entire structure of narco-governance. Space, and the reclamation of space as a political tactic of resistance, and as a political strategy of autonomy is one of the absolutely most important elements of grassroots community-based liberation. Together with the creation of spaces for meeting, organizing, and practicing self-governance, this is where we can see community-based autonomy grow, persist, and flourish.

Community-Based Autonomy

"Nobody in the world, nobody in history, has ever gotten their freedom by appealing to the moral sense of the people who were oppressing them."

— Assata Shakur, Assata: An Autobiography (5)

Autonomy can sound both very romantic and utopian, but in reality it involves a tremendous amount of work, commitment, obligation, discipline, sacrifice, and service to the community. There really is no way to gain half-ass community-based autonomy. The type of struggles for community-based liberation presented in this book, each in its own way, either did require, or continues to require a tremendous amount of work, commitment, obligation, discipline, sacrifice, and service to the community. One of the most powerful forms of real political power is the involvement of thousands of people in a community willing to risk their lives for liberation, and another even more powerful and long-term form of real political power is the participation of thousands of people putting in the work, commitment, obligation, discipline, sacrifice, and service to build grassroots community-based liberation through self-defense, self-determination, and autonomy. This is without a doubt one of the greatest threats to white male Christian supremacy and the corrupt and criminal neoliberal military political economy.

While a tremendous number of Indigenous communities throughout so-called Mexico practice traditional forms of self-governance including community-based self-determination and autonomy, it is important not to romanticize Indigenous identities in general, but rather to take the time and effort to look at specific Indigenous communities, their specific practices, and their specific successes or failures at achieving grassroots community-based liberation. The fact that a community is Indigenous and practices traditional forms of self-governance, does not at all mean that it is engaged in community-based grassroots liberation. Unfortunately political and economic corruption, vulnerability or acquiescence, as well as varying levels of colonization or decolonization, are still strong factors in determining a community's commitment to grassroots community-based liberation. For example several of the paramilitary groups carrying out state sponsored atrocities throughout Mexico, are also Indigenous, some even practicing traditional forms of self-governance. Many Indigenous communities have chosen to align themselves with institutional forms of political, economic, and military power, some purely out of self-interest, others out of duress and under the pressure and vulnerability of precarity.

Conversely it is clear that Indigenous communities who do practice and exercise grassroots community-based liberation through self-determination, self-defense, and autonomy do so with a tremendous amount of risk, work, commitment, obligation, discipline, sacrifice, and service to the community. They are not all shiny, happy people holding hands and dancing *kumbaya*. They are subjected to a constant confrontation with the forces of capital, empire, electoral and institutional forms of governance, and experience vulnerability to crime and corruption. The work is constant and ongoing, and it is not easy work at all. Indigenous identity, worldviews, organizing methods, and structures make it easier for them than for non-Indigenous communities to foment grassroots community-based liberation, however identity alone is not a permanent given anywhere. It is important to recognize that even communities that acquiesce, and submit to colonized and institutional forms of political power and wealth, are victims of the very systems to which they submit themselves.

Comfort and Fear

Two of the greatest barriers to grassroots liberation fomented by the neoliberal military political economy are comfort and fear. Around the world, for the business and political elite and national oligarchs indeed, but even more so for the voting professional class of a society, comfort is a driving force in quelling even mild expressions of solidarity, and to a higher degree, efforts or actions towards community-based grassroots liberation. Comfort keeps populations in developed nations complacent, yet there is always a fear factor even when comfort is present, in the sense that the fear of losing comfort is just as much a factor as the comfort itself. For the working poor, the disenfranchised, and in particular for BIPOC communities, threats of death, violence, incarceration, persecution, unemployment, and homelessness, are all determining factors in shutting down struggles for grassroots liberation. The little comfort that is brought about by employment, housing, running water, hot water, food, and entertainment is enough to keep entire working poor populations from risking any of it by stepping out of line.

Again, one of the most powerful forms of real political power is the engagement of thousands of people in a community willing to risk their lives, liberty, and well-being for liberation, but when it comes to privileged people in general, and privileged people in wealthy countries in particular, even risking comfort seems too much to ask. Grassroots community-based liberation will almost always require risks and sacrifices, particularly of comforts and privileges. It is not enough to simply profess to be an anti-capitalist or anti-imperialist; one has to actively engage in anti-capitalism and anti-imperialism in order to truly stand in solidarity with the oppressed. In order to truly be an anti-capitalist and an anti-imperialist, one has to be ready, willing and able to make sacrifices and take risks of personal comforts and privileges.

Ideological and Infiltrated Provocation & Sabotage

Another very real concern when organizing for grassroots community-based liberation is the possibility of infiltrated provocation within the group or community. Infiltrated provocation takes place when someone who is intentionally working against the community is able to participate in the process of grassroots liberation only to sabotage group efforts through a variety of tactics such as spreading rumors, provoking conflict, derailing collective processes, exacerbating existing conflicts, or luring members to take dangerous, unnecessary, or illegal actions to then incriminate them. Even much more effective than actual infiltrated provocation, however, is the constant fear of infiltrated provocation and the accusations that may occur because of personal differences, ideological differences, or differences of tactics and strategies. It is critically important not to accuse anyone of infiltrated provocation unless there is actual evidence of that fact. That said, one does not need to be an infiltrated provocateur to cause the type of destabilization in a community or organization that renders struggles for grassroots liberation fruitless.

In 2008 the Central Intelligence Agency (CIA) declassified a 1944 document created by the organization's predecessor, the Office of Strategic Service (OSS). The Strategic Services Manual # 3 titled Simple Sabotage Field Manual details simple strategies that an infiltrated provocateur or saboteur can use to simply cause problems, generate conflict, and destabilize organizations, communities, or workplaces. The entire document has since been removed from the CIA website, but can still be found at this link: *https://www.hsdl.org/?view&did=750070*

The Introduction to the Simple Sabotage Field Manual reads as follows:

1. INTRODUCTION

a. The purpose of this paper is to characterize simple sabotage, to outline its possible effects, and to present suggestions for inciting and executing it.

b. Sabotage varies from highly technical coup de main acts that require detailed planning and the use of specially trained operatives, to innumerable simple acts which the ordinary individual citizen-saboteur can perform. This paper is primarily concerned with the latter type. Simple sabotage does not require specially prepared tools or equipment; it is executed by an ordinary citizen who may or may not act individually and without the necessity for active connection with an organized group; and it is carried out in such a way to involve a minimum danger of injury, detection, and reprisal.

c. Where destruction is involved, the weapons of the citizen-saboteur are salt, nails, candles, pebbles, thread, or any materials he might normally be expected to possess as a householder or a worker in his particular occupation. His arsenal is the kitchen shelf, the trash pile, his own usual kit of tools and supplies. The targets of his sabotage are usually objects to which he has normal and inconspicuous access in everyday life.

d. A second type of simple sabotage requires no destructive tools whatsoever and produces physical damage, if any, by highly indirect means. It is based on universal opportunities to make faulty decisions, to adopt a non cooperative attitude and to induce others to follow suit. Making faulty decisions may be simply a matter of placing tools in one spot instead of another. A non.cooperative attitude may involve nothing more than creating an unpleasant situation among one's fellow workers, engaging in bickering, or displaying surliness or stupidity.

e. This type of activity, sometimes referred to as the "human element", is frequently responsible for accidents, delays, and general obstruction even under normal conditions. The potential saboteur should discover what types of faulty decisions and non.cooperation are normally found in his kind of work and should then devise his sabotage so as to enlarge that "margin of error". (6)

The field manual, though clearly outdated, demonstrates the technical existence of a specific infiltrated strategy of provocation and sabotage. Though we know that this is a fact and a potential possibility, it is important to recognize that an individual does not necessarily need to be an infiltrated provocateur or saboteur to cause this type of simple mayhem. Ignorance, laziness, lack of commitment, discipline, or obligations can all lead to similar destabilizing effects without a necessary intention of infiltrated provocation. Sometimes the intention is not infiltrated, but rather stems from an ideological or personal difference. The results however are all the same. It is important to establish limits on destabilization by excluding repeat offenders from areas of risk, or from the entire process for grass roots liberation itself. Asking someone who is consistently destabilizing group or community efforts to leave, does not require accusing them of anything in particular, other than being a problem.

Privilege

Today more than ever it has become absolutely critical to take responsibility and be accountable for our privileges. Though there is a growing rejection of the notion of atoning for privilege altogether from the right wing in particular, even those who are actually taking the time and making an effort to acknowledge their privileges on the left fall far from the true mark of accountability, responsibility, risk, and sacrifice. Sometimes simply acknowledging privilege without taking action to actively atone for it, is the same as asserting the supremacy that said privilege entails. It is not enough to be aware of your privilege and acknowledge it, rather it is about assuming responsibility and taking action. The price of redemption is sacrificing comfort and taking the necessary risks to contribute to the grassroots liberation of others with less privilege than you.

Activist Imperialism

It is, however, important to clarify that if you are a privileged person who has indeed made sacrifices and taken risks in order to contribute to the grassroots liberation of others, then that does not at all mean that you have the right to set the agenda, or that you have a right to speak for or represent any of the others you are supposedly standing and struggling in solidarity with.

There is a political concept that comes from social activism and has over time worked its way into the framework of so-called community organizations and nonprofits, and that concept is one of the key components of what I call activist imperialism. The concept is known as "empowerment."

Our non-profit empowers young Black women to seek leadership and excellence!

This is the most condescending attitude that anyone from within or from outside a community can have towards solidarity and action with and for community members. It is as if activists and non-profits had a monopoly on power, and somehow their work or knowledge was what gave a poor powerless community access to a power it would have otherwise never known. This is bullshit. The community is power. The people in the community are power. The community's ability to collectively exercise its power in the face of adversity is the only true political power that a community has. So in order to challenge this entire notion of empowerment, when it comes to organizing in and with communities, we need to engage in practices, actions and efforts that contribute to self-empowerment. If you are working at a non-profit or so called community organization right now, and you cannot clearly demonstrate how your work is actively contributing to the self-empowerment, self-defense, and self-determination of the community you are trying to serve, than your organization is at the very least ineffectual, and at worst probably part of the problem. This is particularly true of organizations with a working base composed of people from outside the community. An organization from outside a community that is truly invested in that community's grassroots liberation would, over time, write itself completely out of the script and hand over its role as an organization to the community itself. Instead, an overwhelming number of these so-called community organizations and non-profits keep writing themselves back into the script, by creating dependencies as opposed to generating liberation. If you are the Executive Director of a community organization or a non-profit receiving and justifying an exaggerated Executive Director's salary year after year without ever handing over your position of authority within the organization to a local community member, then you in particular are definitely part of the problem.

Peace

Peace is a much more complicated concept than it seems. There are many types of "peace" that are really not peace at all. Too many communities live in a relative peace, which is actually based upon non-confrontation because of threats and vulnerability to violence. This is not peace at all. This type of peace is absolutely based upon submission, and not upon collective liberation. Then there is the very real and palpable peace, in which the privileged few live. They perceive and live in relative peace, tranquility, and comfort; it is painfully clear, however, that the peace, tranquility, and comfort of the privileged few has been, and continues to be built upon the backs, the sweat, and the blood of others. This is by no means peace either. In reality, there can be no peace without dignity, justice, and liberation for everyone, everywhere, all the time. Dignity refers to our daily lives and the work we do to survive. Working for slave wages and surviving on increasing debt dependence can provide a relative peace, but this would be a peace without dignity. Receiving a living wage while being given the ability to build grassroots liberation could potentially bring about peace with dignity. There are entire sectors of society that may be getting a little taste of relative peace, tranquility and comfort, yet without receiving justice for past transgressions and utter violence against their communities throughout history, this again would not be peace at all. Finally, as long as anyone continues to be oppressed and subjugated by systems of power, control and wealth for the few, this would be peace without liberation, which once again is not peace at all.

We are at a critical point in our world's history where each and every single one of us has to ask ourselves what we are willing to do, what we are willing to sacrifice, and what we are willing to risk in order for everyone everywhere to have peace with dignity, justice and collective liberation? It is clear that those who are not willing to do anything, to take any risks, or make any sacrifices to ensure that everyone everywhere has peace with dignity, justice, and collective liberation, are those who benefit the most from white male Christian supremacy and the military political economy of neoliberalism. The peace that they offer is not peace at all either. It is terror.

NOTES

Chapter 1

1. Arundhati Roy, "Public Power in the Age of Empire," *Frontline*, India's National Magazine, October 22, 2004, *https://frontline.thehindu.com/cover-story/article30225132.ece*

2. Andrea Micocci, Flavia Di Mario, *The Fascist Nature of Neoliberalism*, (Rome: Routledge, October 18, 2017), p.15.

3. Edward S, Herman and Noam Chomsky. *Manufacturing Consent: The Political Economy of the Mass Media.* (New York: Pantheon Books, 1988), p. 88.

Chapter 2

1. Stephen E. Ambrose, "Founding Fathers and Slaveholders," *Smithsonian Magazine*, November 2002, *https://www.smithsonianmag.com/history/founding-fathers-and-slaveholders-72262393/*

2. Kathryn Gehred, "Did George Washington's false teeth come from his slaves?: A look at the evidence, the responses to that evidence, and the limitations of history", *Washington Papers*, October 19, 2016, *https://washingtonpapers.org/george-washingtons-false-teeth-come-slaves-look-evidence-responses-evidence-limitations-history/*

3. Constance Grady, "Thomas Jefferson spent years raping his slave Sally Hemings. A new novel treats their relationship as a love story." Vox, April 8, 2016, *https://www.vox.com/2016/4/8/11389556/thomas-jefferson-sally-hemings-book*

4. Dylan Matthews, "Andrew Jackson was a slaver, ethnic cleanser, and tyrant. He deserves no place on our money." Vox, April 20, 2016, *https://www.vox.com/2016/4/20/11469514/andrew-jackson-indian-removal*

5. Vincent Schilling, "The Traumatic True History and Name List of the Dakota 38," (Phoenix: Indian Country Today, December 26, 2020, *https://indiancountrytoday.com/news/traumatic-true-history-full-list-dakota-38*

6. Milton and Rose Friedman, *Free to Choose: A Personal Statement*, New York: Harcourt Brace Jovanovich, 1980.

7. Milton Friedman on Donahue - 1979, Indianapolis: EdChoice, YouTube, August, 26, 2009, *https://www.youtube.com/watch?v=1EwaLys3Zak*

8. Christopher Ingraham, "U.S. spends twice as much on law and order as it does on cash welfare, data show," *The Washington Post*, June 4, 2020, *https://www.washingtonpost.com/business/2020/06/04/us-spends-twice-much-law-order-it-does-social-welfare-data-show/*

9. Aslak Berge, "A Murky Past," Salmon Business, September 13, 2017, *https://salmonbusiness.com/a-murky-past/*

10. Vicky Imerman and Heather Dean, "Notorious Chilean School of the Americas Graduates," School of the Americas Watch SOAW.org Derechos.org, *https://www.derechos.org/soa/chile-not.html*

11. David Parra A, *El Ladrillo: Bases de la Política Económica del Gobierno Militar Chileno,* (Santiago de Chile, Centro de Estudios Públicos Fecha Original 1972, republicado en Junio de 1992).

12. Berge, "A Murky Past."

Chapter 3

1. Zachary Davies Boren, The Telegraph, "Major Study Finds the US Is an Oligarchy," *Business Insider*, April 16, 2014, *https://www.businessinsider.com/major-study-finds-that-the-us-is-an-oligarchy-2014-4?r=MX&IR=T*

2. Katherine Schaeffer, "6 Facts about Economic Inequality in the US," Pew Research Center, February 7, 2020, *https://www.pewresearch.org/fact-tank/2020/02/07/6-facts-about-economic-inequality-in-the-u-s/*

3. José Luis Solís González, "Neoliberalism and Organized Crime in Mexico: The Emergence of the Narco-State in Mexico," *Frontera Norte*, Vol. 25, Núm. 50 Julio-Diciembre de 2013.

4. Simón Sedillo, Radio Fogata, Manovuelta Films, *Guarda Bosques*, 2013, *https://www.youtube.com/watch?v=vIJ_Ld2kvOk*

5. Michelle Alexander, *The New Jim Crow: Mass Incarceration in the Age of Colorblindness*, New York: The New Press, 2011.

Chapter 4

1. History.com Editors, "NAFTA signed into law," March 4, 2010, *https://www.history.com/this-day-in-history/nafta-signed-into-law*

2. Erica Grieder, "NAFTA Was a Bipartisan Effort: Both George H.W. Bush and Bill Clinton deserve credit for the trade deal," *Texas Monthly*, September 30, 2016, *https://www.texasmonthly.com/burka-blog/nafta-bipartisan-effort/*

3. Gómez de Silva Cano, Jorge J., "El derecho agrario mexicano y la Constitución de 1917," Colección INEHRM, 2016. pp. 151-168.

4. Ibid.

5. Diario Oficial de la Federación, DECRETO por el que se reforma el artículo 27 de la Constitución Política de los Estados Unidos Mexicanos, Presidencia de la República. CARLOS SALINAS DE GORTARI, 06/01/1992, *https://www.dof.gob.mx/nota_detalle.php?codigo=4643312&fecha=06/01/1992*

6. Tequio Jurídico A.C., "El PROCEDE en Comunidades Indígenas No Procede," Tercera Impresión, Oaxaca, Agosto 2012.

7. Ibid.

8. Organization of American States - Foreign Trade Information System, North American Free Trade Agreement (NAFTA), 2022, *http://www.sice.oas.org/trade/nafta/naftatce.asp*

9. Jennifer Huizen, "Global trade 101: How NAFTA's Chapter 11 overrides environmental laws," *Mongabay*, 8 November 2016, *https://news.mongabay.com/2016/11/global-trade-101-how-naftas-chapter-11-overrides-environmental-laws/*

10. J.M. Alvarez Contreras; "The USMCA Revisited: The Beginning of the End for Investor-State Dispute Settlement (ISDS) Between Developed Countries ... and Developing as Well?" TDM 3 (2020), www.transnational-dispute-management.com/article.asp?key=2740

11. David J. Lynch and Kevin Sieff, "Trump's tariff threat to Mexico may upend trade deal, undermine the economy," *Washington Post*, May 30, 2019, *https://www.washingtonpost.com/business/economy/trumps-threat-to-hit-mexico-with-tariffs-could-upend-his-trade-deal-and-undermine-the-economy/2019/05/30/876a1de0-8342-11e9-95a9-e2c830afe24f_story.html*

12. Mano Vuelta Films, "El Factor Demarest / the Demarest Factor" (Bilingue English/Español), Mano Vuelta Films 2010, Entrevista Silvia Hernández, You-Tube: *https://youtu.be/Glb3cJJdVYQ*

Chapter 5

1.Violeta Nunez Rodrigues, Adriana Gomez Bonilla, y Luciano Concheiro Borquez, "La tierra en Chiapas en el marco de 'los 20 años de la rebelión zapatista': La historia, la transformación, la permanencia," Argumentos (Méx.) [online]. 2013, vol.26, n.73 [citado 2022-03-18], pp.37-54.

2. School of the Americas Watch, 2003 SOA Country Sheets, Mexico, SOA Watch March 17, 2005, Internet Archive, Wayback Machine, *https://web.archive.org/web/20070119122908/https://soaw.org/new/article.php?id=343#Mexico*

3. Paulina Villegas, "In a Mexico 'Tired of Violence,' Zapatista Rebels Venture into Politics," *New York Times*, August 26, 2017, *https://www.nytimes.com/2017/08/26/world/americas/mexico-zapatista-subcommander-marcos.html*

4. Enlace Zapatista, Zapatista National Liberation Army, January 1994, *https://enlacezapatista.ezln.org.mx/*

5. Human Rights Watch, MEXICO, "Army Officer Held 'Responsible' for Chiapas Massacre; Accused Found Dead at Defense Ministry," June 1995, *https://www.hrw.org/reports/1995/Mexico2.htm*

6. Victor Perera, "Behind the Chiapas Revolt: Corn Gods, Dummy Rifles: Mexico. To the Mayan militants, NAFTA will permanently sever them from their origins. They would be less-than-human men of wood." *The Los Angeles Times*, January 9, 1994, *https://www.latimes.com/archives/la-xpm-1994-01-09-op-10002-story.html*

7. Enlace Zapatista, "First Declaration from the Lacandon Jungle," Zapatista National Liberation Army, January 1994, *https://enlacezapatista.ezln.org.mx/*

8. SOA Watch March 17, 2005, *https://web.archive.org/web/20070119122908/https://soaw.org/new/article.php?id=343#Mexico*

9. Human rights Watch, MEXICO, June 1995, *https://www.hrw.org/reports/1995/Mexico2.htm*

10. "Who killed Luis Donaldo Colosio? 25 years later, Mexicans still wonder," *Mexico Daily News*, March 23, 2019, *https://mexiconewsdaily.com/news/who-killed-luis-donaldo-colosio/*

11. Ibid.

12. Office of the Press Secretary, REMARKS BY THE PRESIDENT (Clinton) AT CINCO DE MAYO EVENT, Mexico Cultural Institute Washington, D.C., May 5, 1994, *https://clintonwhitehouse6.archives.gov/1994/05/1994-05-05-remarks-by-president-at-cinco-de-mayo-event.html*

13. Riorden Roett, CHASE MANHATTAN'S EMERGING MARKETS GROUP MEMO, MEXICO-POLITICAL UPDATE January 13, 1995, *http://www.realhistoryarchives.com/collections/hidden/chase-memo.htm*.

14. Human Rights Watch, Mexico, "Torture and Other Abuses During the 1995 Crackdown on Alleged Zapatistas," February 1, 1996, available at: *https://www.refworld.org/docid/3ae6a85dc.html* [accessed March 19, 2022]

15. Gilberto López y Rivas, "El plan de campaña de 1994 contra el EZLN," *La Jornada*, 4 de febrero de 2011, *https://www.jornada.com.mx/2011/02/04/opinion/025a1pol*

16. SOA Watch March 17, 2005.

17. Enlace Zapatista, Zapatista National Liberation Army, January 1994, *https://enlacezapatista.ezln.org.mx/*

18. López y Rivas, *El plan contra el EZLN.*

19. Ibid.

20. Riorden Roett, Chase Manhattan Memo.

21. Kate Doyle, "Rebellion in Chiapas and the Mexican Military," National Security Archive, January 20, 2004, *https://nsarchive2.gwu.edu/NSAEBB/NSAEBB109/*

22. Ibid.

23. Ibid.

24. SOA Watch March 17, 2005.

25. Comisión Nacional de Derechos Humanos, Insurgencia del Ejército Zapatista de Liberación Nacional (EZLN), *https://www.cndh.org.mx/noticia/insurgencia-del-ejercito-zapatista-de-liberacion-nacional-ezln*

26. Hermann Bellinghausen, "Hostilidad y prepotencia, signos de la PFP en Chiapas," *La Jornada,* 21 de mayo de 2000, *https://www.jornada.com.mx/2000/05/21/pol1.html27*

27. Ñani Pinto, "Persiste hostigamiento paramilitar hacia comunidades zapatistas," Avispa Midia, 10 de enero de 2022, *https://avispa.org/persiste-hostigamiento-paramilitar-hacia-comunidades-zapatistas/*

28. Enlace Zapatista, "Sixth Declaration from the Lacandon Jungle," Zapatista National Liberation Army, January 1994, *https://enlacezapatista.ezln.org.mx/*

Chapter 6

1. History.com Editors, *American-Indian Wars,* November 17, 2019, *https://www.history.com/topics/native-american-history/american-indian-wars*

2. Max Fisher, "How America became the most powerful country on Earth in 11 maps," Vox, May 20, 2015, *https://www.vox.com/2015/5/20/8615345/america-global-power-maps*

3. Robert J. Miller, "The Doctrine of Discovery: The International Law of Colonialism," July 27, 2018, *https://doctrineofdiscovery.org/the-doctrine-of-discovery-the-international-law-of-colonialism/*.

4. Indigenous Values, "Inter Caetera," Doctrine of Discovery Project, July 23, 2018, *https://doctrineofdiscovery.org/inter-caetera/*.

5. Indigenous Values, "Law," Doctrine of Discovery Project , July 30, 2018, *https://doctrineofdiscovery.org/law/*.

6. Ibid.

7. Interview with Jimmy Lee Beason the II, a Native Pahuska from the Eagle Clan of the Osage Nation, and professor in the Indigenous / American Indian Studies Department at Haskell Indian Nations University in Lawrence Kansas, conducted by Simón Sedillo, September 27, 2021.

8. "1898: The Birth of a Superpower," Office of the Historian, Foreign Service Institute, United States Department of State, *https://history.state.gov/departmenthistory/short-history/superpower*

9. Lester D. Langley, *The Banana Wars: United States Intervention in the Caribbean, 1898 – 1934,* Series: Latin American Silhouettes, (Washington D.C. Rowman & Littlefield, November 2001), p. 3.

10. Ashley Pomeroy, *Compensation for Allied Bombing during WW2*, The Straight Dope, September 2012, *https://boards.straightdope.com/t/compensation-for-allied-bombing-during-ww2/634305*

11.Farewell address by President Dwight D. Eisenhower, January 17, 1961, Eisenhower Library. National Archives and Records Administration

Chapter 7

1. SOA Watch March 17, 2005, *https://web.archive.org/web/20070119122908/https://soaw.org/new/article.php?id=343#El%20Salvador*

2. Ibid.

3. Ibid.

4. Ibid.

5. Carolina S. Romero, "Acteal: No la olvidamos ni la olvidaremos jamás," *La Haine*, 24 de agosto de 2009, *https://www.lahaine.org/mundo.php/acteal-no-la-olvidamos-y-la-olvidaremos*

6. School of the Americas Watch, SOA-WHINSEC Graduate Database, Last updated April 6, 2020, *https://soaw.org/category/resources/soa-graduates*

7. Ibid.

8. Simón Sedillo, "SOA Graduate Takes Control of Security in Michoacán, Mexico," *elenemigocomun.net* January 23, 2015, *https://elenemigocomun.net/2015/01/soa-graduate-security-michoacan/* Debate with Lee Rials is located in the comments section of the Indybay.org post of the same article: *https://www.indybay.org/newsitems/2015/01/23/18767414.php*

Chapter 8

1. "1898: The Birth of a Superpower", *https://history.state.gov/departmenthistory/short-history/superpower*

2. Chaz Bufe and Mitchell Cowen Verter, "Dreams of Freedom: A Ricardo Flores Magón Reader," AK Press 2005, Oakland, CA, USA, Edinburgh, Scotland, pp. 368 – 369.

3. Simón Sedillo, Interview with Fernando Lobo, author of *La insurrección transmitida* Oaxaca 2006," Pepitas de calabaza Editorial, Colección AmericaLee, Logroño, España, 2018", Interview conducted on June 9, 2021, exclusively for *Weapons Drugs and Money*

4. Kate Doyle & Jesse Franzblau, Official Report Released on Mexico's "Dirty War," The National Security Archive, November 21, 2006, *https://nsarchive2.gwu.edu/NSAEBB/NSAEBB209/index.htm#informe*

5. U.S. Army Pictorial Center, Psychological Operations in Support of Internal Defense and Development Assistance Programs, Internet Archive, Prelinger Archives, 1968, *https://archive.org/details/0095_Psychological_Operations_in_Support_of_Internal_Defense_and_Dev_07_21_47_00*

6. Doyle & Franzblau discussion.

7. Ibid.

8. Ibid.

9. Ibid.

10. Ibid.

11. Ibid.

12. Ibid.

13. Simón Sedillo, Interview with Griselda Sánchez, June 10, 2021, exclusively for *Weapons Drugs and Money*

14. Dr. Graham H. Turbiville, "Mexico's Multimission Force for Internal Security", Foreign Military Studies Office, Fort Leavenworth, KS. Published for informational purposes on elenemigocomun.net, *https://elenemigocomun.net/wp-content/uploads/2009/03/multimission-internal-security.pdf*

15. Ibid.

16. Ibid.

Chapter 9

1. Boletín de Prensa, Consejo General de Huelga Universidad Nacional Autónoma de México, Ciudad Universitaria, México D.F., 12 de febrero de 2001, Internet Archive, Wayback Machine, *https://web.archive.org/web/20010404091042/http://www.geocities.com/Baja/Mesa/9813/*

2. Simón Sedillo, Interview with Emilia Gomita, June 28, 2021, exclusively for *Weapons Drugs and Money*

3. Simón Sedillo, Interview with Griselda Sánchez.

4. Dr. Graham H. Turbiville, FMSO Information.

5. Simón Sedillo, Interviews with Emilia Gomita and Griselda Sánchez.

Chapter 10

1. Simón Sedillo, Interview with Fernando Lobo.

2. Ibid.

3. José de Jesús Cortés, "Balacera entre transportistas de Oaxaca deja un muerto y heridos," *unotv.com*, Oaxaca, México, 25 de junio de 2019, *https://www.unotv.com/noticias/estados/oaxaca/detalle/registran-balacera-en-tre-transportistas-de-oaxaca-hay-heridos-055109/*

4. Fernando Lobo, *La Insurrección Transmitida, Pepitas de calabaza Editorial, Colección AmericaLee,* Logroño, España, 2018, p.39.

5. Lobo, *La insurrección transmitida,* p. 41.

6. Joel Ortega Erreguerena, "La Asamblea Popular de los Pueblos de Oaxaca. A 15 años de las barricadas," *Revista Común,* Ciudad de México, 14 de junio de 2021, *https://revistacomun.com/blog/la-asamblea-popular-de-los-pueb-los-de-oaxaca-a-15-anos-de-las-barricadas/*

7. Simón Sedillo, Interview with Fernando Lobo.

8. Lobo, *La Insurrección Transmitida,* p.61.

9. Jill Friedberg, *Un Poquito de Tanta Verdad*, Corrugated Films 2007, *https://vimeo.com/ondemand/unpoquitodetantaverdad*

10. Lobo, *La Insurrección Transmitida*, p.71.

11. Lobo. *La Insurrección Transmitida*, pp. 79 -82

12. Lobo. *La Insurrección Transmitida*, pp. 79-82.

13. Lobo, *La Insurrección Transmitida*, pp. 82-83.

14. Simón Sedillo, Interview with Fernando Lobo.

15. Jill Friedberg, *Un Poquito de Tanta Verdad*.

16. Simón Sedillo, Interview with Fernando Lobo.

17. Octavio Vélez Ascencio, "Asesinan en Oaxaca a jefe policiaco acusado de represor," *La Jornada*, 31 de enero de 2008, *https://www.jornada.com.mx/2008/01/31/index.php?section=politica&article=003n1pol*

18. Octavio Vélez Ascencio, "Asesinan en Oaxaca a un ex jefe policiaco acusado de liderar ataques contra la APPO", *La Jornada,* 24 de enero de 2009, *https://www.jornada.com.mx/2009/01/24/index.php?section=politica&article=011n1pol*

19. Octavio Vélez y Agustín Galo, "Oaxaca: ejecutan a porros ligados con las caravanas de la muerte," 29 de octubre de 2010, *https://www.jornada.com.mx/2010/10/30/estados/024n1est*

Chapter 11

1. Simón Sedillo, "The Demarest Factor: The Ethics of Department of Defense Funding for Academic Research in Mexico," elenemigocmun.net, March 25, 2009, *https://elenemigocomun.net/2009/03/demarest-factor/*

2. Ibid.

3. Maximilian C. Forte, "Imperial Instruction: The Human Terrain System's Academic Trainers, Part 1, ZERO ANTHROPOLOGY," May 20, 2010, *https://zeroanthropology.net/2010/05/20/imperial-instruction-the-human-terrain-systems-academic-trainers-part-1/*

4. "Human Terrain Mapping, Current Directives," U.S. Department of Energy, Nov 26, 2019, *https://www.directives.doe.gov/terms_definitions/human-terrain-mapping*

5. American Anthropological Association's Executive Board Statement on the Human Terrain System Project, October 31, 2007, *https://s3.amazonaws.com/rdcms-aaa/files/production/public/FileDownloads/pdfs/pdf/EB_Resolution_110807.pdf*

6. Simón Sedillo, "The Demarest Factor."

7. Ibid.

8. A. John Radsan, "THE UNRESOLVED EQUATION OF ESPIONAGE AND INTERNATIONAL LAW," William Mitchell College of Law, Michigan Journal of International Law, MJIL, Vol. 28, Iss. 3, (2007) - *https://repository.law.umich.edu/mjil/vol28/iss3/5/*

9. Simón Sedillo, "The Demarest Factor."

10. Ibid.

11. Ibid.

12. Ibid.

13. Ibid.

14. Ibid.

15. Ibid.

16. Geoffrey Demarest, Benson Kevin, "Winning Insurgent War: Back to Basics," Foreign Military Studies Office, Leavenworth Kansas, February 4, 2004.

Chapter 12

1. Naomi Adelson, "Represión en el paraíso: La PFP, inocencia en entredicho," *La Jornada*, 4 de marzo de 2001. *https://www.jornada.com.mx/2001/03/04/mas-represion.html*

2. Juan Manuel Venegas, "Traza la PFP frontera entre dos visiones antagónicas," *La Jornada*, Septiembre de 2003, *https://www.jornada.com.mx/2003/09/10/022n1eco.php?printver=1&fly*

3. Jaime Aviles, "Se enfrentan altermundistas y policías," *La Jornada*, 28 de mayo de 2004, *https://www.jornada.com.mx/2004/05/29/003n2pol.php*

4. Centro Nacional de Derechos Humanos, "Represión en San Salvador Atenco," CNDH México, https://www.cndh.org.mx/noticia/represion-en-san-salvador-atenco

5. Fernando Lobo, *La insurrección transmitida*, pp. 135-139

6. Claudia Herrera Beltran, "El gobierno se declara en guerra contra el Hampa; inicia acciones en Michoacán." *La Jornada* 12 de diciembre de 2006. https://www.jornada.com.mx/2006/12/12/index.php?article=014n1pol&section=politica

7. Felipe de Jesús Calderón Hinojosa, *Ley de la Policía Federal*. Nueva Ley publicada en el Diario Oficial de la Federación, Cámara de Diputados, 1 de Junio de 2009, https://www.diputados.gob.mx/LeyesBiblio/pdf/LPF.pdf

8. Ciro Pérez Silva, "Propone Calderón al Congreso crear el mando único policial," *La Jornada*, 7 de octubre de 2012, https://www.jornada.com.mx/2010/10/07/politica/009n1pol

9. Clare Ribando Seelke, Kristin Finklea, "U.S.-Mexican Security Cooperation: The Mérida Initiative and Beyond," Congressional Research Service, June 29, 2017, *https://sgp.fas.org/crs/row/R41349.pdf*

10. Sharyl Attkisson, agent: "I was ordered to let U.S. guns into Mexico," CBS Evening News, March 3, 2011, *https://www.cbsnews.com/news/agent-i-was-ordered-to-let-us-guns-into-mexico-03-03-2011/*

11. Patrick Radden Keefe, "A Billion Dollar Narco Junior Cuts a Deal," *The New Yorker*, April 10, 2014, *https://www.newyorker.com/news/news-desk/a-billion-dollar-narco-junior-cuts-a-deal*

12. EFE, Vicente Zambada, 'El Vicentillo', ya no está en una prisión federal de EUA, *The San Diego Union-Tribune en Español*, 30 de abril de 2021, *https://www.sandiegouniontribune.com/en-espanol/noticias/estados-unidos/articulo/2021-04-30/vicente-zambada-el-vicentillo-ya-no-esta-en-una-prision-federal-de-eua*

13. William Finnegan, "The Drug War and Mexico's Election," *The New Yorker,* July 2, 2012, *https://www.newyorker.com/news/news-desk/the-drug-war-and-mexicos-election*

14. 8 videos de enfrentamientos en la marcha del 2 de octubre, Aristegui Noticias, 3 de octubre de 2013, *https://aristeguinoticias.com/0310/mexico/videos-de-enfrentamientos-en-la-marcha-del-2-de-octubre/?fb_comment_id=698366706859245_91159384*

15. Simón Sedillo, "SOA Graduate Takes Control of Security."

16. Ángel Cabrera, "EPN: Legislativo congeló iniciativas de Mando Único," 24 Horas El Diario Sin Límites, 30 de agosto de 2018, *https://www.24-horas.mx/2018/08/30/epn-legislativo-congelo-iniciativas-de-mando-unico/*

17. Avispa Midia, documental *Oaxaca Ingobernable*, elenemigocmun.net, Subversiones, Jarana Films, 5 de octubre de 2016, *https://avispa.org/documental-oaxaca-ingobernable/*

18. Azam Ahmed and Eric Schmitt, "Mexican Military Runs Up Body Count in Drug War," *New York Times*, May 26, 2016, *https://www.nytimes.com/2016/05/27/world/americas/mexican-militarys-high-kill-rate-raises-human-rights-fears.html*

19. "Mexico faces a test to end torture of women by police and military," Amnesty International, July 12, 2016, *https://www.amnesty.org/en/latest/news/2016/07/mexico-s-faces-a-test-to-end-torture-of-women-by-police-and-military/*

20. Pablo Ferri, "México aprueba la Ley de Seguridad Interior pese al repudio y las protestas dentro y fuera del país," *El País*, 15 de diciembre de 2015, *https://elpais.com/internacional/2017/12/15/mexico/1513305281_940878.html*

21. Jorge Monroy, "AMLO perfila mando único en seguridad," *El Economista*, 4 de octubre de 2018, *https://www.eleconomista.com.mx/politica/AMLO-perfila-mando-unico-en-seguridad--20181004-0003.html*

22. School of the Americas Watch, SOA-WHINSEC Graduate Database, Last updated April 6, 2020, *https://soaw.org/category/resources/soa-graduates*

23. Patricia H. Escamilla-Hamm, "The Guardia Nacional (National Guard): Why a New Militarized Police in Mexico," *Small Wars Journal*, 12, August, 2020, *https://smallwarsjournal.com/jrnl/art/guardia-nacional-national-guard-why-new-militarized-police-mexico*

24. Andrés Manuel López Obrador: ACUERDO por el que se dispone de la Fuerza Armada permanente para llevar a cabo tareas de seguridad pública de manera extraordinaria, regulada, fiscalizada, subordinada y complementaria, SEGOB, Diario Oficial de la Federación, 5 de noviembrede 2020, *https://dof.gob.mx/nota_detalle.php?codigo=5593105&fecha=11/05/2020*

25. "Former Mexican Secretary of Public Security Genaro Garcia Luna Charged with Engaging in a Continuing Criminal Enterprise," The United States Attorney's Office Eastern District of New York, July 30, 2020, *https://www.justice.gov/usao-edny/pr/former-mexican-secretary-public-security-genaro-garcia-luna-charged-engaging-continuing*

26. Mary Beth Sheridan, "Former Mexican defense minister arrested on drug charges in U.S., officials say," *The Washington Post*, October 16, 2020, *https://www.washingtonpost.com/world/former-mexican-defense-minister-arrested-on-drug-charges-in-us-officials-say/2020/10/16/25416d84-0f60-11eb-8a35-237ef1eb2ef7_story.html*

27. Joint Statement by Attorney General of the United States William P. Barr and Fiscalía General of Mexico Alejandro Gertz Manero. The United States Department of Justice, Office of Public Affairs, November 17, 2020, *https://www.justice.gov/opa/pr/joint-statement-attorney-general-united-states-william-p-barr-and-fiscal-general-mexico*

28. Nina Pullano, "U.S. Moves to Drop Charges against Mexico's Former Defense Secretary," Courthouse News Service, November 17, 2020, *https://www.courthousenews.com/us-moves-to-drop-charges-against-mexicos-former-defense-secretary/*

29. Tom Phillips, "Outrage after Mexico exonerates ex-defense minister in drug case," *The Guardian*, January 15, 2021, *https://www.theguardian.com/world/2021/jan/15/salvador-cienfuegos-mexico-exonerated-drug-case*

30. Christopher Sherman and Mark Stevenson, "Mexico says U.S. 'fabricated' charges, releases evidence," *AP News*, January 15, 2021, *https://apnews. com/article/mexico-elections-crime-arrests-drug-trafficking-a54eb-46084fd31fa06f5a840eafafa86*

31. James Fredrick, "Mexico's Suit against U.S. Gun Companies May Seek More Than Court Win," *National Public Radio*, August 7, 2021, *https://www. npr.org/2021/08/07/1025636092/mexico-lawsuit-united-states-gun-com-panies-analysis*

32. Summary of Action Plan for U.S.-Mexico Bicentennial Framework for Security, Public Health, and Safe Communities, Fact Sheet, U.S. Department of State, January 31, 2022, *https://www.state.gov/summary-of-the-ac-tion-plan-for-u-s-mexico-bicentennial-framework-for-security-pub-lic-health-and-safe-communities/*

33. Ryan Devereaux, "The U.S. Is Organizing a $5 Million Gun Sale to Mexican Forces Accused of Murder and Kidnapping," *The Intercept*, October 6, 2021, *https://theintercept.com/2021/10/06/mexico-weapons-sale-biden-mur-der-kidnapping/*

Chapter 13

1. "Elites and Organized Crime: Introduction, Methodology, and Conceptual Framework," InSight Crime, Internet Archive, Wayback Machine, April 25, 2016, *https://www.insightcrime.org/images/PDFs/2016/Introduction_Sec-tion_Elites_Organized_Crime*

2. 2018 Country Reports in Human Rights Practices: Mexico, Bureau of Democracy, Human Rights, and Labor, U.S. Department of State, *https:// www.state.gov/reports/2018-country-reports-on-human-rights-practices/ mexico/*

3. Drug Money Laundering, Strategic Findings, National Drug Threat Assess-ment 2006, National Drug Intelligence Center, January 2006 *https://www. justice.gov/archive/ndic/pubs11/18862/money.htm*

4. Nick Robinson, Harvard Law School Center, "Declining Dominance: Lawyers in the U.S. Congress," November/December 2015, *https://thepractice.law. harvard.edu/article/declining-dominance/*

5. Doyle and Franzblau discussion.

6. "Block the Vote: How Politicians are Trying to Block Voters from the Ballot Box," American Civil Liberties Union aclu.org, August 17, 2021, *https://www.aclu.org/news/civil-liberties/block-the-vote-voter-suppression-in-2020/*

7. Andrew Witherspoon and Sam Levine, "These maps show how Republicans are blatantly rigging elections," *The Guardian*, November 12, 2021, *https://www.theguardian.com/us-news/ng-interactive/2021/nov/12/gerrymander-redistricting-map-republicans-democrats-visual*

8. Lee Drutman, "How Corporate Lobbyists Conquered American Democracy," *The Atlantic*, April 20, 2015, *https://www.theatlantic.com/business/archive/2015/04/how-corporate-lobbyists-conquered-american-democracy/390822/*

9. Christine Mahoney, "Why lobbying in America is different," *Politico*, June 4, 2009, *https://www.politico.eu/article/why-lobbying-in-america-is-different/*

10. "Revolving Door, Overview," Open Secrets, *https://www.opensecrets.org/revolving/*

11. Libby Watson, "What is shadow lobbying? How influence peddlers shape policy in the dark," *Sunlight Foundation*, April 19, 2016, *https://sunlightfoundation.com/2016/04/19/what-is-shadow-lobbying-how-influence-peddlers-shape-policy-in-the-dark/*

Chapter 14

1. "A History of the Drug War," *Drug Policy Alliance*, 2022, *https://drugpolicy.org/issues/brief-history-drug-war*

2. Dan Baum, "Legalize it All: How to win the war on drugs," *Harper's Magazine*, April, 2016, *https://harpers.org/archive/2016/04/legalize-it-all/*

3. German Lopez, "The war on drugs, explained," Vox, May 8, 2016, *https://www.vox.com/2016/5/8/18089368/war-on-drugs-marijuana-cocaine-heroin-meth*

4. Pedro Rios, "For 25 years, Operation Gatekeeper has made life worse for border communities," *The Washington Post*, October 1, 2019, *https://www.washingtonpost.com/outlook/2019/10/01/years-operation-gatekeeper-has-made-life-worse-border-communities/*

5. Ryan Devereaux, $5 Million Gun Sale

6. Claudia Herrera Beltran, "El gobierno se declara en guerra contra el Hampa; inicia acciones en Michoacán," *La Jornada*, 12 de diciembre de 2006. *https://www.jornada.com.mx/2006/12/12/index.php?article=014n1pol&section=política*

7. Ribando and Finklea discussion

8. "México tramita en EE UU la compra de armamento por 5.5 millones de dólares," *El País*, 3 de agosto de 2021, *https://elpais.com/mexico/2021-08-03/mexico-tramita-en-ee-uu-la-compra-de-armamento-por-55-millones-de-dolares.html*

9. "Neither Rights nor Security: Killings, Torture, and Disappearances in Mexico's 'War on Drugs,'" Human Rights Watch 2011, *https://reliefweb.int/sites/reliefweb.int/files/resources/Full_Report_2842.pdf*

10. Genaro Garcia Luna charged with criminal enterprise.

11. Maureen Meyer, "Mexico Supreme Court Overturns Controversial Security Law," Washington Office on Latin America, November 15, 2018, *https://www.wola.org/2018/11/mexico-supreme-court-overturns-controversial-security-law/*

12. Iñigo Guevara Moyano, "Mexico's National Guard: When Police are Not Enough," Wilson Center, Mexico Institute, January 2020, *https://www.wilsoncenter.org/sites/default/files/media/uploads/documents/Mexico%27s%20National%20Guard.pdf*

13. Associated Press, "Mexican cartels are turning to meth and fentanyl production," National Public Radio, December 21, 2021, *https://www.npr.org/2021/12/21/1066163872/mexican-cartels-turning-to-meth-and-fentanyl-production*

Chapter 15

1. "International Narcotics Control Strategy Report," U.S. Department of State, Report, Bureau of International Narcotics and law Enforcement Affairs, March 2, 2021, *https://www.state.gov/2021-international-narcotics-control-strategy-report/*

2. "To Murder in Mexico: Impunity Guaranteed," *Animal Politico*, *https://www.animalpolitico.com/kill-murder-mexico/*

3. "Homenaje a Peribán," *Tejemedios*, 24 de junio de 2014, *https://www.youtube.com/watch?v=mwflOL95eNw*

4. Ibid.

Chapter 16

1. Kenneth Pletcher, "Opium Wars, Chinese History," britannica.com, *https://www.britannica.com/topic/Opium-Wars*

2. Erin Blakemore, "America's First Multimillionaire Got Rich Smuggling Opium," History.com, August 22, 2018, *https://www.history.com/news/john-jacob-astor-opium-fortune-millionaire*

3. Alexandra Hall, "The New Brahmins," *Boston Magazine*, May 15, 2006, *https://www.bostonmagazine.com/2006/05/15/the-new-brahmins/*

4. Linda Poon, "Opium Dens Are a Terrible Theme for Bars." The anti-immigrant history behind these spaces should make you reconsider casting the stereotypical drug den as the inspiration for a lounge. *Bloomberg CityLab*, Government, May 31, 2017. *https://www.bloomberg.com/news/articles/2017-05-31/the-problem-with-opium-den-themed-bars-and-restaurants*

5. Gardiner Harris, "Fort Knox Vaults Harbor Millions in Opium, Morphine – Stockpile Held For Emergencies." *The Seattle Times*, September 16, 1993, https://archive.seattletimes.com/archive/?date=19930916&slug=1721425

6. Fact Sheet from the U.S. Mint obtained through FOIA Request #2017-09-205, Release Date April 6, 2018, *https://www.governmentattic.org/30docs/VisitBullionDepositFtKnox_2017.pdf*

7. Roberts, Joyce, "VIETNAM VETERANS AND ILLICIT DRUG USE," 2017. Electronic Theses, Projects, and Dissertations. 548. *https://scholarworks.lib.csusb.edu/etd/548*

8. National Institute on Drug Abuse, Opioids, Opioid Overdose Crisis, National Institute on Drug Abuse Advancing Addiction Science, *https://nida.nih.gov/drug-topics/opioids/opioid-overdose-crisis*

9. "Lobbyists, 2021, Pharmaceuticals/Health Products," *Open Secrets*: Following the Money in Politics, *https://www.opensecrets.org/federal-lobbying/industries/summary?id=H04*

10. Jay Hancock, "Drug Trade Group Quietly Spends 'Dark Money' To Sway Policy and Voters," KHN July 30, 2018, *https://khn.org/news/drug-trade-group-quietly-spends-dark-money-to-sway-policy-and-voters/*

11. Scott Higham, Lenny Bernstein, Steven Rich and Alice Crites, "Drug industry hired dozens of officials from the DEA as the agency tried to curb opioid abuse," *Washington Post*, December 22, 2016, *https://www.washingtonpost.com/investigations/key-officials-switch-sides-from-dea-to-pharmaceutical-industry/2016/12/22/55d2e938-c07b-11e6-b527-949c5893595e_story.html*

12. Scott Higham and Lenny Bernstein, "The Drug Industries Triumph over the DEA," *Washington Post*, October 15, 2017, *https://www.washingtonpost.com/graphics/2017/investigations/dea-drug-industry-congress*

13. Bill Whitaker, "Meet 60 Minutes DEA Whistleblower," Interview with DEA Investigator Joseph Rannazzisi, *60 Minutes*, October 17, 2017, *https://www.cbsnews.com/news/meet-60-minutes-dea-whistleblower/*

14. "U.S. Drug Overdose Deaths Remain High," Centers for Disease Control and Prevention, Maps and Graphs, 2021, *https://www.cdc.gov/drugoverdose/deaths/index.html*

15. Erin McCormick, "Historically tragic: Why are drug overdoses rising among Black and Indigenous Americans?" *The Guardian*, February 17, 2022, *https://www.theguardian.com/us-news/2022/feb/17/black-native-americans-fentanyl-deaths-rise-opioid-crisis*

16. Opioid Settlement Tracker, "The Curious Case of the Cherokee Nation," January 30, 2020, *https://www.opioidsettlementtracker.com/blog/cherokee*

17. Gabrielle Emanuel and Vanessa Romo, "Pharmaceutical Executive John Kapoor Sentenced to 66 Months in Prison in Opioid Trial," National Public Radio (NPR), January 23, 2020, *https://www.npr.org/2020/01/23/798973304/pharmaceutical-executive-john-kapoor-sentenced-to-66-months-in-prison-in-opioid*

18. Brian Mann, "The Sacklers, Who Made Billions from OxyContin, Win Immunity from Opioid Lawsuits," *National Public Radio* (NPR), September 1, 2021, *https://www.npr.org/2021/09/01/1031053251/sackler-family-immunity-purdue-pharma-oxcyontin-opioid-epidemic*

19. Steve Inskeep and Brian Mann, "Judge rejects Purdue Pharma's opioid settlement that would protect Sackler family," *National Public Radio* (NPR), December 17, 2021, *https://www.npr.org/2021/12/17/1065083175/judge-rejects-purdue-pharmas-opioid-settlement-that-would-protect-sackler-family*

20. Brian Mann, "Sackler Family Transferred Money To Swiss Bank Accounts, New York AG Says," *National Public Radio* (NPR), September 14, 2019, *https://www.npr.org/2019/09/14/760794331/sackler-family-transferred-money-to-swiss-bank-accounts-new-york-ag-says*

21. Will Fitzgibbon, "As American Public Turned to Opioids, OxyContin's Founder Tapped a Private Swiss Bank," International Consortium for Investigative Journalists, October 22, 2018, *https://www.icij.org/investigations/swiss-leaks/as-american-public-turned-to-opioids-oxycontins-founder-tapped-a-private-swiss-bank/*

Chapter 17

1. "HSBC was born from one simple idea – a local bank serving international needs," HSBC Company History, *https://www.about.hsbc.it/our-company/company-histor*

2. Jean-Louis Conne, "HSBC: Chinese for making money," *Le Monde diplomatique*, Maritime business and the opium trade, February 2010, *https://mondediplo.com/2010/02/04hsbc*

3. Ibid:

4. Statement of Facts, Deferred Prosecution Agreement (DPA) between the United States Department of Justice, Criminal Division, Asset Forfeiture and Money Laundering Section; the United States Attorney's Office for the Eastern District of New York and the United States Attorney's Office for the Northern District of West Virginia (collectively, the Department) and HSBC Bank USA, N.A. (HSBC Bank USA); and HSBC Holdings plc (HSBC Holdings), Department of Justice, Office of Public Affairs, December 11, 2012, *https://www.justice. gov/sites/default/files/opa/legacy/2012/12/11/dpa-attachment-a.pdf*

5. Francine McKenna, "HSBC wasn't prosecuted because it was too big to fail," House committee, MarketWatch, July 11, 2016, *https://www.market-watch.com/story/house-committee-says-hsbc-wasnt-prosecuted-due-to-too-big-to-jail-fears-2016-07-11*

6. Dominic Rushe and Jill Treanor, "HSBC's record $1.9bn fine preferable to prosecution, U.S. authorities insist," *The Guardian*, December 11, 2012, *https://www.theguardian.com/business/2012/dec/11/hsbc-fine-prosecu-tion-money-laundering*

7. Alan Zibel and Brent Kendall, "Banks May Be Too Large to Prosecute," *Wall Street Journal*, March 6, 2013, *https://www.wsj.com/articles/BL-WB-37939*

8. Aruna Viswanatha, "Ex-DOJ criminal chief Breuer returns to Covington & Burling," *Reuters*, March 28, 2013, *https://www.reuters.com/article/jus-tice-breuer-idINL2N0CJ1OC20130328*

9. C. Ryan Barber, "Finalist for White Collar/Regulatory Litigation Department of the Year," *The American Lawyer Magazine*, December 20, 2017, *https:// www.law.com/americanlawyer/2017/12/20/the-regulator-whisper-ers-covington-burling-finalist-for-white-collarregulatory-litigation-depart-ment-of-the-year/?slreturn=20220224150128*

10. Jill Treanor, "Swiss authorities raided the Geneva, Switzerland offices of HSBC," *The Guardian*, February 18, 2015, *https://www.theguardian.com/ news/2015/feb/18/hsbc-swiss-bank-searched-as-officials-launch-money-laundering-inquiry*

11. "HSBC to pay 40M Swiss francs in Geneva money-laundering probe," *Reuters* with *CNBC*, June 4, 2015, *https://www.cnbc.com/2015/06/04/hsbc-to-pay-40m-swiss-francs-in-geneva-money-laundering-probe.html*

12. Brett Wolf, "U.S. Treasury anti-laundering head to join HSBC: sources," *Reuters,* April 26, 2016, *https://www.reuters.com/article/us-banks-money-laundering-hsbc-idUSKCN0XN2W7*

13. BuzzFeed News. HSBC Monitor Quarterly Update, U.S. Department of Justice report to U.S. District Judge Ann M. Donnelly, March 31, 2017, *https://www.documentcloud.org/documents/7213513-BuzzFeed-News-HSBC-Monitor-Quarterly-Update.html*

14. HSBC Holdings plc, "Expiration of 2012 Deferred Prosecution Agreement," December 11, 2017, *https://www.hsbc.com/news-and-media/media-releases/2017/hsbc-holdings-plc-expiration-of-2012-deferred-prosecution-agreement*

15. "Justice Department Announces Deferred Prosecution Agreement with HSBC Private Bank (Suisse) SA," United States Department of Justice, Office of Public Affairs, December 10, 2019, *https://www.justice.gov/opa/pr/justice-department-announces-deferred-prosecution-agreement-hsbc-private-bank-suisse-sa*

16. *Leopold v. U.S. Dep't of Justice*, Civil Action No.: 19-3192, January 13, 2021, *https://casetext.com/case/leopold-v-us-dept-of-justice-3*

17. "Alleged Money Launderers for Mexican Cartels Indicted," Department of Justice U.S. Attorney's Office for the Southern District of California, November 16, 2021, *https://www.justice.gov/usao-sdca/pr/alleged-money-launderers-mexican-cartels-indicted*

18. Anthony Cormier, Jason Leopold, Tom Warren, Scott Pham, John Templeton, Jeremy Singer-Vine, Richard Holmes, Michael Sallah, Tanya Kozyreva, and Emma Loop, "The Untold Story of What Really happened After HSBC, El Chapo's Bank, Promised to Get Clean," BuzzFeed in Collaboration with the International Consortium of Investigative Journalists, September 21, 2020, *https://www.buzzfeednews.com/article/anthonycormier/hsbc-money-laundering-drug-cartels*

19. "Press Release: Wachovia Enters into Deferred Prosecution Agreement," The United States Attorney's Office, Southern District of Florida, March 17, 2010, *https://www.justice.gov/archive/usao/fls/PressReleases/2010/100317-02.html*

20. Cormier, et al. The untold story of HSBC promises

21. International Consortium of Investigative Journalists, "Global banks defy U.S. crackdowns by serving oligarchs, criminals and terrorists," September 20, 2020, *https://www.icij.org/investigations/fincen-files/global-banks-defy-u-s-crackdowns-by-serving-oligarchs-criminals-and-terrorists/*

Chapter 18

1. "Finding Aid, Holocaust-Era Assets," Military Agency Records, *https://www.archives.gov/research/holocaust/finding-aid/military/part-1-notes.html*

2. Timothy L. O'Brien, "Chase Reviews Nazi-Era Role," *The New York Times*, November 7, 1998, *https://www.nytimes.com/1998/11/07/world/chase-reviews-nazi-era-role.html*

3. "About BIS - overview," Bank for International Settlements, *https://www.bis.org/about/index.htm?m=1_1*

4. Adam LeBor, "How bankers helped the Nazis," *Sydney Morning Herald*, August 1, 2013, *https://www.smh.com.au/business/how-bankers-helped-the-nazis-20130801-2r1fd.html*

5. Gregg Fields, "The Tower of Institutional Corruption: The Bank for International Settlements in the Nightmare Years," Harvard University's Edmond J. Safra Center for Ethics, July 2, 2013, *https://ethics.harvard.edu/blog/tower-institutional-corruption*

6. Agustín Carstens - General Manager, "About BIS, governance and organization," *https://www.bis.org/about/bioac.htm*

7. Uzan, Marc. "Bretton Woods: The Next 70 Years," (PDF). Econometrics Laboratory - University of California, Berkeley, *https://eml.berkeley.edu/~eichengr/Bretton-Woods-next-70.pdf*

8. Ibid.

9. "Nixon and the End of the Bretton Woods System, 1971–1973," U.S. Department of State, Office of the Historian, Milestones, 1969-1976, *https://history.state.gov/milestones/1969-1976/nixon-shock*

10. Will Kenton, "International Monetary Fund," *Investopedia*, 2020, *https://www.investopedia.com/terms/i/imf.asp*

11. Will Kenton, "World Bank," *Investopedia*, 2021, *https://www.investope-dia.com/terms/w/worldbank.asp*

12. Robert Lensink, "Structural Adjustment in Sub-Saharan Africa," Longman Group United Kingdom, February 1, 1996

13. Howard White, "Adjustment in Africa," *Development and Change,* 1996, Vol. 27, issue 4, *https://econpapers.repec.org/article/bladevchg/v_3a27_3 ay_3a1996_3ai_3a4_3ap_3a785-815.htm*

14. Walden Bello, "Deglobalization: Ideas for a New World Economy," *Global Issues*, June 1, 2004, p. 43.

Chapter 19

1. Simòn Sedillo,"Self-Determination and Self-Defense in Cherán, Micho-acán," *elenemigocomun.net*, *https://elenemigocomun.net/2013/01/ self-determination-defense-cheran/*

2. Ibid.

3. *Celebrating Seven Years of Self Governance in Cherán*, August 1, 2018, *https://www.youtube.com/watch?v=oDspeScGZrQ*

4. *Guarda Bosques,* Manovuelta Films, *https://www.youtube.com/ watch?v=vIJ_Ld2kvOk*

5. Ibid.

6. *Caminando Hacia la Autonomía*, TV Cherán, *https://www.youtube.com/ watch?v=XNFyREo3c68*

7. *Guarda Bosques,* Manovuelta Films

8. *Caminando Hacia la Autonomía,* TV Cherán

9. Ibid.

10. *Guarda Bosques*, Manovuelta Films

11. *Caminando Hacia la Autonomía,* TV Cherán

12. *Guarda Bosques,* Manovuelta Films

13. Ibid.

14. *Seven Years of Self Governance*, TV Cherán

15. *Guarda Bosques*, Manovuelta Films

16. Ninx Salvaje and Regina López, "Cherán community says no to single police command," March 17, 2016, *https://elenemigocomun.net/2016/03/cheran-no-single-police-command/*

17. "Indigenous Self Determination Threatened in Michoacán," elenemigocomun.net, August 19, 2013, *https://elenemigocomun.net/2013/08/indigenous-self-determination-threatened-michoacan/*

Chapter 20

1. Rolando Pacheco & Simón Sedillo, "Workshop on Mesoamerican Indigenous Principles of Unity and Resistance," National Conference on Organized Resistance (NCOR), American University, Washington, DC, 2005.

2. Assata Shakur, *Assata: An Autobiography*, Lawrence Hill Books, 1988, p. 260.

3. Assata Shakur, *Autobiogaphy* (02), p. 152.

4. Assata Shakur *Autobiography* (03), p. 181.

5. Assata Shakur *Autobiography* (04), p. 139.

6. "Simple Sabotage Field Manual," Homeland Security Digital Library, United States. War Department. Strategic Services Unit, Original publication 1944, *https://www.hsdl.org/?view&did=750070*

Glossary

Academic Industrial Complex - All educational institutions, but particularly higher learning institutions such as colleges and universities, their administrators and professors, and the industries they work with or feed into directly and indirectly. In countries like the United States and Chile, for example, the private higher education industry also includes its own student debt industry which stands aside from the Banking Industrial Complex because of its relationship to higher education.

Acculturation - The stripping of an individual or groups culture, in order to replace it or merge it with another culture.

Activist Imperialism - The imposition by activists of ideas about change in a community or their belief that they know best, without consulting the community.

Agents of neoliberalism - The institutions, industries, nations, and people who benefit the most from the neoliberal military political economy.

Agribusiness - The business of industrial agriculture.

Agricultural Industrial Complex - Agribusiness and the government policies around it; this industrial complex is included in the Business Industrial Complex but is vast enough in its political and economic power, scope, and influence to be designated as its very own complex.

Americanism - (According to Merriam-Webster), an attachment or allegiance to the traditions, interests, or ideals of the United States.

Anarchism - (According to Merriam-Webster), a political theory holding all forms of governmental authority to be unnecessary and undesirable and advocating a society based on voluntary co-operation and free association of individuals and groups.

Anglicanism - White male Christian beliefs, particularly associated with England.

Assimilation - (According to Wikipedia), the process in which a minority group or culture comes to resemble a society's majority group or assume the values, behaviors, and beliefs of another group whether fully or partially.

Asymmetric threats (warfare) - (According to Britannica), unconventional strategies and tactics adopted by a force when the military capabilities of belligerent powers are not simply unequal but are so significantly different that they cannot make the same sorts of attacks on each other. Guerrilla warfare, occurring between lightly armed partisans and a conventional army, is an example of asymmetrical warfare. Terrorist tactics, such as hijackings and suicide bombings, are also considered to be asymmetrical, both because they tend to involve a smaller, weaker group attacking a stronger one and also because attacks on civilians are by definition one-way warfare. War between a country that is both able and willing to use nuclear weapons and a country that is not would be another example of asymmetrical warfare.

Atrocities - (According to Merriam-Webster), shockingly bad or atrocious acts, objects, or situations.

Austerity Measures - Stern or severe policies of cutting government spending and increasing taxes.

Authoritarian - (According to Merriam-Webster), of, relating to, or favoring blind submission to authority, for example, 'someone had authoritarian parents'; of, relating to, or favoring a concentration of power in a leader or an elite not constitutionally responsible to the people, for example, 'an authoritarian regime.'

Autonomy- (According to Merriam-Webster), the quality or state of being self-governing, especially the right of self-government.

Banking Industrial Complex - All banks and international financial institutions, as well as financial regulatory agencies and institutions, chambers of commerce, international trade and investment, the stock market, and monetary regulating institutions. It is important to note that banks usually hold controlling interest in most transnational corporations as well, and are the largest holders and purveyors of private property in the world. One way or another, banks and financial institutions also hold and benefit from all business activity, be it public or private, legitimate or criminal.

Billionaire Industrial Complex - May not be considered an industrial complex in itself by other analysts; however, in addition to benefiting from one or another of the other industrial complexes, these 2755 billionaires merit their own personal mention because of the amount of wealth and power concentrated among such a small number of individuals in the world.

Bipartisan - (According to Merriam-Webster), marked by or involving cooperation, agreement, and compromise between two major political parties.

BIPOC - Black Indigenous & People of Color.

Black Operations - (According to Wikipedia), a covert or clandestine operation by a government agency, a military unit or a paramilitary organization; can include activities by private companies or groups. Key features of a black operation are that it is secret and it is not attributable to the organization carrying it out. Such secrecy is often needed for deniability, due to the sometimes illegal or unethical nature of such operations.

Business Industrial Complex - Transnational corporations and the business industries in which they engage. This is the most diverse of the industrial complexes in that it includes all of the manufacturing industries, such as weapons, transportation, consumer goods, electronics, chemicals, pharmaceuticals, paper, printing and publishing, plastics, industrial equipment, furniture and fixtures, building materials, fashion, sporting goods, toys, household goods, etc. It would also include the entire food and animal feed industry, such as agriculture, food processing, food packaging, food storage and transportation, etc. There is also the entire media communications industry, including telecommunications, TV, film and video, photo, radio, newspapers magazines and books etc. The Business Industrial Complex is such a giant that it has to be broken down into several smaller parts in order to be digested, however when treated as its own entire independent industrial complex, we can fathom the vastness of its political and economic power, scope, and influence.

Business Political Elite - Wealthy business and political interests working in coordination to maintain wealth and power

Capitalism - A financial or economic system for making money by any means necessary.

Capitalist imperialism -The taking of land, labor, and resources by force for money and power.

Civil disobedience - (According to Merriam-Webster), refusal to obey governmental demands or commands especially as a nonviolent and usually collective means of forcing concessions from the government.

Civilian - (According to Merriam-Webster), a person not on active duty in the armed services or not on a police or firefighting force.

Climate Crisis - (According to Wikipedia), a term describing global warming, climate change, and their impacts.

Cold War - (According to Wikipedia), a period of geopolitical tension between the United States and the Soviet Union and their respective allies, the Western Bloc and the Eastern Bloc, which began following World War II and lasted for more than 40 years, from March 12, 1947 to December 26, 1991.

Colonialism - (According to Merriam-Webster), the domination of a people or area by a foreign state or nation: the practice of extending and maintaining a nation's political and economic control over another people or area.

Commandeer - (According to Merriam-Webster), to take arbitrary or forcible possession of something.

Commerce - (According to Merriam-Webster), the exchange or buying and selling of commodities on a large scale involving transportation from place to place.

Communal Ownership - (According to Merriam-Webster), the ownership of land or other property by a community so that each member has a right to use the property or a portion of it.

Communal property - Collectively owned property, in direct opposition to private property ownership.

Communism - (According to Merriam-Webster), a system in which goods are owned in common and are available to all as needed; a theory advocating the elimination of private property.

Community-based - The process of making collective decisions by the majority if not by all community members.

Community-Based Autonomy - The process of collective self-governance by the majority if not all community members.

Community-Based Liberation - The process of collective struggling for liberation by the majority if not all community members.

Community-Based Self-Defense - The process of defending a community by the majority if not by all community members.

Community-Based Self-Determination - The process of community decision-making by the majority if not by all community members.

Community Rights - The collective rights of an entire community and not just those of individuals within the community.

Conservative - (According to Merriam-Webster), the principles and policies of a Conservative party; the Conservative party. Disposition in politics to preserve what is established or a political philosophy based on tradition and social stability, stressing established institutions, and preferring gradual development to abrupt change specifically; a philosophy calling for lower taxes, limited government regulation of business and investing, a strong national defense, and individual financial responsibility for personal needs (such as retirement income or health-care coverage).

Conspicuous - (According to Merriam-Webster), obvious to the eye or mind.

Consumerism - (According to Merriam-Webster), the theory that an increasing consumption of goods is economically desirable; a preoccupation with and an inclination toward the buying of consumer goods.

Corporate - (According to Merriam-Webster), having qualities such as commercialism or lack of originality associated with large corporations or attributed to their influence or control.

Corruption - (According to Merriam-Webster), dishonest or illegal behavior especially by powerful people such as government officials or police officers.

Counterinsurgency - (According to Merriam-Webster), organized military activity designed to combat insurgency.

Counterintelligence - (According to Merriam-Webster), organized activity of an intelligence service designed to block an enemy's sources of information, to deceive the enemy, to prevent sabotage, and to gather political and military information.

Criminalize - (According to Merriam-Webster), to make illegal; to turn into a criminal or treat as criminal.

Currency - Currency today is basically just money. Formally it is a "recognized unit of exchange," but when we say currency, we basically mean money. Today there are new types of money or currency such as digital currency, frequent flier miles, and corporate bucks, etc. For purposes of this discussion, think about money in terms of bills, like a dollar bill, or a 20 peso bill. Nationally, money works because the government of a country and the people of that country basically agree that a valueless piece of paper, does indeed have an actual value.

Decentralized autonomous direct actions - Direct actions carried out by group or individuals with no form of centralized coordination or command.

Declassified documents - Documents that are no longer considered to be secret, though at some point they were classified as secret.

Democracy - (According to Merriam-Webster), government by the people; rule of the majority.

Democratization - Although the literal meaning is to make democratic, in reality and in particular with regards to U.S. foreign policy, democratization is more often than not associated with the imposition of the U.S. military political economy of neoliberalism.

Democrats in the USA - (According to Merriam-Webster), a member of the Democratic party of the United States.

Deniable Atrocities - Outrages such as extrajudicial executions, kidnappings, beatings, rape, and torture carried out against a civilian population in such a way that governments, police, or the military can deny involvement in and/or responsibility for them, once committed. These barbarous actions are used to dissuade social, political, or economic opposition.

Depoliticize - (According to Britannica), to change something so that it is no longer influenced or controlled by politics.

Deregulation - (According to Merriam-Webster), the act or process of removing restrictions and regulations.

Devaluation - (According to Merriam-Webster), an official reduction in the exchange value of a currency by a lowering of its gold equivalency or its value relative to another currency; a lessening especially of status or stature.

Dignity - (According to Merriam-Webster), the quality or state of being worthy, honored, or esteemed.

Direct action - A physical action taken for a political or social end.

Dirty War (Mexico) - (According to Wikipedia), a reference to the Mexican theater of the Cold War, an internal conflict in the 1960s and 1980s initiated by the Mexican PRI-ruled government under the presidencies of Gustavo Díaz Ordaz, Luis Echeverría and José López Portillo, backed by the U.S. government, against left-wing student and guerrilla groups.

Disappearances - Acts carried out by unofficial paramilitary and official government forces from the Dirty War era up to now. During the Dirty War it was particularly political dissidents who were apprehended without any sort of judicial process, never to be seen again. Today it seems that anyone can disappear in Mexico for any number of reasons, many with no direct connection to any political or criminal activity whatsoever. During the official Dirty War era throughout Latin America, some of the disappeared people ended up in secret prisons or concentration camps (sometimes for years on end) with absolutely no paperwork, no tracking system, no access to attorneys, and absolutely no way of being found by family members or friends. Others were permanently disappeared, with absolutely no trace of them, or their bodies ever again. Disappearances are acts of terror not necessarily intended for the disappeared. Disappearances are acts of terror more specifically intended for those left behind, the family and friends of the disappeared. Disappearances are intended to terrorize entire communities if not entire countries into submission and silence. Disappearances are about controlling entire populations with fear.

Displace - (According to Merriam-Webster), to remove from the usual or proper place, specifically; to expel or force to flee from home or homeland.

Disposable Variable - One or more persons or things deemed discardable or worthless.

Doctrine of Discovery - (According to Wikipedia), a concept of public international law expounded by the United States Supreme Court in a series of decisions, most notably *Johnson v. M'Intosh* in 1823. Chief Justice John Marshall explained and applied the way that colonial powers laid claim to lands belonging to foreign sovereign nations during the Age of Discovery. Under it, European Christian governments could lay title to non-European territory on the basis that the colonizers travelled and "discovered" said territory. The doctrine has been primarily used to support decisions invalidating or ignoring aboriginal possession of land in favor of modern governments, such as in the 2005 case of *Sherrill v. Oneida Nation*.

Domesticate - (According to Merriam-Webster), to adapt an animal or plant over time, especially by selective breeding. from a wild or natural state to life in close association with and to the benefit of humans.

Dominant media narrative - The portrayal assigned to a given story by the mainstream media.

Due Diligence - (According to Merriam-Webster), the care that a reasonable person exercises to avoid harm to other persons or their property.

Economic Liberalism - A political and economic ideology derived from strong support for a market economy based on individual lines and private property in the means of production. Economic liberals tend to oppose government intervention and protectionism in the market when it inhibits free trade and open competition, but support government intervention to protect property rights and resolve market failures. Economic liberalism has been generally described as representing the economic expression of classical liberalism until the Great Depression and rise of Keynesianism.

Economics - (According to Merriam-Webster), a social science concerned chiefly with description and analysis of the production, distribution, and consumption of goods and services.

Economic System - (According to Wikipedia), a system of production, resource allocation and distribution of goods and services within a society or a given geographic area. It includes the combination of the various institutions, agencies, entities, decision-making processes and patterns of consumption that comprise the economic structure of a given community.

Ecosystem - (According to Merriam-Webster), the complex of a community of organisms and its environment functioning as an ecological unit.

Ejido - (According to Merriam-Webster), a system of communal land tenure in Mexico.

Electoral Politics - A system of politics based upon elections.

Emerging threats – While asymmetric threats to the national security of the United States assessed by the Foreign Military Service Office (FMSO) refer to guerrilla armies and terrorist organizations, emerging threats are not clearly defined, but by deduction, can be taken to mean social movements, particularly urban or indigenous social movements.

Empire - (According to Britannica), a group of countries or regions controlled by one ruler or one government.

Environmentalism - The work of protecting the natural environment from anything that would cause it harm.

Espionage - (According to Britannica), the things that are done to find out secrets from enemies or competitors; the activity of spying.

Ethnicity - (According to Britannica), of or relating to races or large groups of people who have the same customs, religion, origin, etc.

Euro - (According to Britannica), a monetary unit used by countries of the European Union since 1999.

Exonerate - (According to Britannica), to prove that someone is not guilty of a crime or responsible for a problem, bad situation, etc.

Expansionism - (According to Britannica), the belief that a country should grow larger; a policy of increasing a country's size by expanding its territory.

Exploit - (According to Britannica), to use someone or something in a way that helps you unfairly.

Export - (According to Britannica), to send a product to be sold in another country.

Expropriate - (According to Britannica), to take someone's property; used especially when a government takes property for public use.

Extralegal - (According to Merriam-Webster), not regulated or sanctioned by law.

Extractivism - (According to Wikipedia), the process of extracting natural resources from the Earth to sell on the world market. It exists in an economy that depends primarily on the extraction or removal of natural resources that are considered valuable for exportation worldwide. Some examples of resources that are obtained through extraction include gold, diamonds, lumber and oil. This economic model has become popular in many Latin American countries, and is becoming increasingly prominent in other regions as well.

Extrajudicial Execution - (According to Wikipedia), the killing of a person by governmental authorities without the sanction of any judicial proceeding or legal process, other than in lawful military and police operations. Political, trade union, dissident, religious and social figures are often targeted.

Extramural - (According to Merriam-Webster), existing or functioning outside or beyond the walls, boundaries, or precincts of an organized unit (such as a school or hospital).

Fair Wage or Living Wage - (According to Wikipedia), the minimum income necessary for workers to meet their basic needs. This is not the same as a subsistence wage, which refers to a biological minimum. Needs are defined to include food, housing, and other essential necessities such as clothing.

Fascism - (According to Merriam-Webster), a political philosophy, movement, or regime (such as that of the Fascisti) that exalts nation and often race above the individual and that stands for a centralized autocratic government headed by a dictatorial leader, severe economic and social regimentation, and forcible suppression of opposition.

Financial - (According to Britannica), relating to money.

Financial Institutions - (According to Wikipedia), sometimes called banking institutions, these are business entities that provide services as intermediaries for different types of financial monetary transactions. Broadly speaking, there are three major types of financial institutions: 1. Depository institutions - deposit-taking institutions that accept and manage deposits and make loans, including banks, building societies, credit unions, trust companies, and mortgage loan companies. 2. Contractual institutions - insurance companies and pension funds. 3. Investment institutions - investment banks, underwriters, and other different types of financial entities managing investments.

Fogata - Literally means campfire, but in Cherán, Michoacán particularly refers to campfire barricades as community-based self-governing organizing spaces.

Food Manufacture Industrial Complex - Part of the Business Industrial Complex but vast enough in its political and economic power, scope, and influence to be designated as its very own Industrial Complex.

Foreign Currency Reserves - (According to Investopedia), a currency that is held in large amounts by governments and other institutions as part of their foreign exchange reserves. These reserve currencies usually become the international pricing mechanisms for commodities traded on the global market such as oil, natural gas, gold, and silver, causing other countries to hold this currency to pay for these goods. Currently, the U.S. dollar is the primary reserve currency in the world, kept not only by American banks but by other countries.

Foreign Investment - (According to Investopedia), a practice that involves capital flows from one country to another, granting foreign investors extensive ownership stakes in domestic companies and assets. Foreigners have an active role in management as a part of their investment or an equity stake large enough to enable the investor to influence business strategy. A modern trend leans toward globalization, in which multinational firms have investments in a variety of countries.

Foreign Policy - (According to Britannica), general objectives that guide the activities and relationships of one state in its interactions with other states. The development of foreign policy is influenced by domestic considerations, the policies or behavior of other states, or plans to advance specific geopolitical designs.

Freedom of Information Act (FOIA), USA - (According to Wikipedia), a federal law that requires the full or partial disclosure of previously unreleased information and documents controlled by the United States government upon request. The act defines agency records subject to disclosure, outlines mandatory disclosure procedures, and defines nine exemptions to the statute. The act was intended to make the functions of U.S. government agencies more transparent so that the American public could more easily identify problems in government functioning and put pressure on Congress, agency officials, and the president to address them. The FOIA has been changed repeatedly by both the legislative and executive branches.

Freely floating fiat currencies - (According to Investopedia), government-issued currencies not backed by a commodity such as gold. Fiat money gives central banks greater control over the economy because they can control how much money is printed. Most modern paper currencies, such as the U.S. dollar, are fiat currencies.

Free market - (According to Wikipedia), a system in which the prices for goods and services are self-regulated by buyers and sellers negotiating in an open market without market coercions. In a free market, the laws and forces of supply and demand are free from any intervention by a government or other authority other than those interventions that are made to prohibit market coercions.

Free trade - (According to Wikipedia), a trade policy that does not restrict imports or exports. It can also be understood as the free market idea applied to international trade. In government, free trade is predominantly advocated by political parties that hold economic liberal positions, while economic nationalist and left-wing political parties generally support protectionism, the opposite of free trade.

General Assembly - (According to Wikipedia), an official meeting of the members of an organization or of their representatives.

General Strike - (According to Wikipedia), a form of protest for social or political goals in which participants cease all economic activity, such as, working, attending school, shopping, going to the movies, etc. General strikes are organized by large coalitions of political, social, and labor organizations. General strikes might exclude care workers, such as teachers, doctors, and nurses, since these people leaving their jobs could lead to harm. General strikes may include rallies, marches, boycotts, civil disobedience, non-payment of taxes, and other forms of direct or indirect action.

Geneva Convention on the Rules of War - (According to Wikipedia), four treaties, and three additional protocols that establish international legal standards for humanitarian treatment in war. The singular term Geneva Convention usually denotes the agreements of 1949, negotiated in the aftermath of the Second World War (1939-1945), which updated the terms of the two 1929 treaties and added two new conventions. The Geneva Conventions extensively defines the basic rights of wartime prisoners (civilians and military personnel), establishes protections for the wounded and sick, and provides protections for the civilians in and around a war-zone; moreover, the Geneva Convention defines the rights and protections afforded to non-combatants.

Genocide - (According to Britannica), the deliberate and systematic destruction of a group of people because of their ethnicity, nationality, religion, or race. The term, derived from the Greek *genos* ("race," "tribe," or "nation") and the Latin *cide* ("killing"), was coined by Raphael Lemkin, a Polish-born jurist who served as an adviser to the U.S. Department of War during World War II.

Geopolitics - (According to Merriam-Webster), a study of the influence of such factors as geography, economics, and demography on the politics and especially the foreign policy of a state.

Gerrymandering - (According to Merriam-Webster), the practice of dividing or arranging a territorial unit into election districts in a way that gives one political party an unfair advantage in elections.

Gestapo - (According to Wikipedia), the *Geheime Staatspolizei* (Secret State Police, abbreviated Gestapo) was the official secret police in Nazi Germany and in German-occupied Europe.

Global Financial System - (According to Wikipedia), the worldwide framework of legal agreements, institutions, and both formal and informal economic actors that together facilitate international flows of financial capital for purposes of investment and trade financing.

Globalization - (According to Wikipedia), the process of interaction and integration among people, companies, and governments worldwide. Globalization has accelerated since the 18th century due to advances in transportation and communication technology. This increase in global interactions has caused a growth in international trade and the exchange of ideas, beliefs, and culture. Globalization is primarily an economic process of interaction and integration that is associated with social and cultural aspects. However, disputes and diplomacy are also large parts of the history of globalization, and of modern globalization. Economically, globalization involves goods, services, data, technology, and the economic resources of capital.

Government Intervention - (According to Wikipedia), an economic policy position favoring government intervention in the market process with the intention of correcting market failures and promoting the general welfare of the people. An economic intervention is an action taken by a government or international institution in a market economy in an effort to impact the economy beyond the basic regulation of fraud, enforcement of contracts, and provision of public goods and services.

Grassroots - (According to Merriam-Webster), the basic level of society or of an organization especially as viewed in relation to higher or more centralized positions of power.

Healthcare and Pharmaceuticals Industrial Complex - the entire healthcare industry, including hospitals, clinics, private practices, doctors, nurses, and administrators as well as the entire pharmaceutical industry, biomedical engineering, and research and development industries.

Hinder - (According to Merriam-Webster), to make progress slow or difficult.

Horizontal Power Structures - A reference to people organized collectively and in unity for a common objective and/or against a common threat or enemy. Power that comes from below, from poor people, from workers, from students, from communities, from Indigenous peoples in a horizontal manner, like a large crowd of people or a machete making a path.

Human Rights - (According to Britannica), a basic right such as the right to be treated well or the right to vote, which many societies believe every person should have. Human rights often refer to individual rights and not to collective or communal/community rights.

Human Terrain Mapping or Human Terrain Systems (HTS) - (According to Wikipedia), a United States Army Training and Doctrine Command (TRADOC) support program employing personnel from the social science disciplines, such as anthropology, sociology, political science, regional studies, and linguistics, to provide military commanders and staff with an understanding of the local population (i.e. the "human terrain") in the regions in which they are deployed.

Human Trafficking - (According to Wikipedia), the trade of humans for the purpose of forced labor, sexual slavery, or commercial sexual exploitation for the trafficker or others. This may encompass providing a spouse in the context of forced marriage, or the extraction of organs or tissues, including extraction for surrogacy and ovary removal. Human trafficking can occur within a country or transnationally. Human trafficking is a crime against the person because of the violation of the victim's rights of movement through coercion and because of his or her commercial exploitation. Human trafficking is the trade in people, especially women and children, and does not necessarily involve the movement of the person from one place to another.

Imperialism - (According to Wikipedia), a policy or ideology of extending rule over people and other countries, for the purpose of extending political and economic access, power and control, often through employing hard power, especially military force, but also soft power. While related to the concepts of colonialism and empire, imperialism is a distinct concept that can apply to other forms of expansion and many forms of government involving the forcible taking of land, labor, and resources for power and control.

Import - (According to Merriam-Webster), to bring from a foreign or external source.

Impunity - (According to Merriam-Webster), exemption or freedom from punishment, harm, or loss.

Immunity - (According to Britannica), special protection from what is required for most people by law.

Indigenous - (According to Merriam-Webster), of or relating to the earliest known inhabitants of a place and especially of a place that was colonized by a now-dominant group.

Indigenous ("Indian") Reservation USA - (According to Wikipedia), an area of land held and governed by a federally recognized Native American tribal nation whose government is accountable to the U.S. Bureau of Indian Affairs and not to the state government in which it is located. Some of the country's 574 federally recognized tribes govern more than one of the 326 Indian reservations in the United States, while some share reservations, and others have no reservation at all. Historical piecemeal land allocations under the Dawes Act facilitated sales to non-Native Americans, resulting in some reservations becoming severely fragmented, with pieces of tribal and privately held land being treated as separate enclaves. This jumble of private and public real estate creates significant administrative, political and legal difficulties.

Industrial complex - (According to Wikipedia), a socioeconomic concept whereby businesses become entwined in social or political systems or institutions, creating or bolstering a profit economy from these systems. Such a complex is said to pursue its own financial interests regardless of, and often at the expense of, the best interests of society and individuals. Businesses within an industrial complex may have been created to advance a social or political goal, but mostly profit when the goal is not reached. The industrial complex may profit financially from maintaining socially detrimental or inefficient systems.

Insurgency - (According to Wikipedia), a violent, armed rebellion against authority waged by small, lightly armed bands who practice guerrilla warfare from primarily rural base areas. The key descriptive feature of insurgency is its asymmetric nature: small irregular forces face a large, well-equipped, regular military force state adversary. Due to this asymmetry, insurgents avoid large-scale direct battles, opting instead to blend in with the civilian population (mainly in the countryside) where they gradually expand territorial control and military forces. Insurgency frequently hinges on control of and collaboration with local populations.

Intelligence - (According to Britannica), secret information that a government collects about an enemy or possible enemy.

Inter Caetera - (According to Wikipedia), a papal bull issued by Pope Alexander VI on May 4, 1493, which granted to the Catholic Monarchs King Ferdinand II of Aragon and Queen Isabella I of Castile all lands to the "west and south" of a pole-to-pole line 100 leagues west and south of any of the islands of the Azores or Cape Verde islands.

Internal Security - (According to Wikipedia), the act of keeping peace within the borders of a sovereign state or other self-governing territories, generally by upholding the national law and defending against internal security threats. Responsibility for internal security may range from police to paramilitary forces, and in exceptional circumstances, the military itself.

Intervention - (According to Wikipedia), the military offensive or invasion of a sovereign state.

Investment - (According to Britannica), the act of using money to earn more money; the act of investing money.

Invisible hand - (According to Merriam-Webster), a hypothetical economic force that in a freely competitive market works for the benefit of all.

Irrefutable - (According to Britannica), not able to be proved wrong; not capable of being refuted.

Irregular Warfare - (According to Wikipedia), as defined in United States joint doctrine, "a violent struggle among State and non-State actors for legitimacy and influence over the relevant populations." Concepts associated with irregular warfare are older than the term itself.

Isolationism - (According to Britannica), the belief that a country should not be involved with other countries; a policy of not making agreements or working with other countries.

Keynesian economics, protectionism - (According to Merriam-Webster), the economic theories and programs ascribed to John M. Keynes and his followers; specifically, the advocacy of monetary and fiscal programs by government to increase employment and spending.

Labor - (According to Merriam-Webster), the expenditure of physical or mental effort especially when difficult or compulsory, for example "was sentenced to six months at hard labor"; the services performed by workers for wages as distinguished from those rendered by entrepreneurs for profits; or human activity that provides the goods or services in an economy.

Laissez-faire - (According to Merriam-Webster), a doctrine opposing governmental interference in economic affairs beyond the minimum necessary for the maintenance of peace and property rights.

Land Baron - (According to Merriam-Webster), a baron is a man who possesses great power or influence, and so we surmise that a land baron is a man who possesses great power of influence through the ownership or control of large pieces of land. This is an approximate translation for the Spanish language term *cacique*.

Left - (According to Merriam-Webster), those professing views usually characterized by a desire to reform or overthrow the established order, especially in politics, and usually by advocacy of change in the name of the greater freedom or well-being of the common man; a radical as distinguished from a conservative position.

Legalese - (According to Merriam-Webster), the specialized language of the legal profession.

Legal Industrial Complex - Overlaps with the prison industrial complex but also includes the wide variety of lawyers outside of the criminal justice system. It also overlaps with the Political Industrial Complex in terms of legislation and public policy and regulations.

Legislation - (According to Merriam-Webster), the action of legislating; specifically, the exercise of the power and function of making rules (such as laws) that have the force of authority by virtue of their promulgation by an official organ of a state or other organization.

Legislative - (According to Merriam-Webster), having the power or performing the function of legislating; belonging to the branch of government that is charged with such powers as making laws, levying and collecting taxes, and making financial appropriations.

Liberal (in the world) - (According to Merriam-Webster), a theory in economics emphasizing individual freedom from restraint and usually based on free competition, the self-regulating market, and the gold standard.

Liberal (in the USA) - (According to Merriam-Webster), a political philosophy based on a belief in progress, the essential goodness of the human race, the autonomy of the individual, and the protection of political and civil liberties; specifically, such a philosophy considers government as a crucial instrument for the amelioration of social inequities, such as those involving race, gender, or class(More specifically, it is associated with everything to the left of the Republican political party, including the Democrats, civil rights, human rights, social programs, multiculturalism, identity politics, environmentalism, equality, and a very watered down version of socialism.

Liberation - (According to Britannica), the act or process of freeing someone or something from another's control; the act of liberating someone or something.

Liberation theology - (According to Wikipedia), a Christian the-ological approach emphasizing the process of gaining freedom for the oppressed. In certain contexts, it engages socio-economic analyses, with "social concern for the poor and political libera-tion for oppressed peoples." In other contexts, it addresses other forms of inequality, such as race or caste.

Lobby - (According to Merriam-Webster), to conduct activities aimed at influencing public officials and especially members of a legislative body on legislation.

Low Intensity Warfare - (According to Wikipedia), a military con-flict, usually localized, between two or more State or non-State groups that is below the intensity of conventional war. It involves the State's use of military forces applied selectively and with re-straint to enforce compliance with its policies or objectives. The term can be used to describe conflicts in which at least one or both of the opposing parties operate along such lines.

Mainstream Media - (According to Wikipedia), a term and abbre-viation used to refer collectively to the various large mass news media that influence many people, and both reflect and shape prevailing currents of thought. The term is used to contrast with alternative media. It is often used for large news conglomerates, including newspapers and broadcast media that underwent successive mergers in many countries. The concentration of media ownership has raised concerns of a homogenization of viewpoints presented to news consumers. Consequently, the term mainstream media has been used in conversation and the blogosphere, sometimes in oppositional, pejorative or dismissive senses, in discussion of the mass media and media bias.

Mando Unico - In Mexico, this Spanish language term is a refer-ence to a single command for all military and police.

Manifest Destiny - (According to Wikipedia), a widely held cultural belief in the 19th-century United States that American settlers were destined to expand across North America. (More specifi-cally, Manifest Destiny was the U.S. American expression of the Doctrine of Discovery.)

Marginalize - (According to Britannica), to put or keep some-one in a powerless or unimportant position within a society or group.

Marxism - (According to Britannica), the political, economic, and social theories of Karl Marx including the belief that the struggle between social classes is a major force in history and that there should eventually be a society in which there are no classes.

Media Industrial Complex - Telecommunications (cell phone and internet), TV, film and videos, photos, radios, newspapers, maga-zines, and books, etc.

Mesoamerica - (According to Wikipedia), a historical region and cultural area in southern North America and most of Central America. It extends from approximately central Mexico through Belize, Guatemala, El Salvador, Honduras, Nicaragua, and northern Costa Rica. Within this region pre-Columbian societies flourished for more than 1,000 years before the Spanish coloni-zation of the Americas.

Mestizo - (According to Wikipedia), a term used both for the ra-cial classification of a person with a combined European and Indigenous American ancestry, and also for people who are cul-turally/ethnically combined regardless of ancestry. The Spanish language term was used as an ethnic/racial category for mixed-race castes that evolved during the Spanish Empire. Although, broadly speaking, *mestizo* means someone of mixed European/ Indigenous heritage, the term did not have a fixed meaning in the colonial period. (More specifically, *mestizo* is just a pretty way of identifying the result of the colonial rape of Indigenous people.)

Militant - (According to Merriam-Webster), aggressively active, as in a cause.

Militarism - (According to Wikipedia), the belief or desire of a government or a people that a State should maintain a strong military capability and use it aggressively to expand national interests and/or values. It may also imply the glorification of the military and of the ideals of a professional military class and the predominance of the armed forces in the administration or policy of the State.

Military Industrial Complex - All weapons and weapons technology manufacturers, all armed forces and police, all private military police and security contractors, and the local, state, and federal governments that employ them. (It is simultaneously part of the Business Industrial Complex and the Political Industrial Complex.)

Military Political Economy - A system of money and power that relies heavily on militarism for achieving political and economic goals or interests.

Monetary Hegemony - (According to Wikipedia), an economic and political concept in which a single State has decisive influence over the functions of the international monetary system.

Monetary System - (According to Wikipedia), the manner in which a government provides money in a country's economy. Modern monetary systems usually consist of the national treasury, the mint, the central banks and commercial banks.

Monopoly - (According to Britannica), complete ownership or control of something.

Municipality - (According to Britannica), a city or town that has its own government to deal with local problems.

Narco - Of or relating to organized crime and narcotics cartels, in particular throughout so-called Latin America.

Narco-Business - "Legitimate" business activity which is heavily influenced or controlled by organized crime and narcotics cartels.

Narco-Governance - "Legitimate" government activity which is heavily influenced or controlled by organized crime and narcotics cartels.

Narco-Paramilitarism - The arming and training of civilian individuals by an organized crime or narcotics cartel for the purposes of social and political control of a region.

Narco Violence - Violence associated with organized crime and narcotics cartels.

Natural Resource Extraction Complex – The mining of raw materials, related to biodiversity, lumber and water, gas, and oil, is also included in the Business Industrial Complex but is vast enough in its political and economic power, scope, and influence to be designated as its very own industrial complex.

Neoliberalism - A system of military-political economy that prioritizes and enforces the interests of wealthy and powerful nations, their transnational corporations, financial institutions, and some very wealthy and influential individuals.

Non-Governmental Organization (NGO) - (According to Wikipedia), an organization that generally is formed independently from government. Such organizations are typically non-profit entities, and many of them are active in humanitarianism or the social sciences; they may also include clubs and associations that provide services to their members and others.

Non-Profit - (According to Wikipedia), a legal entity organized and operated for a collective, public or social benefit, in contrast with an entity that operates as a business aiming to generate a profit for its owners. A non-profit is subject to the non-distribution constraint: any revenues that exceed expenses must be committed to the organization's purpose, not taken by private parties. An array of organizations are non-profit, including some political organizations, schools, business associations, churches, social clubs, and consumer cooperatives. Non-profit entities may seek approval from governments to be tax-exempt, and some may also qualify to receive tax-deductible contributions, but an entity may incorporate as a non-profit entity without securing tax-exempt status.

Non-profit NGO Industrial Complex - The non-profit Non-Governmental Organization Industrial Complex includes all non-profits and NGOs, their executive officers, their staff, their funders, the government agencies and philanthropic organizations that they are associated with, and all of their activities. Although a lot of very good work is being done by many non-profits and NGOs, the non-profit and NGO phenomenon is an integral component of the neoliberal military-political economy.

Oligarchy - (According to Wikipedia), a form of power structure in which power rests with a small number of people. These people may or may not be distinguished by one or more characteristics, such as nobility, fame, wealth, education, and corporate, religious, political, or military control.

Outsourcing - (According to Investopedia), the business practice of hiring a party outside a company to perform services or create goods that were traditionally performed in-house by the company's own employees and staff. This is a practice usually undertaken by companies as a cost-cutting measure. As such, it can affect a wide range of jobs, ranging from customer support to manufacturing to administrative work in the back office. Outsourcing was first recognized as a business strategy in 1989 and became an integral part of business economics throughout the 1990s. The practice is subject to considerable controversy in many countries. Those opposed argue that it has caused the loss of domestic jobs, particularly in the manufacturing sector. Supporters say it creates an incentive for businesses and companies to allocate resources where they are most effective, and that this business practice helps maintain the nature of free-market economies on a global scale.

Pacifism - (According to Britannica), the belief that it is wrong to use war or violence to settle disputes.

Papal Bull - (According to Wikipedia), a type of public decree, letters patent, or charter issued by a pope of the Catholic Church. It is named after the leaden seal (bulla) that was traditionally appended to the end in order to authenticate it.

Paramilitarism - The use of armed civilians who receive training, support, and financing, or simply impunity from official entities such as a political party, a government administration, the police, or the military. A paramilitary organization may also be generated and supported by non-governmental institutions including corporations, banks, or individuals such as wealthy local land owners and the political elite as well. Such forces use violence to carry out social, political or economic objectives against a target civilian population that is either considered a disposable variable, a barrier, or a direct threat to a given political, economic, or military interest. The primary purpose and function of paramilitarism is to generate and exploit what are known as "deniable atrocities." That is to say, its forces carry out atrocities such as extrajudicial executions, kidnappings, beatings, rape, and torture against a civilian population in such a way that governments, police, or the military can deny involvement in and/or responsibility for those atrocities once committed. These atrocities are used to dissuade social, political, or economic opposition. A key calling card of paramilitarism is the implementation of its atrocities with total impunity. It is impunity of this nature that further delegitimizes governments and their justice systems all together. When a paramilitary group is generated from a local population to cause internal conflict in a target region, oftentimes ideological, political, religious, cultural, geographic, or social differences between opposing groups are exploited to generate violent confrontations. A common end result of the deniable atrocities carried out by heavily armed paramilitaries around the world is the formalized militarization, policing, and criminalization of a community, organization, group, or individual being targeted.

Patriarchy - (According to Wikipedia), an institutionalized social system in which men dominate over others, but can also refer to dominance over women specifically; it can also extend to a variety of manifestations in which men have social privileges over others to cause exploitation or oppression, such as through male dominance of moral authority and control of property. Some patriarchal societies are also patrilineal, meaning that property and title are inherited by the male lineage.

People of Color - (According to Merriam-Webster), persons whose skin pigmentation is other than and especially darker than what is considered characteristic of people typically defined as white.

Political dissident - (According to Britannica), someone who strongly and publicly disagrees with and criticizes the government.

Political Industrial Complex - The intricate systems of local, state, and federal institutional governments of nation-states, and their political parties around the world. A critical analysis of this complex has to include a critique of electoral politics in and of itself, political parties and their candidates, and institutional forms of governance as a whole as well, but in particular, centralized forms of institutional governance. This industrial complex is in essence omnipresent and includes virtually all the other industrial complexes within it; however, it contains within itself factors such as campaign financing, gerrymandering, voter suppression, lobbying, and a legal and legislative framework, which together are the bases for the legitimized institutional political corruption of all the other industrial complexes.

Porro - A paid and protected student or non-student thug, who, along with his cohorts, belongs to an organization much like a syndicate or union that functions within a public education framework. Members are paid and compensated in various ways for carrying out acts of violence against student organizers, particularly at student protests. They can generally be associated with right-wing conservative political alliances within Mexico's political parties, in particular the Institutional Revolutionary Party (PRI) and the National Action Party (PAN). These associations, in addition to providing payment for services, also provide protection from prosecution or sanctions from the administration for said violent services rendered.

Precarity - (According to Wikipedia), a hazardous existence, lacking in predictability, job security, and material or psychological welfare.

Prison Industrial Complex - The entire prison industry, both private and public, as well as the entire justice system including the courts, the police, bail bonds, and probation and parole industries.

Private property - (According to Wikipedia), a legal designation for the ownership of property by non-governmental legal entities.

Privatization - (According to Investopedia), a process in which a government-owned business, operation, or property becomes owned by a private, non-government party. Note that privatization also describes the transition of a company from being publicly traded to becoming privately held. This is referred to as corporate privatization.

Privilege - (According to Wikipedia), social privilege is a theory of special advantage or entitlement, used to one's own benefit and/or to the detriment of others. Privileged groups can be advantaged based on education, social class, caste, age, height, nationality, geographic location, disability, ethnic or racial category, gender, gender identity, neurology, sexual orientation, physical attractiveness, and religion. This is generally considered to be a theoretical concept used in a variety of subjects and often linked to social inequality. It is also linked to social and cultural forms of power. It began as an academic concept, but has since been invoked more widely, outside of academia. This subject is based on the interactions of different benefits within certain situations. Furthermore, it must be understood as the inverse of social inequality, in that it focuses on how power structures in society aid societally favored people, as opposed to how those structures oppress others.

Propaganda - (According to Wikipedia), communication that is primarily used to influence or persuade an audience to further an agenda that may not be objective and whose authors may be selectively presenting facts to encourage a particular synthesis or perception, or using loaded language to produce an emotional rather than a rational response to the information that is being presented. Propaganda can be found in news and journalism, government, advertising, entertainment, education, and activism and is often associated with material that is prepared by governments as part of war efforts, political campaigns and health campaigns that may be related to revolutionaries, big businesses, ultra-religious organizations, the media, or certain individuals known as "soapboxers."

Prosperity - (According to Wikipedia), flourishing, thriving, good fortune and successful social status. It often refers to the production of profuse wealth with a plenitude of factors such as happiness and health.

Provocateur - (According to Wikipedia), an agent provocateur is a person employed to act undercover to entice or provoke another person to commit an illegal or rash act.

Proxy war - An armed conflict between two State or non-State actors acting at the instigation or on behalf of other parties that are not directly involved in the hostilities. In such a war, there must be a direct, long-term relationship between external actors and the belligerents involved, which usually takes the form of funding, military training, arms, or other forms of material that assist a belligerent party in sustaining its war effort.

Psychological operations - (According to Wikipedia), known by many other names or terms, including Military Information Support Operations (MISO), Psy Ops, political warfare, "Hearts and Minds", and propaganda, such practices "denote any action that is practiced mainly by psychological methods with the aim of evoking a planned psychological reaction in other people." Various techniques are used, and are aimed at influencing a target audience's value system, belief system, emotions, motives, reasoning, or behavior. They may induce confessions or reinforce attitudes and behaviors favorable to the originator's objectives, and are sometimes combined with black operations or false flag tactics. They are also used to destroy the morale of enemies through tactics that aim to depress troops' psychological states. Target audiences can be governments, organizations, groups, and individuals, and are not just limited to soldiers. Civilians of foreign territories can also be targeted by technology and media so as to cause an effect in the government of their country. There is evidence of psychological warfare throughout written history. In modern times, such measures have been used extensively. Mass communication allows for direct communication with an enemy populace, and therefore has been used in many efforts. Social media channels and the internet allow for campaigns of disinformation and misinformation performed by agents anywhere in the world.

Public Corruption - (According to Wikipedia), dishonest or illegal behavior, especially by powerful people such as government officials or police officers.

Quantify - (According to Britannica), to find or calculate the quantity or amount of something.

Racialize - (According to Merriam-Webster), to give a racial character to someone or something; to categorize, marginalize , or regard according to race.

Ratified - (According to Britannica), a treaty, agreement, etc. made official by signatures or vote.

Repression - (According to Britannica), the act of using force to control someone or something.

Republicans in the USA - (According to Merriam-Webster), members of the Republican Party of the United States.

Revolving Door - (According to Wikipedia), a situation in which personnel may move between roles as legislators and regulators, on one hand, and members of the industries affected by the legislation and regulation, on the other, analogous to the movement of people in a physical revolving door. In some cases, the roles are performed in sequence, but in certain circumstances they may be performed at the same time. Political analysts claim that an unhealthy relationship can develop between the private sector and government, based on the granting of reciprocated privileges to the detriment of the nation, and can lead to regulatory capture.

Right - (According to Britannica), political groups that favor traditional attitudes and practices and conservative policies; the position of people who favor traditional attitudes and practices and conservative policies of the political Right.

Sabotage - (According to Britannica), the act of destroying or damaging something deliberately so that it does not work correctly.

Saboteur - (According to Britannica), a person who destroys or damages something deliberately; a person who performs sabotage.

Self-defense - The act of fending for oneself or one's community without support from any official entity.

Self-determination - The right of peoples to decide what is in their own best interest.

Shadow Lobbyists - Unregistered lobbyists working for lawyer/

lobbyist firms as consultants, advisors, or specialists through a loophole known as the Daschle Loophole, named after Tom Daschle, who worked as an unregistered lobbyist for years until registering just recently.

Socialism - (According to Merriam-Webster), any of various economic and political theories advocating collective or governmental ownership and administration of the means of production and distribution of goods.

Socioeconomic - (According to Britannica), of, relating to, or involving a combination of social and economic factors.

Sovereignty - (According to Britannica), the independent authority and right of a country, or presumably of an Indigenous nation, to govern itself.

Stipulate - (According to Merriam-Webster), to specify as a condition or requirement in an agreement or offer.

Strategy - (According to Britannica), a careful plan or method for achieving a particular goal, usually over a long period of time.

Structural Reforms or Structural Adjustment - (According to Investopedia), a set of economic reforms that a country must adhere to in order to secure a loan from the International Monetary Fund and/or the World Bank. Structural adjustments are often a set of economic policies, including reducing government spending, opening to free trade, and so on.

Subjugate - (According to Britannica), to defeat and gain control of someone or something by the use of force; to conquer and gain the obedience of a group of people, a country, etc.

Subsidy - (According to Britannica), money that is paid, usually by a government, to keep the price of a product or service low or to help a business or organization to continue to function.

Superpower - (According to Merriam-Webster), an extremely powerful nation.

Surveillance - (According to Merriam-Webster), close watch kept over someone or something.

Sustainable - Able to be maintained without being completely used up or destroyed; the involvement of methods that do not completely use up or destroy natural resources; and/or the ability to last or continue for a long time.

Systematic - (According to Merriam-Webster), methodical in procedure or plan

Systemic - (According to Merriam-Webster), fundamental to a predominant social, economic, or political practice.

Tactic - (According to Britannica), an action or method that is planned and used to achieve a particular goal.

Tariff - (According to Britannica), a tax on goods coming into or leaving a country.

Tax Abatements - An amount by which a tax is reduced.

Terminology - (According to Britannica), the special words or phrases that are used in a particular field.

U.S. Military Attaché - (According to Britannica), an atttaché is a person who works at an embassy as an expert on a particular subject, so it could be assumed that a U. S. Military Attaché is a U.S. expert on military affairs.

Vertical Power Structure - A regime with a strict hierarchy and domination of one over the other.

Vichy Regime - (According to Wikipedia), the common name of the French State (État français) headed by Marshal Philippe Pétain during World War II. The regime was authoritarian, xenophobic, anti-semitic, corporatist and traditionalist in nature. Officially independent, it adopted a policy of collaboration with Nazi Germany, which occupied its northern and western portions before occupying the remainder of Metropolitan France in November 1942. Though Paris was ostensibly its capital, the Vichy government established itself in the resort town of Vichy in the unoccupied "Free Zone" (zone libre), where it remained responsible for the civil administration of France as well as its colonies.

Voter suppression - (According to Wikipedia), a strategy used to influence the outcome of an election by discouraging or preventing specific groups of people from voting. It is distinguished from political campaigning in that campaigning attempts to change likely voting behavior by changing the opinions of potential voters through persuasion and organization, activating otherwise inactive voters, or registering new supporters. Voter suppression, instead, attempts to reduce the number of voters who might vote against a candidate or proposition. The tactics of voter suppression range from minor changes that make voting less convenient, to physically intimidating and even physically attacking prospective voters, which is illegal. Voter suppression can be effective if a significant number of voters are intimidated or disenfranchised.

Wage - (According to Britannica), an amount of money that a worker is paid based on the number of hours, days, etc., that are worked.

Whistleblower - (According to Merriam-Webster), one who reveals something covert or who informs against another; an employee who brings wrongdoing by an employer or by other employees to the attention of a government or law enforcement agency.

White supremacy - (According to Wikipedia), the belief that white people are superior to those of other races and thus should dominate them. The belief favors the maintenance and defense of any power and privilege held by white people. White supremacy has roots in the now-discredited doctrine of scientific racism and was a key justification for European colonialism. It underlies a spectrum of contemporary movements including neo-Confederates, neo-Nazism and the so-called Christian Identity movement.

Wire Transfers - (According to Investopedia), an electronic movement of funds via a network that is administered by banks and transfer service agencies around the world. Wire transfers involve a sending and receiving institution and require information from the party initiating the transfer, such as the receiver's name and account number. These transmissions don't actually involve the physical exchange of cash, but are settled electronically. Types of wire transfers include those facilitated between domestic banks and international ones.

World Reserve Currency - The dominant foreign reserve currency used globally. Today's currency of this type is the U.S. Dollar.

Ya basta - **Enough is Enough.**

Index

www.ingramcontent.com/pod-product-compliance
Lightning Source LLC
Chambersburg PA
CBHW062114020426
42335CB00013B/961